MEMOIRS OF

Ace Mariner, Salvor, Yachtsman

I was brought into the world in 194: bomb on Bournemouth, that notable n something about it, but rather I in some cases keep thinking about whether the bang has impacted me!

My soonest memories are of the ocean, the water at the edge of our nursery. At three years old I was in medical clinic to have my informative supplement out. I was taken from the ward to the working performance center completely cognizant, in light of the fact that in those days there was no great infusion to spread one out. I have as of late made a similar outing and the working performance center for this completely developed grown-up was an overwhelming spot, what it resembled to a three-year-old who realized they planned to cut him open I can't envision. I have the vividest memory of a brilliant light above me and an extraordinary beast of a man pushing this elastic cover over my face. I can smell the elastic right up 'til today. I shouted in degraded dread for I thought they were killing me.

I was in emergency clinic for a very long time. My folks nicknamed me their Belsen youngster for the revulsions of the inhumane imprisonments had arisen. It is hard to accept I was ever thin, not to mention skeletal, for I have forever been fat.

My folks were, I assume, wealthy, although we never seemed to have any money and the lament was always the lack of it; but I suspect that is the same in every household however rich or poor! I was talking about this the other day with my mother to find out what she thought our position in society was.

"And I guess you would say we were upper working class," I said.

"No center with regards to us, my dear," she answered, in a tone which brooked no answer, and that pretty much aggregates it up.

I am perched on my yacht in Tahiti composing this and England appears to be far, far away; and the England of my adolescence appears, on schedule, as incredible as the distance I am currently away. Anything anybody could say England is rich, the streets are brimming with vehicles and the shops are loaded with goods.

In 1946 England was on her knees monetarily, reflected in the apportioning then set up. A great deal of things which are currently important for life were just not accessible or were completely proportioned. Despite the fact that I didn't know anything about it, being excessively youthful, I felt the impacts. Britain was dark and shabby.

In 1948, when I was five, I had red fever. It was an awful experience for a five-year-old, since I was shipped off a segregation medical clinic and for quite some time lived in a glass confine. My folks, when they visited, could just wave from outside the glass; no much love. I wouldn't leave my teddy bear behind, later all he had been my main sidekick, and I kicked up such a fight that they disinfected him so I could bring him home.

We resided in Lilliput, Poole, in the area of Dorset. Our home, *Waterfront was on the water's edge sitting above Brownsea Island in Poole harbor*, an unspoiled spot to reside for a youngster who clearly had salt water in his veins. The ocean, goodness the ocean, it has been my first love, giving me my residing and given me my most noteworthy pleasures.

The house was two-storeyed, with a carport and a serious enormous nursery with lavender along the short drive. The lavender sticks in my memory since I was either pushed or fell into it so often.

The ocean was at the front of the house. At high water the ocean side was covered and the water lapped against the ocean divider. At the point when the tide was out there was too beautiful, gooey, tacky, Poole mud to play in.

Boats have been with me for my entire life. Whenever I first went out all alone (regardless of whether it was with or without authorization I don't recollect that) I wound up got by the dock that ran out down tide of the house. I was attempting to cruise. The main boat that I possessed was a little, level lined paddling boat around 6 feet since quite a while ago painted red – "Redshell". My senior sibling, Donald, claimed a much unrivaled boat called "Cockleshell", predominant in that she was a cruising dinghy. She is included in Eric Hiscox's first book Cruising Under Sail. The two boats were worked at Newmans in Poole, the yacht yard my dad was the manager.

I went to a 'woman school' run by old – all things considered, she appeared to be old to me – Bertha Brown in Canford Cliffs. The main thing I recollect was being told I was utilizing the India-elastic the incorrect way. The special lady speedily did it the same way and unsettled the paper like me.

My mom used to cruise with a Miss Brotherton who lived with her dad in Canford Cliffs. They had a major house with a huge nursery on the bluff sitting above the ocean. She was a huge woman and to me appeared to be exceptionally serious; however I at times went to the house, and the elderly person used to take me for a drive in his Rolls-Royce, which extraordinary fun.

In 1951 my dad turned into the supervisor of the Berthon Boat Yard in Lymington and we moved to Brockenhurst. Why anybody needs to live in Brockenhurst I can't think, except if they should be close to the rail line station. Every one of the quick trains to London, aside from the Bournemouth Belle, halted at

Brockenhurst, so it is a rich worker station.

My folks leased a huge house on the little stream that gets down to Lymington, inverse the Balmer Lawn Hotel. The house – presently transformed into pads – was claimed by Jack Giles, the renowned yacht fashioner of Laurent Giles and Partners. My dad worked with Mr. Giles before the conflict when the Vertue Class yacht was planned and again during the conflict, on the smaller person submarine design.

I went to the neighborhood state school with Edward, my more youthful sibling, and despised it. It was not extremely far away and we bicycled there and back a long time before weighty traffic. The feature of my visit was getting heat-stroke and being extremely debilitated. I was sleeping for a really long time in my obscured room – for the house was large enough for all of us to have our own rooms. As of now there were four of us: Donald, my senior sibling by three years; Edward, my more youthful by year and a half; and Malcolm, who was brought into the world in 1947.

The stream, which probably been a bad dream for my folks, was a wellspring of endless fervor to us. It overwhelmed in winter and was almost dry in summer. The banks in many spots were intensely lush so brimming with monsters and beasts – indeed, the new woods horse or a stag can be a terrifying spirit to a youthful child.

My first business adventure with Donald was at Mavis, which was the name of the house. In the spring primroses filled in abundance along the street and in the timberland. The thought was for us to pick and offer lots of the blossoms to improve our pitiful pocket cash. I wound up picking the blossoms and selling them yet Donald wound up with the money!

We were just there a year prior to my folks had the favorable luck to observe Thorns Beach and purchase the leftover 33 years of a 99-year rent from Beaulieu Estate. My mom was in assets for her mom had as of late died.

My granddad and grandma on my mom's side lived in Stawell Village, Somerset, close to Bridgewater. Indeed my granddad, clearly, claimed its vast majority. They resided in the Manor, a three-storeyed house fronting the street going through the town. My uncle, my mom's oldest sibling, resided in another three-storeyed house – Manor House. My Godfather, my mom's most youthful sibling, resided further up the town on a slope in the Rosary, a house possessed by my mom who offered it to him when he married.

The ranch laborers resided in ranch cabins generally claimed by my granddad; and Nellie, the family servant, resided inverse the Manor in one more house claimed by him. All the nobility houses and church were on one side of the road

going through the town, while the homestead laborers houses, pressing station and studios were on the other. One of my cousins currently resides in Nellie's old house, an indication of the huge changes in the public arena since the war!

We every so often visited my grandparents, a three-hour drive from either Poole or Lymington, and I at times remained, when my grandma was as yet alive. She was exceptionally enthused about caravanning. I delighted in remaining in the parade which she kept on the slope inverse Manor House. It neglected Sedgemoor underneath and the River Parrett to one side – a brilliant view on an unmistakable day.

She conferred one piece of intelligence which I have always remembered. "Do not forget, Ian, God is always watching you even when you are alone." What underhandedness I had been up to for this injury to have been caused I to don't know!

My granddad, in spite of the fact that I didn't understand it at that point, was a well known man, particularly in yachting circles. He cruised his yacht "Emmanuel," a 30-foot gaff shaper, across the Atlantic in 1936. He was the primary man to cruise independent from Ireland to Newfoundland and it pulled in much consideration at that point. The family house on the opposite side of the slope from Stawell was offered to pay for the boat.

Just before the conflict he crossed the Atlantic with my auntie, and afterward on across the Pacific to New Zealand. They couldn't finish the arranged circumnavigation since war broke out. He had to sell the yacht "Caplin" and got back to England by dealer transport. My auntie returned three years later.

He was a standoffish and forcing man to me and, as indicated by my mom, would generally rather avoid youngsters. My central memory of him is stepping down the town in his in addition to fours with an enormous strolling stick, looking neither to the left or the right. In the Manor I was really peaceful so as not to irritate him.

After the conflict he did no seriously cruising, taking up natural science as a side interest and being a Labor Council part. I especially recall him one day in the lounge area finding a seat at the table – presently in the place of my sibling Edward – concentrating on a plant in a magnifying lens, the sun gushing through the window. I was totally silent so as not to upset him.

THORNS BEACH

Thorns Beach was a heaven on earth for youngsters, and I am starting to think as old as moderately aged grown-up. Thistles is stowed away down more than two miles of un-metalled street on the bank of the Solent. Its 30 sections of land is fronted by 300 yards of private ocean side, out of reach to the public except if they trespass. There was a five-section of land plantation, the Barn and five houses over the street; a five-section of land field, a swamp, a walled garden, a bandstand and four houses underneath the street. The rest was woodland.

When we originally showed up there was no mains water or power. Power was provided by our own generator arranged in the walled garden. The garden was run by two gardeners who just about paid for their wages by the produce produced – luxuries, such as early strawberries, being sent to Covent Garden for sale.

We previously lived in the Barn, which initially had been the pens and coachroom. The helpers lived previously. It was a gigantic wooden house: the coachroom being used to house dinghies in the winter; a large stone-flagged kitchen with a coal fired Aga enabling us to eat in the warmth; a dining-room with the table from Stawell for formal occasions; a play room; and a work room for my mother. There were seven rooms higher up – one for every one of us four young men, my folks' room, a space for the live in housekeeper young lady and an extra space for visitors. There were two restrooms and a latrine with a bowl ground floor. Outside there were pens for four or five ponies, and carports for ten engine vehicles! My mom would generally rather avoid it for it was not by the ocean, which was 100 yards away.

It was about this time that my sister, Maureen, was conceived. She just lived nine months. My sister was in medical clinic for a brief time, and it was an awful evening when my dad let me know she had kicked the bucket and would not be returning home. The memorial service was a miserable issue, with old Mrs Cook from the homestead following us to the burial ground out in the country.

That was the finish of the Barn. On the ocean front there were three huge rooms, all that was left of a 55-room home. The first home was worked by a Mrs Peach who kept ponies in the Barn. Groups from London played in the bandstand behind the house, while 35 workers took care of the guests.

There was a street between the house and the ocean side and, so the story goes, Lord Montagu used to drive his vehicles along the street now and again joined by King Edward. Sadly, Mrs Peach protested the vehicles, saying it terrified the ponies. The vehicle driving didn't stop so Mrs Peach had every one of the ponies shot and left. The rent was sold on to the Constants, who used to possess a drifter delivering organization. Tragically, Mrs Constant tried to avoid the tin home so Mr Constant had everything pulled down, aside from three rooms, and constructed a two-storeyed house nearby with regards to a large portion of a mile away.

The three excess rooms were tremendous however there were no typical workplaces. My folks based on a restroom, two latrines, a cookroom in one of the rooms and a parlor toward the front. The house was raised around 3 feet off the ground and was worked of wood with layered iron outside and on the rooftop. It is arranged in a little inlet practically impalpable from the beginning plainly noticeable from the air, and consequently is shielded from the common westerly breezes. It is the main house along the shore without twofold coated windows. In the late spring of 1952 we moved in and have been there from that point onward. (Sold in 2005 later my mom died.)

The perspectives from the parlor resemble pictures in Wordsworth's 'Daffodils' in my inner consciousness. You can nearly see out to The Needles in the West and Cowes, Isle of Wight, in the East. The view is always showing signs of change with ships, yachts, ships, fishing boats, an intermittent warship, a pull, in some cases with a tow, dinghies, kayaks – truth be told practically any sort of art you wish to name – passing down the Solent with the lovely landscape of the Isle of Wight as the setting. The foreshore is, obviously, in a consistent condition of progress with the tide consistently moving, so at whatever point one looks it is changed. At the point when the mud and shingle are revealed there are consistently birds taking care of winter and summer. The tones are continually changing with the climate – sun and downpour, cloud or part cloud, wind or calm.

As a little fellow the spot was a nonstop wellspring of marvel. There was a genuinely new thing to find: the bamboo forest; the old lily lake; the stone nursery, stowed away down the back drive; the wood, with every one of its bushes and rhododendrons; the trench, where the old link ran; the swamp, with its possible risk of falling into the water; and, obviously, the mud; the plantation; the green field; the little plantation by the sewerage siphoning station; the Windmill behind the outdated house; the foreshore with its junk at high water, and the mud and kelp, shakes and pools at low water; the walled garden, a never-ending wellspring of revelation with its developing of vegetables, the nursery, the seedling outlines with their glass covers; the generator room with its loud motor; the bungalows with their various inhabitants; and the dinghies around the ocean; swimming in the mid year – a genuine paradise.

SCHOOL

I went to the neighborhood town school at Beaulieu which I despised considerably more than the spot at Brockenhurst. Edward and I needed to walk the one and a half miles to the primary street to get the school transport, and back again in the early evening. I expect in the event that it was pouring my mom drove us! The school was controlled by a savage head instructor who delighted in beating, and he singled out a dark kid who appeared to get it each day.

Donald, presently 11, was at the Dragon School in Oxford, the school my dad had gone to when he was a kid. I was expected to go there and I was unable to stand by. I'm frequently informed that I kept in touch with the superintendent, Jock Lynham, who was there with my dad, and inquired as to whether I could come early. He concurred. My initial term was the late spring of 1952, and my 10th birthday celebration was during the term.

Teddy Hicks was my housemaster. He was later to be a renowned yachtsman and when Yachtsman of the Year.

Donald had been in a similar house, so my folks realized the Hicks well. Teddy gave off an impression of being a severe taskmaster yet I couldn't say whether this was actually the situation. I once did an excursion with him and his significant other Phil – who didn't actually like boats – from Teddington Lock to Lymington in his Dragon "Gerda". "Gerda" was an exceptionally popular boat, having been cruised across the North Sea from Norway. The main memory I have of this outing is being nauseous and awakening to observe that Teddy and Phil had paddled the yacht from Beachy Head to Newhaven in a quiet. I felt so embarrassed that I had not made a difference! I guess I was ten or eleven at this time.

The Dragon was a novel school. There were not many principles thus the discipline was great. What rules there were basically complied! The experts were completely called by their monikers: Jock the director; Hum, his dad, was still near and cared for the Sunday administration; Chris Jacques was Jacko, structure expert of Upper One, which dazed statures I never accomplished; Mike Gover, Gov, was accountable for Upper Two A, which is just about as high as I came to. Gover later became representative dean numerous years later I left along with Keith Ingram, Inky. Mr Plummer, Plum, had the following house up the street from Teddy. Mr Parnell, Parny, took me for topography and field undertakings. I last saw Parny at my Godson's affirmation. Mr Barroclough, Putty Nose, took me for something yet, more significantly, he took me – alongside Nigel Forman, one of a handful of the companions I made – to see the beginning of the Tall Ships Race from Start Point. We went through the night with Nigel's folks in their house

at Torquay.

When I moved to School House Ma Kay was the lady. Mrs Senior didn't have a moniker and took me for music illustrations, at which I had no ability at all. I presume she didn't a lot of care to show somebody who was so useless.

Morning petitions were held in the Old Hall, which was there when my dad was. Then, at that point, there was the focal corridor with study halls beginning around it. The sing-tune toward the finish of term was held in the hall.

The New Hall was utilized for school plays – Shakespeare in the late spring and Gilbert and Sullivan in the colder time of year terms. Much as I needed to I never made it in a school play! There were homerooms on the ground floor and the corridor was previously. I once read one of the illustrations at a Sunday administration, and had a little part in a film which was made.

The mid year term was awesome. The River Cher, which ran at the lower part of the broad school grounds, was my cherished spot. When in School House, rather than the virus plunge promptly in the first part of the day taken by Jock, we got down to the waterway for bare swimming. When the garments test was passed, we were permitted alone somewhere around the river.

I was nothing but bad at cricket, being fat. Teddy Hicks began a cruising group and I cruised for the school.

Donald was currently at the Dragon when Edward turned up along these lines, for a term or two, there were three of us at the school. We saw the guardians at half term just, despite the fact that I accept you were permitted out multiple times a term, however petroleum apportioning was in power. It was with extraordinary energy that we used to stand by at the lower part of Bardwell Road and watch for the car.

My folks had a parade which they stopped in a quarry – a lot less expensive than an inn and more exciting.

Donald continued to Canford. I think my folks figured we should be at isolated schools. Hugo Moresby White – sometime down the road to become second Sea Lord
– whose father my dad knew, continued from the Dragon to Pangbourne Nautical College. Hugo turned up one day wearing his uniform and I figured, that looks great, I would like something very similar. My mom, who consistently needed one of us to follow her dad into the Royal Navy, energized me thus my destiny was fixed. I went to Pangbourne.

It was numerous years after the fact, at a Royal Cruising Club yearly supper, that I heard my mom tell Richard Devitt, the grandson of the originator, that they had committed an error. But it is no good blaming circumstances, least of all   parents

who are doing all that can be expected. What's more, obviously, at that stage I didn't realize it was a slip-up. North of thirty years after the fact I got my old fashioned reports and on opening the first, understood that, for sure it was a misstep. I was extremely individualistic to be a decent Naval Officer

I never made companions effectively, and not very many at that. I just recall

Nigel Forman and Andrew Scorah from the Dragon yet I stayed aware of neither in the wake of leaving, despite the fact that I kept in touch with Nigel when he turned into a MP and when he was made individual private secretary to Lord Carrington, yet I never gotten an answer! I had even remained with him at Torquay with his folks to watch the beginning of the tall boats race. I realize Teddy Hicks was very appalled with him when he was at Oxford for remaining in Linton Lodge, the inn close to the school run by Tony Retty! I have no clue about what befallen Andrew.

BOATS

My mom possessed "Mary Helen", a six-ton gaff shaper my dad planned and worked with the returns of their wedding presents in 1936. She spent the conflict in a mud billet in the Beaulieu River however they currently cruised her each mid year cruising to France. Not long before the conflict they traveled west around Great Britain to Norway and back through Holland, for which my mom had been granted the RCC Challenge Cup – the primary woman to win this cup. It was not won by one more individual for 50 years.

We cruised with my folks except if cultivated out – whether or not we enjoyed it. Fortunately I preferred it thus do every one of my siblings. So the ocean, boats and cruising have been and keep on being, an immeasurably significant piece of my life. I'm staying here in Tahiti on my 39 feet yacht composing this, having begun to cruise around the world!

The main boat I possessed was "Redshell", and how she took her life I don't have the foggiest idea. I realize I had her at Thorns Beach. The main thing about my next boat was that she was a legitimate cruising dinghy. My dad requested two Lymington Scows 11 feet 6 inches since a long time ago worked at the Berthon, one for myself and one for my senior sibling Donald. "Titwillow" was mine and she was painted yellow and I cherished that boat. She was given to me on my eighth birthday celebration which was in the late spring of 1951. Throughout the late spring she was kept around the ocean at Thorns where I cruised her. In the colder time of year she was kept in the Barn where I painted her.

The following year I visited Beaulieu River and Lymington River, yet Lymington was defaced by the Isle of Wight ships which seemed colossal in the tight waterway. The bogs toward the west were met by Pyewell Creek and assuming the tide was elevated sufficient I could cruise through to Tanners Lane and Pitts Deep close to most of the way to Thorns. It was extraordinary amusing to cruise through the bogs, with the smell of the esparto grass, and assuming the tide was not elevated enough, the smell of the mud.

In the Easter occasions I used to gather seagulls' eggs and offer them to

Fishy Foot, the fishmonger. On breezy days, with a reasonable breeze, I would go through the springs causing a colossal wash in the restricted channel, particularly in the event that the tide was not full, envisioning I was a privateer getting away from the Navy, or a bootlegger outsailing the Revenue Cutter. On more settled days I would once in a while take a cookout and skim through the creeks.

I initially cruised across the Solent when I was ten. The Solent is a narrow stream between the Isle of Wight and the central area and being restricted, the tides are solid. With a westerly wind and ebb tide the ocean rapidly gets up the renowned Solent cleave. I think my folks were exceptionally bold and in this day and age of rules and guidelines, I would figure they would be thought of as reckless. I heard in later years that they would once in a while be seen at the club paying special mind to me on a harsh day. I didn't know anything about it; taking everything into account, assuming I was permitted to do something I was relied upon to do it properly.

I cruised all around the Solent and to Cowes for frozen yogurts. They were the creamiest I have ever eaten.

Newtown was an intriguing spot to investigate. When I was in Newtown and the climate weakened the breeze expanding such a lot of that at the thin entry I understood it was too unpleasant to even think about cruising home. I enrolled nearby assistance to leave the dinghy, some way or another got myself to Yarmouth and captured the ship to Lymington – all with no cash! I generally conveyed cash with me later that incident!

Lymington was the really thrilling waterway to cruise in light of all the traffic, even in those days prior to the marinas. Each 30 minutes or so I needed to battle with the ships. The Royal Lymington Yacht Club held their late spring regatta wherein I used to take part. My dad monitored the Berthon yard dispatch as a salvage boat. On one race where the course took us out into the Solent there was a new breeze. I was eleven or twelve right now and I lifted the middle plate when running downwind. My dad advised me to put it down to stop the rolling yet in my endless youthful insight I knew better and inverted. What a dishonorable finish to the race, yet it was the main time I at any point inverted my flatboat. I sailed in pretty strong winds, even reefing at times, and often had to bail but they were remarkably seaworthy dinghies.

There was a day regatta at Hurst Castle at which I dashed, and at Yarmouth, Isle of Wight. I once cruised over for the race just to think that it is dropped because of the terrible climate, so cruised back again to Lymington in disgust.

PANGBOURNE 1956 – 1960

Pangbourne was a finished and utter culture shock from the opportunity at the Dragon School and the opportunity of cruising in the Solent, with the obligation and confidence it brought. I entered a universe of rules and guidelines, cadet skippers who could and beat other young men, frivolous guidelines, regalia and all the technicality it involved, of being right or more all of adjusting, resembling other young men. But I was not like other boys, I was me. Other young men didn't claim their own boats, and I would have rather not adjust. I was fat and joined with my dissention, I was the butt of much harassing 'inside my own companion bunch', as per the report.

We used to pass via train to the Dragon School however for my initial term at Pangbourne my folks drove me. I can recall the energy. I needed to go to this school, I needed to enlist in the Navy, I needed to do well.

Port Jackson, the house we all were in for the primary year, was set in the most exquisite grounds right down the slope from the principle school. When my folks left the facade of civilisation was off and I entered the universe of discipline authorized by the more established young men with the full simultaneousness of power. It was an outsider and totally unusual reality where everybody was viewed as dumb, or that was the way it seemed.

'Accers', the early morning run, was a bad dream. Whatever the climate, when the cornet sounded at 06:30 you had three minutes – or was it five? – to awaken, dress in running stuff and march outside, there to be told by a cadet chief or cadet commander where to run. They would follow on a bike. I was not a quick sprinter and would in general raise the backside. All things considered, assuming the kid in control felt cruel he, for the sake of discipline, would arrange the last kid home to go round once more. This made you late for everything. Somebody must be last yet, obviously, the saying was to ensure it was not you. Somewhat like whipping the last man off the yard in the times of sail.

Once home you were hosed somewhere around the cadet chief with a virus hose and on the off chance that he was feeling lively he would point the solid fly at your private parts, which you were not permitted to secure with your hands. The virus water bit was a walk in the park, being utilized to Jock's virus water plunge, however the different was more hard to deal with. It was all for the sake of hardening you up for the afflictions of life – to be men, to be pioneers in the perishing days of the British Empire. It was the last pant of a framework that had stood the realm well, yet turned out to

be a chronological error in this day and age; the domain was at that point dead and its framework antiquated. Possibly I ought not say anything negative, I made due. Regardless of whether I needed to take care of business I wouldn't; it be able to was past the point of no return I was there, and my folks were making huge penances to send me to a respectable public school.

Survive I did. Regardless of whether coincidentally or plan, I can't say. Assuming that you can't beat them go along with them and adjust, and this I did to make due – however solely after much torment and exertion. Most likely it very well may be said the framework worked for my situation, surely my life would have been unique on the off chance that I had gone to a typical school.

In my first year I needed to box, whether or not I needed to. I didn't. I have consistently believed enclosing to be absolutely savage a humanized society. All things considered, being fat, I was a heavyweight thus got thumped in the ring by an all around created senior kid and the supposed match was halted before the end by the chief administrator. That is the unparalleled time in my life I have boxed.

After a year in Port Jackson under 'Minnie' Beat the housemaster – who I never knew, apparently in light of the fact that I kept out of true difficulty – I moved to Hesperus Division. The housemaster there was an altogether different pot of fish. His name was Holland and his epithet was The Brute. What's more he was not called The Brute to no end. He administered the house by dread and nobody got away somewhere around one beating while in his home. Mine was fourteen days before I left in my last term, yet I am in front of myself.

The divisional structure was a substantial monster with substantial floors and cold as transgression in winter with those older style, upstanding, iron, steam radiators. I once visited Alcatraz, the scandalous island jail in San Francisco Bay. Remaining in the old lounge area, having strolled round the jail, I had the most incredibly horrendous inclination that I had been there previously; and it was some time before I understood that it was Pangbourne.

The Brute used to lurk around evening time to discover individuals talking later lights out and beat the hell out of them, or if nothing else this is the thing that he appeared to do. Consistently there was a report – or possibly it was at regular intervals – from the experts accountable for each subject and assuming you got an adequate number of betas it was a beating. Regularly the casualties were beaten in the evening and when it was over in would come The Brute to take evening petitions. He was a tall man with a solid face and he strolled with his head jabbed forward.

The mid year term was awesome. The school possessed various Fireflies and cruising was viewed as a game, so I got an opportunity to dominate. The cruising was controlled by Bobby Aitken, helped by Cecil Rogers who possessed National 12 12-foot dinghies. The boats were kept on the bank of the Thames close to the school paddling boat storage. It was on the arrive at where the popular Swan Inn is arranged, referenced in Jerome K Jerome's Three Men in a Boat.

The cruising extended one's cruising capacity, whatever amount of wind was blowing, since it was so fluky with trees on one bank and a slope over the other. Bobby Aitken was a lot of the coordinator. A diminutive man who clamored about while Cecil – who was not exceptionally fit, his blue face parting with his heart condition – was simply there giving directions in a sharp voice.

On my subsequent summer, when I ought to have made the primary group, one of those school fiascos happened. The rowers consistently thought to be the mariners to be sissy and wet, while the mariners believed the rowers to be all muscle and no mind! I was manning with Ewen Tailyour, later of Falkland popularity. An eight was simply pulling off the bank when Ewen emulated the cox in a falsetto voice which I idiotically replicated. Ewen was the Captain of Sailing so I got the fault. The Executive Officer Ronny Hoyle, who was responsible for paddling, heard us. There was nothing but toxicity among Hoyle and Aitken and I was prohibited from the stream for the mid year. Bobby either would not or couldn't do anything about it so I had no cruising that mid year thus passed up the shot at being Captain of Sailing in my the previous summer. Rodney Pattisson, later of Olympic notoriety, whom I consistently beat hustling, was chief. How significant school praises appeared at that point, and what destroying disillusionment when one passed up a great opportunity! The following year I made the school group and was granted my colours.

On my the previous summer The Brute would not make me skipper of the house group since I had not been advanced, making boss cadet chief Rae, who was futile, commander all things considered. I took steps to decline to cruise for the house which, presumably, irritated The Brute. God, how it hurt!

I was entered for a Royal Naval Scholarship at 15 years old and needed to go to London for the meeting. My folks set up for me to remain with Roger Pickney who was an unmistakable individual from the RCC. I went to London via train in my uniform and observed my direction to the level, which was an energy in itself having beforehand simply been to London in transit to remain with my Godmother. He took me out to supper at a Greek café which caused me to feel exceptionally developed up.

The following day I gave an account of board HMS Wellington, sat some sort of knowledge test and in the early evening was met by three men. I bombed so horrendously that I was not needed to go for the few days of movement tests. After thirty years I read the report Pangbourne shipped off the Naval

Authorities and knew why the meeting was a particularly exercise in futility –
I got no opportunity. Possibly it has ended up being all embracing to improve
things however at the time I was profoundly disillusioned and viewed myself
as a disappointment. The youthful, or possibly I felt, hurt and agony
comparably much as the grown-up! Numerous years after the fact my most
youthful sibling James won a Royal Naval Scholarship, so honor is fulfilled
the extent that the family is concerned.

***

Founder's Day was tHe large event for march work. We were prepared up
in our walking and tidied up our shoes so you could brush your hair in the
reflection on the toe cap. I would sit tight for the incredible day with much
anxiety that I would not accomplish something terrible like fall over or weak
or turn the incorrect way. A noticeable individual from nautical life would be
the visitor of honor. The one I especially recall was Captain Sorrell, who was
commander of the Queen Mary and had docked her in New York without a
pilot or pulls – which was viewed as an extraordinary accomplishment. He,
would deliver a discourse, and the commander administrator would give a
discourse and afterward the prizes would be given. I really won a prize, or
possibly two, for 'industry', never for being first.

People like Ian Phillips, who was attractive, one of the most amazing
looking individuals I have at any point met, splendid at sport and never
appeared to need to put forth an attempt academically, normally won. I was a
'plodder'. The main thing I was great at, and truly appreciated, was cruising;
however in those days you were unable to get by out of sailing.

Was I cheerful? Did I partake in my school days? To be completely honest I
truly don't know for I don't know what satisfaction is. In any case it was a
perseverance test to get by, yet when I weakened and the companion bunch
harassing halted I endured it. What stands apart most to me is that I needed to
accomplish, to be among awesome, however just wound up top of the
subsequent division. The one region where I accomplished – cruising – I
came out top, despite the fact that Hoyle's self-assertive restricting still
annoys even later every one of these years.

I went to an old young men's gathering supper a few days ago, the first time
in quite a while, (which says a ton regarding how I felt about the school) and
sat near Ewen Tailyour. At the point when I helped Ewen to remember the
scene with the rowers he claimed not to recall at the same time, later the wine
had streamed somewhat more, he did

recollect and apologized. What's more I feel better accordingly. Wretched,
truly, yet that is life!

***

My last term – the late spring of 1960 – was a bad dream. I was not advanced, which I figured I ought to have been. Many of my term intake were already promoted but I, in my own mind, considered I was as good as them if not better but I was only in the Merchant Navy form and the top people went into the Navy, then the Army, then Civilian Life and lastly into the Merchant, even though the place was founded for training officers for the Merchant Navy.

Devitt and Moore were a renowned cruising transporting organization in their day. They ran a cadet transport and later established Pangbourne Nautical College to prepare young men to become officials in the Merchant naval force. On the off chance that you put responsible for such a foundation disregarded Royal Navy chiefs, what do you anticipate? Commander Lewis was the chief administrator as of now and he had an unprintable moniker. He had the common lush's bronzed coloring – or perhaps I am being low and it was a heart condition – I can just compose what I thought and felt at the time.

As I found when I got the old reports from Pangbourne, my card had been well and genuinely checked. I had grumbled to my folks that we were not being shown maths appropriately on the grounds that the expert was sick or debilitated and just a more seasoned kid was taking us. The class was a ruins and I was adapting nothing. Being that sincere youthful young adult who needed to get on it was not sufficient. My folks properly grumbled to the school. The Director of Studies, a dry old stick called Topliss, who used to smoke a line, examined. Despite the fact that he concurred with me, Authority was not going to concede I was correct so my folks were palmed off with a misleading statement letter and, all the more critically, I was set apart as an agitator. In those days you essentially didn't groan, not least when you had a resigned Royal Naval taskmaster at the helm.

***

Two of the advantages I accomplished were a bike and the utilization of a senior kid's room at the highest point of the division. Two cadet commanders were found savoring the Red Lion bar and had been disrated. The Brute called me in and said that my advantage of utilizing this room – quite critical to a student, both for 'face' and to move away from the hurly-stout of the gunrooms, or diversion rooms in non military personnel speech – was removed. I was

stunned with shock and fought overwhelmingly Be that as it may much good it did me. The Brute had not yet beaten me, I up until this point had dodged his stick. It was so absolutely unreasonable and crooked. I was the 'great' kid, I had done nothing out of sorts, yet here were two young men who had been advanced and disrupted the guidelines and I was getting the discipline for it. It cast a total cover over my last term and the embarrassment of getting back to the gunroom, the sniggers and looks. However, I actually had my bicycle and used to go for long rides.

My folks came up on a Saturday to take me out – I assume there had been no cruising coordinate – and consolidated it with a visit to the Dragon School where my sibling Malcolm was a senior kid. We got back from Oxford and were eating at the lodging in Streatley by the River Thames. My dad needed to complete his wine so we would not be back by the 20:00 cutoff time, but senior young men with consent were permitted out till 21:00. I had not requested this consent in spite of the fact that, being in my last term, was qualified for this advantage. I was back before 21:00 and my dad said, "On the off chance that there is any issue advise Mr Holland to give me a ring."

Some weeks after the fact The Brute called me into his review and said, "Mr Stephens," – who was the representative housemaster – "lets me know he saw you in the inn at Streatley later 20:00. You didn't have authorization to be out that late." And he snorted, his stock-in-exchange, and puffed on his pipe.

"That is right, sir, and I am sorry for not having gotten consent for the additional hour however we had not relied upon to be simply late. My dad demands that you ring him assuming there is any issue," I considerately replied.

He snorted and excused me. At first I was unable to see what I had fouled up however understood that it may have been more judicious to have my dad to come in when I was dropped off. I had failed to remember the principal rule of endurance – 'assuming you encroach a standard, but idiotic, cover your arse!'

The Brute's snort foretold inconvenience however I expected he would ring my dad. The term delayed however The Brute's snort actually irritated. He was the previous expert in the specialty of dread, and the more I didn't hear anything from him the more terrible my dread became. It resembled Kafka's clever The Trial – what wrongdoing had I perpetrated? Nobody would tell me and I was being attempted without knowing what the wrongdoing was.

I envisioned a wide range of situations and the most noticeably terrible one was that he would remove my bike. I was profoundly miserable in this, my last term. Its one redeeming quality was my bike since it gave me opportunity of a sort and obviously, 'face' among the youngsters. The strain became agonizing and like the

screw-up in The Trial, I was prepared to submit to anything.

Finally the call came and I turned up at his review. The entryway was closed. I thumped. Quietness. Will I thump once more, has he heard? The

Brute truly was a definitive in executing mental fear.

I had nearly worked up determination to thump again for there was no good reason for estranging him.

"Enter."

I heard the snort. I opened the entryway and went in. He was sitting in his rocker confronting the entryway. I shut the entryway behind me and remained to consideration before him. There was no pipe.

"I will beat you for rudeness," he said.

No introduction, nothing, he had got me. In any case, as in The Trial, The Brute might have done anything to me and it would not have made a difference for the one thing that truly made a difference was as yet mine – my bike. I was so assuaged I practically grinned, however my face remained unchanged.

"Take out your shirt from your pants and twist around that chair."

It was nearly with enthusiasm that I went along. He took a little run and managed the primary stroke. My head was singing 'I actually have my bicycle' as the subsequent stroke fell, and afterward the third, and afterward the fourth, 'heck, it will be six however I couldn't care less, I have my bicycle,' the fifth and afterward the last 6th stroke fell.

"You can go now," he grunted.

I turned, looked at him without flinching and said, "Thank you, sir, goodnight, sir."

He dropped his eyes looking so amazed that I thought he planned to say something, it was clearly not the response he was anticipating. I immediately left, getting my shirt into my pants. I was 17 and later reprimanded myself for not having battled him, however I was so assuaged at keeping my bike. I never told my folks. It was reputed the Brute beat a kid for being late back while his folks were as yet outside the structure, I surely accepted it true.

It was fourteen days to the furthest limit of term and the days hauled into an unfathomable length of time. In the end I went down to the town and called my folks to come and remove me before I went frantic. This, in itself, was a wrongdoing. You were not permitted to phone without the housemaster's consent. I was because of get my first boat together with British India in half a month and I was unable to stand fooling around with the triviality of Pangbourne, particularly later the Brute's mental success.

***

My dad consistently believed Captain Lewis to be a messy person. I couldn't say whether they had some conflict, possibly it was the maths. At any rate I was brought in to see Captain Lewis, probably for him to wish me well for the future, and his splitting words were, "Don't allow your dad to make statements against me," and right up 'til the present time I never knew what it was all about.

My folks came to get me four days before the finish of term. The Brute never bid farewell and the last time I saw him he was leaving round the edge of the structure as we drove up the drive. Perhaps he thought I planned to whine to my dad about the beating, yet I was extremely diminished to stress over that. He was killed in a fender bender (or possibly he kicked the bucket of malignant growth) around seven years after the fact, and when I heard I didn't grieve. I as of late read his sparkling tribute in an old duplicate of the school magazine and didn't perceive the man I knew as my housemaster or divisional tutor.

And so I left Pangbourne with its monumental principle building set on the highest point of a slope with the most brilliant perspectives over miles of untainted open country, trees and green fields; its own sublime grounds; the lengthy drive, along the edges of which – toward the start of the late spring term – were floor coverings of bluebells; the forest, where secret student trysts occurred; the radiantly continued to play fields, where fights between the schools were battled in rugby and cricket; and, most importantly, the stream with its cruising and paddling on a delightful stretch of the Thames. It was 36 years before I visited the stream once more. The boat shelter was there, the whaler and a dispatch yet it was not the equivalent. There were no individuals. Where was the enthusiasm, the hurt, the seriousness, the endeavoring to accomplish, the outright need of overcoming the other individual cruising; the triumphant? I cruised for the school in the Public School Boys' Championships on the Gareloch in Scotland, close to Glasgow. It was held in Dragons and Garelochs. I did well two years running and was expected to go for my last year. Be that as it may, my dad said I ought to go to the ocean on the date indicated by British India and my mom contended I should cruise for the school. My dad won.

***

I was 17 and two months old when I left school and entered the grown-up world, and it was practically from one predicament into something worse. However at that point, such is reality and it is dependent upon you how you manage what life tosses at you. A close buddy of my folks, General Richardson, when he was old and visually impaired later a functioning life – including cruising – once said to me, "Ian, your folks have given you the devices to prepare you forever. You are an informed individual; I can't tell you a

game-plan is correct or wrong, it's dependent upon you to settle on that choice. You realize what is good and bad, yet when you have chosen stay with it."

CADET 1960

I joined the British India Steam Navigation Company Limited (BI) cadet transport "Chindwara", and it was a misstep! This was another world however one that I was not ready to acknowledge in light of the fact that the efficient harassing of first travelers was off-base with a capital W. I couldn't simply acknowledge what was occurring and leave it. The Dragon School and Pangbourne had instructed me that and it had been supported by General Richardson. I settled on my strategy and followed it through.

The harassing began the first or second night in London when the senior cadets returned from the bar. Every one of the main travelers were rousted out of their bunks and arranged along the bulkhead. A kid, well young fellow truly, all around constructed and intense, called T was the most noticeably terrible, he punched everybody ordinarily in the chest. I truly can't recall the amount it hurt, it was the embarrassment. Pangbourne had been an extreme spot somehow, and I basically was not ready to be thumped by a lot of inebriated bums. Not every one of the senior cadets partook, but rather the individuals who didn't never really halted it. It went on constantly we were in London and was known as Sports Nights. Once adrift it stopped.

The boat was on BI's East African run. Barclays District and Colonial Bank (DCO) were solid on that coast. My dad knew the director of the bank, and the chiefs of the different branches were cautioned I was coming. In Port Sudan the commander of the boat got a message that a vehicle would get me – which it did – and off I went to supper. This treatment, much agreeable however it was for me, didn't charm me to different cadets ready, in particular the senior bullies.

In Massawa the domineering jerks returned inebriated from the massage parlors and a 'genuine' Sports Night occurred. We were all rousted out and, later the underlying beating, secured in the drying room with the hotness turned up. There were 12 of us in a tiny hot space and Massawa was a hot spot without being in a drying room. I attempted to awaken the remainder of the primary travelers to retaliate. There were enough of us to take on the harassers however I was unable to convince them, despite the fact that one of them had been at Pangbourne with me yet in an alternate division. His name was J and he was very gorgeous. We were exclusively removed from the drying room and went through the wet towel test of endurance – stripped with the exception of undies. Once back in the drying room I again attempted to stir most of them to retaliate, yet to no avail.

The 'sports' continued for quite a while and wound up with us holding tight a line to see who endured longest prior to tumbling off and getting more towel flicking. Sooner or later J's clothing was pulled off and it is possible that he or another person had to put an aggravation fluid on his genitals.

I kept in touch with my folks clarifying what was happening and got some information about it. They did. They went to see the executive of BI – they had a presentation from an individual director.

Meanwhile we perspired our direction down the coast – cooling was a thing of things to come – visiting Aden, Mombasa, Zanzibar, Dar Es Salam and Tanga. Every one of the spots were British, the 'undeniable trend' – the well known Macmillan words in South Africa – had not blown on this coast yet. The ports were completely run by the British and the key posts were totally held by ostracizes, even down to the boat's stevedore foreman.

How very much run the ports were run. Everything worked, and great stacking and releasing occasions were acquired by the African work. I was taken out by the Bank Managers in both Mombasa and Dar Es Salaam. They all had heaps of workers and later the cadetship it was incredible to be looked out for. Later Tanga the "Sports Nights" halted. My folks visit to the Chairman had produced results. When different Cadets found who had blown the whistle, I was shipped off Coventry. The other first travelers on torment of a beating were taboo to converse with me. It is very hard to live peacefully, the main correspondences were directions from the senior cadets about work and such expendables as "be careful with the shackle from a lofty position" or "we will toss you over the edge in the channel" and different implications of a rough demise. "The Brute's" mental preparing in dread might have helped me for I endure the journey flawless. A Mr Spanton joined the boat in Gibraltar to research my charges and I was met by him. I don't have the foggiest idea about the result of this enquiry however I was moved to another boat. Again out of a sizzling griddle into a much more profound fire.

DARA 1962

I was to join the deck traveler transport "Dara" in Bombay. My dad took me to the air terminal which was another experience for myself and I think for my dad. My gear was horribly overweight that I needed to repack on the floor at the air terminal and he took a large portion of my stuff back home. The airplane was the cutting edge state-of-the-art stream a Boeing 707. I watched with alert as we removed, the wings fluttering in the breeze here and there while the extraordinary planes under moved from one side to another. I thought my last second had come and the thing would separate on the ground, yet lift she did and flew me to Bombay through various stops on the way.

Nothing in my past pre-arranged me for India, under twenty years later freedom, the commotions, the hotness despite the fact that it was winter, the crowds of individuals, the ghettos, the destitution, the smell and the bums. I made it a standard for life never to provide for a transient on the guideline in the event that you provided for one you ethically will undoubtedly provide for all. Who were you to play God. It is said you either love India or disdain her, there is no in the middle. I adored her. Similarly as indeed, as it would have been hard to have stayed in any case. It was totally not quite the same as Africa.

The "Dara" was a deck traveler boat of 5,000 gross tons and she conveyed around 1,500 travelers at hand, a few hundred in second class and 30-odd in top of the line. The cadets, alongside all the European officials, ate in the top notch cantina – an alternate world from the cadet ship.

There were just two of us and I imparted the lodge to the next cadet, Josh Grimwood. The lodge was arranged on the official's deck down a short back street from the central official's lodge, a long ways from the quarters on the "Chindwara." Josh, an European Kenyan from the white high countries, was the extreme senior cadet. We managed everything sufficiently well, and he was truly adept at giving me the general tour for I was still green notwithstanding the journey to East Africa.

Here we were, youthful officials under preparing rather than student healthy sailors (ABs) to work the boat. The main time I had been on the extension of the "Chindwara" was as student officer to guide her. Here my station – going all through port – was on the scaffold wearing whites. My occupation was to pick up the phone and transfer the orders from the chief and direct and review the scaffold ringer book – a really capable occupation for a 17-year-old!

We even had a 'kid' to care for us, clean the lodge, clean our uniform shoes, and ensure we had clean whites from the clothing. Domestics dealt with! Somewhat unique in relation to England.

***

Captain Elson was a man of not many words. Boss Officer Jordan was a slim man yet I had even less to do with him than the skipper. Josh, being the senior cadet, managed the mate. The second, third and fourth officials were the watch keeping officials and I possibly saw them when I was at my stations entering and leaving port. I predominantly saw the third official whose station was likewise on the bridge.

There were two radio officials – an old man and a youngish second – to sort out the remote telecommunication and tap all messages in Morse code. We had barely anything to do with the architects who lived in discrete convenience rearward on the boat deck. The cadets had their own table in the main cooled place on the boat – the top notch eating cantina. The remainder of the team were Indian. I should learn 'Malim Sahib's Hindustani' yet lament to say I never did.

The "Dara" – alongside the three sister ships "Dumra", "Dwarka" and "Daressa" – ran a week after week administration from Bombay to Basra by means of Karachi and inlet ports, here and there calling at two ports in a single day. Despite the fact that I didn't know it at that point, I was serving a perishing organization on courses made conceivable by the realm, additionally in its passing knell.

It was with much fear that I went to the scaffold for my first stations. Josh had showed me around the extension and how the phones functioned – by setting a dial for whom one wished to address and wrenching a handle. The extension appeared to be packed with the pilot – still, there was an Englishman – his Indian collaborator; the skipper; the third official; myself; and two secunnies, one to control and the other to get things done, lift or lower signals or calm the secunny in the driver's seat. The commander's kid was consistently available for espresso, tea or cold beverages for the Burrah Sahibs.

I was in a funk to begin with. The boat must be moved out of the harbors and through the lock doors into the harbor. There were various orders to transfer and reports to be produced using forward and rearward, yet I before long got into its swing and started to live it up. This was the spot I needed to be – on the extension at the control place! I was needed to record each motor development, so stayed alive and alert the entire time.

Stations going all through Bombay consistently consumed most of the day, and once out of the dock we went close by Ballard Pier to stack the travelers and mail.

Ballard Pier was close to the 'Doorway to India', the extraordinary opening representing section into India. The flight of the week by week mail boat to Basra was an occasion. The boats were the best way to get around a large portion of the Persian Gulf right now so we were a significant connection between India, Pakistan, Oman, Gulf States, Saudi Arabia, Kuwait and Iraq for the voyaging public. The boats were in every case loaded with passengers.

Sailing day from Ballard Pier was a day of rushing about. The yells and chatter of many individuals with their spouses, kids and workers; the calls of the watchmen conveying the gear, colossal groups on their heads; and the road merchants peddling their wares.

The cadets stacked the mail. Indeed, we conveyed nothing, we directed it –

along with the second official who was in control. To lose a mail sack was unthinkable.

There was a constant flow of humankind getting on by means of the paths; yells and now and again fights as men marked out piece of the deck for the journey. Obviously, the more special went inferior and appreciated lodges. Europeans were not permitted to go at hand. Five star came on board by a different corridor where the obligation secunny kept watch.

The tween decks, where the deck travelers resided, appeared to be a type of uproar to me on my first Gulf trip. There were two holds forward in the ship – both for traveler things and for freight – and the winches were working at maximum speed swinging the freight on board by the derricks, the stevedores perspiring in the holds stowing it.

Finally everybody and everything was ready; the boat was completely bunkered and watered; the outing to the cash transformer finished, for there was a decent worker trading Indian rupees into Gulf rupees and up the Gulf the alternate way round; not that I had wealth to spend. My first year adrift I was paid £3 each month which emerged from the Bond my dad paid for me to be apprenticed to BI.

The pilot was on the extension; the pulls made quick front and rearward; the passages were put aground; and, with much yelling, moaning and waving from the travelers ready and the families left shorewards, the boat moved off the billet. She was turned and the pulls were given up. With a keep going impact on the boat's foghorn, the "Dara" steamed out to the ocean through the bustling harbor bungled by country make with their worn out sails or on the other hand assuming that there was no wind with their teams working at enormous ranges, all loaded down with freight for exchanging all over the coast and when the storm was reasonable for East Africa. We passed

secured ships hanging tight for a billet – the structures of Bombay to starboard – thus out into the Arabian Sea and up the coast to Karachi and being the North East storm the climate approved of a quiet sea.

The boat adrift was her very own universe and, aside from the clamor of the diesel motors, it was very tranquil. Assuming that my obligations brought me down to the tween decks there was the persistent prattle from the many travelers nearby and it was once in a while hard to traverse the decks on the grounds that the travelers spread themselves and their belongings.

The ocean routine was extremely wonderful. We took care of the rafts and really look at the stuff, water and food – not that we at any point expected to utilize them. We changed into whites for all dinners and were relied upon to be in the cantina on schedule. When off the clock I examined and worked at the correspondence course we were relied upon to complete.

The distances between the ports were very short, particularly in the Gulf, so we were in and out of port most days. I especially recollect Dubai since we moored off, as we accomplished for most ports in the inlet back then. The travelers were taken aground by barge towed by a pull, however we went shorewards in the specialist's dispatch and arrived in the spring. The creek was full of dhows loading and unloading their cargoes; on the port side, entering the creek, were the stalls and shops where duty free goods of all kinds could be purchased. Dubai was the focal point of gold sneaking to India.

We put in a couple of days in Basra, being the other terminal port from Bombay, yet there was not a ton to do shorewards for an impecunious cadet. Bombay was significantly more fun with swimming at Breach Candy – the swimming club where young ladies may be met. The club in those days was for Europeans only.

I figured out how to get a sail or two at the Royal Bombay Yacht Club in Seagulls employed from the club, however it was costly for myself and I needed to tip the boatman who ran for me. The tides run unequivocally in Bombay so neighborhood information was helpful.

Josh acquainted me with the enjoyments of the enclosures in Grant Road where Ladies of the Night sat in banished windows showing as quite a bit of their products as they suspected important to captivate you inside and test them – for an expense, obviously. A lot of brew was devoured ready, before my first outing to Grant Road, on the grounds that there was preclusion in Bombay around then. You expected to sign on as a heavy drinker before you could get a license to buy liquor. That was outlandish for me on the grounds that my arrangements disallowed me from drinking cocktails or going into places with a history of shameful behavior. Josh was the coordinator for provisions of lager on board.

***

I was in the Seaman's Club one Saturday feeling dejected. Bombay was quite far from home and the world I presently resided in was altogether different from England. A man fired up a discussion which at last found time for the absence of liquor. He said he lived in a condo with bunches of liquor and welcomed me up. He appeared to be a fair sort so I acknowledged, thinking nothing didn't wander anything acquired. Indeed, to spare the nitty-gritty details I dropped – regardless of whether from a lot of drink or in light of the fact that something was slipped into my beverage I don't have a clue. At the point when I came to I observed myself to be exposed in bed with my new 'companion' playing out an exceptionally personal assistance on me, a horrifying presence. I was astonished, stunned and loaded up with disdain. I jumped up, dressed and ran from the level. At the point when I returned to the boat Josh inquired as to whether I was okay, obviously, I was unable to let him know what happened in that level. He was an extreme East African. There was nobody I could converse with, so I hefted the responsibility around with me. I showered and showered to attempt to feel clean, to purge myself of the shame.

***

It was April 1961 when I began my fourth journey soon after the episode with the man. The climate was starting to warm up in the Gulf. The "Dara" was moored off Dubai releasing freight and passengers.

During the evening the breeze expanded and a freight transport hauled its anchor and crashed into us on the port side. There was a lot yelling and anarchy, yet the main harm was to the raft arranged between the forward holds. Notwithstanding, the breeze proceeded to increment and Captain Elson took the boat to the ocean to brave the tempest, taking various Dubai stevedores with us.

It was harsh when we turned in. I moved into the top bunk, Josh resting in the last one. At around 04:00 I was awoken by the fire chimes ringing. It was still unpleasant, the boat was rolling and pitching. Josh said it seemed like a crisis and we better outfit and go to our fire stations. The lights were not working so we dressed rapidly by the light of a light and left the lodge into the alleyway.

We met the third official who said, "There is a fire on B deck. Go to your stations."

We went to our fire station, gathering the breathing device coming, down to B deck. B deck, which was one of the traveler decks, was

complete chaos. There were individuals going around in different conditions of dress yelling and shouting, the commotion intensified by the thunder of the fire which illuminated the region – the light rising and falling in power. One man was going around shouting with blood all down his front. Josh wore the breathing mechanical assembly and attempted to get to the crisis stopped fuel valves on the motor room bulkhead on the starboard side of B deck however was driven back by the flares. Looking along B deck there was an unholy sparkle, the smoke concealing it like a mist. There could have been no other lighting.

Josh said, "This is really sad, we would be advised to go to our boat station."

We battled our direction back through the bumping, shouting, freezing travelers to our boat station which was between the two rearward holds, a light our main light. It was as yet dim and the boat was moving dead in the water.

We let go of the fusses and lashings off the boat so we could swing it out for bringing down. Josh advised me to get in light of the fact that this was my boat and I was accountable for it. I hopped ready and Josh brought the boat down to embarkation level. What a frenzy! The most grounded travelers amassed on board.

"Lower away, Josh!" I yelled, "the boat is now full and more are attempting to get on board."

He could see what was going on and brought down the boat into the water. Tragically, a vacant boat floated by from the boat deck forward of our position. The travelers all went to the side of my boat and it inverted. I wound up in the waters of the Persian Gulf. It was as yet dim and very harsh. The consuming boat floated away from me and I was all alone. I don't have a clue what befallen the travelers from my boat.

I considered my position. The boat was floating excessively quick for me to swim back to her. I was not wearing a daily existence coat – it had not entered my head to carry it with me from the lodge. Fortunately I was a solid swimmer and passed the Award of Merit in Lifesaving at Pangbourne. I was still completely dressed so removed my shoes and dungarees. In my scramble to leave the lodge I didn't put on any clothing. Without the dungarees it was much more straightforward to swim yet I kept my shirt on. There was not a lot of I could do with the exception of float and pause, a periodic wave breaking over my head. I was separated from everyone else with my contemplations yet I was not apprehensive. Goodness youth, immortal.

It began to gradually get light and I saw what I thought was a shark's balance not far away from me. I thought this was my discipline for the occurrence with the man, and the ocean water was the last chemical. I was currently spotless again.

I watched the balance and later what appeared to be an unfathomable length of time, I understood that it was

not moving and a little later that the balance was truth be told a human body grasping a paddle. The liberating sensation that I was not going to pass on was very overpowering. I swam to the oar.

There was a body on the paddle and I put my arm around her. It was lighter now and I could see she was not wearing a daily existence coat. Her face was in the water a great deal of the time, the waves washing over it, her hair a dark mass whirling around her head and I couldn't say whether she was alive or dead. Later it turned out to be totally light she tumbled off the paddle and vanished. I guess I had been in the water for 90 minutes at this point. I have frequently contemplated whether I ought to have done more to attempt to save her, yet would she say she was at that point a body? Had I been clutching a carcass for the last hour?

In the sunlight I saw a raft close by, and forsaking my paddle, I swam to the boat. When jumping on board one of the travelers saw my absence of base dress and mercifully provided me with some shorts to make me good, for there were a couple of ladies in the boat. The associate purser thankfully gave over charge of the boat to me. It was still harsh and the raft was rolling awkwardly so I convinced the group and a couple of travelers to man the paddles and keep the bow into the breeze and ocean. It made it significantly more agreeable for everyone.

Some time later it was starting to get blistering as the sun rose in the sky. A big hauler showed up nearby and I trained the rowers to push. We advanced over to the boat, which had halted in the water with the corridor down. I told the associate purser I didn't think there was any utilization attempting to get the ladies off first and just let the men go as they would. We came close by the corridor and a sensibly coordinated disembarkation resulted. The men went first followed by the ones who were increased the corridor by the Japanese group when necessary.

Once the boat was vacant I found a man sleeping in the lower part of the boat, face down. I had a go at energizing him however it was without much of any result so figured out how to turn him over onto his back. It was then I understood it was a cadaver, the string eyes. I figured the family would need the body so figured out how to convince the Japanese to accept the cadaver and put him in the cooler. I at last came on board myself and the raft was set adrift.

The travelers were obliged and I was given a lodge in the team quarters. One kind team part provided me with a container of whisky which I drank, scratching out the consuming ghastliness of B deck; the frenzy; the man with blood all down his front; the shouting; the thunder of the flares; the envisioned, yet very genuine looking shark's balance; the cadaver in the water; lastly, the carcass in the lifeboat.

The Japanese big hauler took us to Bahrain where an exceptionally perturbed specialist scolded me for welcoming the body on board.

"I figured the family would need it, sir," I replied.

"Do you understand the difficulty you have caused me just to get it aground, let alone out of Bahrain? You ought to have hurled it over the edge or left it in the raft," he said.

***

The "Dara" mIsfortune was the greatest peacetime catastrophe to strike a British boat since the "Titanic" and pulled in world consideration in the

Press. I can't think why I couldn't speak with my folks albeit, back then, it was anything but a question of simply getting the phone beneficiary. I, for reasons unknown, was left off the rundown of survivors and it was three days after the fact before my folks were told I was protected. It was numerous years after the fact before I was told by a sibling the awful end of the week it had been sitting tight and wanting for fresh insight about me.

I remained in a lodging in Bahrain where the BOAC air team remained; was kitted out with a negligible of dressing; gave with a visa 'unique lost adrift'; lastly, joined the "Aronda" for the journey back to India. I gave proof to the Preliminary Enquiry held in Bombay where I was told not to discuss my encounters to others. I flew home for my fourteen days 'survivor leave'.

Johnathen Priest, my closest companion at school who was still there, had kept in touch with me while I was on the "Dara". He let me know that Captain Lewis had assembled the entire school and enlightened them that the bits of gossip zooming around concerning harassing on the cadet transport "Chindwara" were totally false and I was a liar.

Toby Hickman, who was on the East African coast simultaneously as the "Chindwara" on a Clan Line transport, was on leave. I had complained to him about the bullying when we met up in Mombasa and he said that he would rouse his 'white' crew and come over to beat up the bullies! I asked him if he would accompany me to Pangbourne and lend moral support so that I could confront the captain-superintendent. He concurred and I acquired my folks' vehicle and we headed to the school. I finished my driving assessment half a month prior to joining BI.

***

I observed Captain Lewis on Big Side watching a cricket match. It was a fine,

radiant day and the green, all around kept grass appeared the whites of the cricketers; an extremely English scene. He was sitting in a rocker and I went dependent upon him. Despite the fact that I had left the school, there were butterflies in my stomach.

He said, "I hear you excelled on the "Dara", Tew."

"Thank you, sir," I answered and continued, "I'm told you assembled the entire school and called me a liar, saying that there was no harassing on the "Chindwara". I guarantee you, sir, that all that I said was true."

"Goodness, I trust you, Tew, however that isn't the point. The great name of the Merchant Navy was in question, taking everything into account, and for the benefit of everyone I needed to scotch the rumours."

I checked out him in dismay. "We were educated here at Pangbourne to be straightforward and honest regardless, yet you were ready to lie and darken my name for the purported great of the Merchant Navy."

"Indeed, and great day to you." He finished the conversation.

I could scarcely trust my own ears and left in a condition of shock. Chief Lewis RN Retired had quite recently subverted what I thought the ethos and educating and character working of the Nautical College, Pangbourne, was about. Toby nearly questioned me. I had no dealings with the school for north of thirty years, not so much as a letter. Today is an altogether different spot from all records - well it would not have made due assuming it had not changed.

We feasted at the Swan Inn and I drove Toby back to Sandbanks, which is only the opposite side of Bournemouth. It being exceptionally late when we showed up, I went through the evening and slept late. I was not famous when I returned the vehicle to my folks; they needed to recruit a taxi to take my most youthful sibling to school.

AFTER DARA: 1962-1964

My survivor leave was soon finished and I traveled to Calcutta to join a boat of which Henry Severs was the expert. He was boss official of the "Chindwara" on my first outing so I was not really in quite a while decent books! The drive in from the air terminal was a culture shock, even later Bombay, the destitution was miserable. The Hooghly River ran quick and brown yet I didn't see it. I fell debilitated and was hospitalised.

The Woodlands Nursing Home was to be my home for more than two months. For part of the time I was in a state of unconsciousness and I had both a day and a night medical caretaker to care for me. I was cognizant when my bladder wouldn't work and the lady utilized a catheter without grease or sedative. I shouted in misery. It didn't work and she said I would need to be worked on. I was in sadness later my two weeks in a state of unconsciousness and truly scared. The little night nurture brought things into her hands. She put me in a hot shower where my water works began to work again and there were no more issues. I was soon recuperating and when I was released I joined the "Okhla". I never realized what wasn't right with me.

The "Okhla" was docked in Kidderpore Dock and she was old. She was a five-incubate freight transport with split convenience, driven by a steam all over motor. There were two holds forward of the officer's accommodation and saloon; another hatch number three; then the engineers' cabins surrounding the engine and boiler room; with another two hatches aft for and five. The cadet's lodge was on the port side at the forward finish of the architect's convenience; outside, inside 2 feet of the finish of the top bunk, was an open steam winch. At the point when it was working, the entire lodge shivered and shook, the commotion making discussion nearly impossible.

Peter Thomas was the other cadet and he was higher ranking than me. At the point when I showed up ready I was stunned to think that he is sitting in the lodge in his clothing, however any traveler transport thoughts were immediately dissipated. The boat was hot as damnation and it was the stature of the South West storm, so it was hot as well as wet and tacky as well!

Peter Thomas – whose guardians worked in Rhodesia – was a great chap, and we managed everything well together. Skipper Elson from the "Dara" had taken over as the expert however was quiet and removed. His significant other was with him. Donald, the main official, was a short perky Australian yet being the lesser cadet I had little dealings with him from the start. The subsequent official was a huge, happy fellow

and we managed everything well together. I used to drink illicit brew with him. The third official was a tall, slender man called Ricky, who some of the time drank extensive amounts of liquor and was somewhat of a wild kid shorewards. At the point when he was drinking I here and there got roped in as a drinking companion.

Calcutta was a city of fierce differences: vomited destitution close by extensive abundance; ghettos close by forcing pilgrim structures. The roads were overflowing with individuals and cabs without any brakes. The waterway was occupied with a great deal of nation make traffic continually going with the tide, the ones loaded up with blocks were particularly weighty to clear when there was no wind. There were heaps of little paddling boats shipping individuals forward and backward across the quick running sloppy river.

At specific seasons there was a drag – like the Severn bore in England – when an immense tsunami came thundering up the waterway on the start of the flood clearing all before it. Assuming that the specialist had any sense any BI boat would be securely restricted inside a dock.

The Calcutta Swimming Club – Europeans just – was a social place. I once saw a gigantically hefty man in the changing rooms being dressed by his kid and thought that was the lifestyle choice, truly being looked out for hand and foot!

We left Calcutta for Rangoon in Burma. The Irrawaddy River was nearly pretty much as fascinating as the Hooghly yet not close to as long. There were still some old European Hooghly pilots left with their own conveyors and cook, however in Burma every one of the Europeans had gone and the pilot was Burmese. We secured to floats in the stream and started stacking rice for Mauritius.

We were in Rangoon for about a month and took a full burden. Peter and myself were put on freight watch and at whatever point freight was being stacked from the scows close by, one of us was on the job. The significant thing about rice was to ventilate it appropriately and it was our particular obligation to ensure the stevedores didn't hold back on putting the wooden box ventilators at normal stretches among the bags.

Our other primary obligation, aside from being at hand and watching out for everything, was to put the electric lights for freight work around evening time and watch that the stevedores didn't crush them. When working freight there was constant commotion from the open steam winches – slow, when hurling up a heap on the association buy between two derricks; and quick and shaking as the heap was permitted to drop into the hold or the vacant sling put over the side into the barge.

Even however the "Okhla" was just a freight transport without any travelers, there was appropriate silver assistance in the cantina. We needed to change into clean whites before dinners and to be on schedule. We ate at our own table, clean white decorative liners and napkin.

The shore-going dispatch was driven by steam. There was a smaller than normal message right up the alley which the coxswain used to move. *Ding and the steam motor would go on; ding and it would be halted; and ding ding would be toward the back.* The boat had been worked before the First World War, however was as yet in amazing running order.

Rangoon – confined from the world for a really long time – was exceptionally run down, the wonderful frontier structures in a condition of decay and exposed of paint. The old Strand Hotel more likely than not been wonderful in its day yet was currently a shell of its previous magnificence. All things considered, you could get cold beer.

The Mission to Seamen claimed a club house out on the lakes which was minimal utilized. I convinced the padre to allow me to take out the cruising boat they claimed – with the boatman – and went through numerous a glad evening time cruising in the blistering sun longing for the Solent and Thorns Beach.

I visited the glorious Shwedagon Pagoda with its very shocking perspectives over the Irrawaddy River, and the encompassing fields sparkling in the fieriness of the sun. The higher I climbed, the better the view, and at the top the gold leaf on the pagoda sparkled and sparkled in splendid sunshine.

The old "Okhla" could just oversee 11 bunches most extreme – all things considered, say 10½ – be that as it may, profound loaded, she drew an agreeable wash on the waterway banks when we withdrew down stream. When clear of the sloppy waters and solid tides of the delta, we steamed through the unmistakable blue ocean in fine climate to Mauritius. Peter and I were put on span watches with the officials, which I completely delighted in. I stood the eight to twelve with Ricky taking a sun sight in the first part of the day and working out the early afternoon position subsequent to shooting the sun at its pinnacle. The night watch hauled somewhat on the sea journey, however Ricky for the most part gave me a lager at 12 PM in his lodge. He weeped over his destiny that he was on anti-microbials and couldn't drink – the aftereffect of a wild night shorewards. He before long compensated for it whenever he was relieved! Any off the clock time was spent considering on the grounds that Captain Elson anticipated that we should be in the know regarding our correspondence courses.

Mauritius was an excellent island in the Indian Ocean, south of the equator, pristine and remote from the world. There was no air terminal, so the main method for transport to the island was by transport. With the gift of Captain Elson, no

question supported by his significant other, a party was held in Port Louis on board the boat. A many individuals turned up and the cadets were permitted to join in. Every one of the officials and ourselves were adroitly wearing 'Red Sea rig' – long blue uniform pants, white shirt with epaulets and cummerbund. The end result of the party was that the cadets and officials were welcome to go through the end of the week at the place of one of the visitors on the opposite side of the island around the ocean. I was one of the fortunate ones to go and spent an ideal end of the week swimming and celebrating. I became hopelessly enamored with the girl of the house yet it was to no end. I compared with her for certain years and sent Christmas cards for some more, however it turned into an uneven affair.

***

We left Mauritius in counterweight for East Africa. The Indian group would not perfect the hold bilges, so Donald requested Peter and I to do it. What a task it was! The bilges were loaded with aging rice which must be uncovered, alongside the greatest cockroaches I have at any point found in my life. Assuming you remained on the enormous ones they would convey you a couple of yards prior to capitulating. The smell was overwhelming and I was happy when we wrapped up. What a difference - eating our suppers wearing clean whites served by our boy!

On the East African journey we went on the 'nut' run. I don't know whether it was so named on account of the freight we conveyed (cashew nuts) or the psychological condition of individuals on board!

Captain Elson left the boat, Donald was advanced acting expert and I was advanced acting third official. I was 18, being paid as an official, and subtly exceptionally pleased with myself. Peter was moved to a home line transport for leave thus passed up a great opportunity. The following time I saw Peter was a few years after the fact. He was in medical clinic in the United Kingdom and his head was shaven. He was incapacitated all down one side and couldn't play his guitar appropriately or scarcely talk. The cerebrum cancer from which he endured had been worked on and he went through radiation therapy, however it had left him somewhat disabled. He recuperated enough to fly out to Rhodesia however fell down and died on the landing area before his parents.

***

I delighted in being third official, and the acting second official loaned me a couple of epaulets. On the coast we stacked a full freight of nuts for India, the last port being Mombasa. Notwithstanding my deck watch I needed to make the freight arrangement and it must be prepared before we cruised, so cruising day was a frenzy. It was a help to be once again adrift and standing the eight to twelve watch all alone, the elderly person possibly being on the scaffold assuming there was a gust or one more boat on a

consistent bearing.

We released every one of the nuts in Cochin and another skipper joined so I returned to being a cadet, which was very little fun. In Bombay I was moved to the deck traveler transport "Kampala", so starting my long excursion home for the "Dara" enquiry.

The "Kampala" was around 10,000 tons gross and conveyed a little more than 1,000 travelers – the deck travelers all having bunks. There were a lot more first and second class.

Together with the "Karanja", the boats ran a month to month administration from Bombay by means of the Seychelles which didn't have an air terminal, to East Africa, ending at Durban in South Africa. They were the fundamental connection between the two mainlands before the coming of air travel killed them off. The three journeys I made were extremely lovely during the fine climate of the North East storm. Time in port, aside from Bombay and Durban, was short to keep up the mail plan. In Durban, Garner Lynham – the sibling of Jock Lynham, dean of the Dragon – used to take me out. He had been an orange manor proprietor yet was currently retired.

In Mombasa I joined the home line 12-traveler transport "Chilka". Why the home line ships were so not quite the same as Eastern assistance I don't have a clue, yet they were. Everybody was substantially more unsettled, cadets were to be kept in their place and there was little fraternization with the officials. I was senior cadet and the main official was a smaller than usual martinet. The expert was 'Granny' Vincent who was quite pleasant.

In Tanga the other cadet and myself employed a vehicle and drove for a day up country, which was fun and invigorating. The journey home was harsh in the Mediterranean and we painted the cantina one night off the shoreline of Portugal.

The "Dara" enquiry was held in London and the disaster area magistrate was Porgies. Gerald Darling was the QC addressing BI. On the day I was to give proof my dad accompanied me to London. I was very nearly nineteen years of age however it was an overwhelming encounter to sit up there before a many individuals and answer inquiries regarding the misfortune and what I did or didn't do.

After the enquiry I traveled to Calcutta and joined the "Bulimba" – a new, quick, present day, cooled freight transport on the India-Australia run. I was the senior cadet, which I enjoyed, and interestingly adrift indeed in my life, involved my own lodge. or then again room. Irene Theabold, a first cousin, used to live in India and she had given me a prologue to the executive of Metal Box. His enchanting Indian spouse used to welcome out to formal evening gatherings and

dance evenings at the Tollygunge Club, an exceptionally prevalent club right external Calcutta.

The Gemmels used to welcome me out for cruising at the Barrackpore Sailing Club where we cruised Enterprises on the Hooghly. It was believed to be perilous to fall in the Hooghly in view of dead bodies, thus cruising had just barely begun and was for the more strong. Nobody appeared to experience any evil impacts of an upset. I some of the time actually dealt with a sail in Rangoon yet the mission boat turned out to be exceptionally run down with no maintenance.

We were typically not extremely long in Penang or Port Swettenham, where we got palm oil in the profound tanks. It was the cadet's responsibility to ensure the profound tanks were perfectly spotless and to screen the temperature during the journey. In Singapore I used to go out with Peregrine Bruce whose guardians lived in Lymington and whose father was a notable yachtsman. He had a MG sports vehicle, which was enjoyable. On the Australian coast there were parties in Perth, Adelaide, Melbourne and Sydney – the young ladies typically from the nearby medical clinics – and a boozy, hot time was had by all!

I was cheerful on that boat. I played extension with the commander, AB Stephens; the central official, Mr Fullager; and the third official. I drank whisky with the other two while the third mate was a teetotaller. It was a wonderful raced to be on, the boat was very new, I really focused in, and life was pretty good.

My ocean time for second mates was practically up and I joined the home

line transport "Woodarra". There was a similar frightening contrast between home line and Eastern assistance. She was an exceptionally quick boat – a greatest speed of 20 knots
– worked for the fleece exchange, however it was anything but a cheerful journey, and I was happy to get off in London. I had been away from England for well north of a year so was happy to be once again at Thorns and meet my family.

SECOND MATE'S TICKET

I went to the School of Navigation at Warsash to read up for my subsequent mate's authentication. Warsash was on the opposite side of Southampton Water from Thorns Beach, so was extremely advantageous for me. I went through the ends of the week Ocean Racing on "Daiquiri", a Nicholson 36 skippered by Nicholas Edmiston, who was more youthful than me. I was 20 that summer.

On the Lyme Bay race, running back from the imprint under spinnaker in thick climate, there was a cry at hand, "Breakers ahead!"

"Luff!" I yelled and ran on deck.

I was the pilot and understood that it was the tide race off Portland Bill. We cruised round it, having dropped the spinnaker and carried on to the completion. It had been a disturbing moment.

Nineteen 65 was a Fastnet year and Nicholas entered. The group – we were all novices back then – was essentially upset having cruised all late spring together, so it was with high expectations when we got going from Cowes. My senior sibling, Donald, was cruising with Ren Clarke in one of the Quivers and I figured he may effectively be the victor. I was as yet the pilot and took my sextant with me – the times of GPS were in the far off future. We finished a decent 6th in our group, having been the most youthful team ever in the Fastnet, and that was the last Ocean Race I participated in. I guess conditions plotted against me taking part again and, to be totally honest, much as I partook in the season dashing with Nicholas, my heart was not in it. I favored cruising.

I passed every one of the assessments for second mates, incorporating my orals with the impressive Captain Freaker. I was a certified official in the Merchant Navy at 21 years old, and very satisfied with myself.

***

BI was a withering organization, just like the entire British Merchant Navy – not that I understood it at that point. As its name suggested BI was restricted with India thus, as the Indians utilized their 'autonomous' muscles and began growing their own armadas, organizations like BI declined. I don't think the board was exceptionally astute in searching out new exchanges.

Assuming the Greeks could do it I don't have the foggiest idea why we were unable to have done as such, or maybe custom was so profoundly instilled they were unequipped for rolling out the extreme improvements important to make due and in the occasion they didn't, being totally consumed by P&O.

BI had 50 boats as of now, down from a general all out of 250 in its prime, yet had 250 second mates. The possibilities for advancement were not by and large great and I was excessively goal-oriented to need to stay a lesser official for quite a long time, so I kept in touch with different transportation organizations and ultimately acknowledged a proposal from Ellermans.

I flew out to Gibraltar with Captain Fairhurst and different officials and joined the "City of Oxford", a 12-traveler freight transport, on the Canada-India run as third official. The team, as in BI, were all Indian. The boat was run especially as a BI home line transport rather than Eastern assistance; junior officials were not permitted to utilize the bar or hobnob with the passengers.

We released and stacked round the Indian coast yet were changed to home line so wound up back in the UK rather than Canada. I had requested to cruise on a Canada-India run transport with the goal that I could get my ocean time in as fast as could really be expected. I needed to sit for my first mate's declaration, and leave didn't count for ocean time.

I did one more two outings as third mate to India and East Pakistan, Chalna and Chittagong on the new freight in particular "City of Worcester", joining her in Birkenhead and leaving in Liverpool. I made a UK seaside stumble on one of the enormous four, the "City of Durban", and afterward joined the "City of Poona" for an excursion to the Far East as junior second officer.

This outing truly expanded my perspectives in a bigger number of ways than one. East of Singapore was an alternate world. We called at Bangkok – that really opened my eyes in the world of the erotic! Labuan and Jesselton in East Malaysia; Sandakan and Tawau in Borneo; then to Hong Kong.

Navigating among the reefs of Borneo was fun, however most likely a bad dream for the expert. As we were going into Hong Kong a shrewd traveler transport was leaving and I figured I would wouldn't fret joining that company.

We continued to Taiwan where the clinical guidelines necessitated that a glass tube be embedded into the backside to check whether you were experiencing typhoid, or whatever illness! This incited shock among the officials, yet it was very basic – no glass tube, no shore leave. The bait of outlandish Chinese ladies won!

The outing to Hong Kong truly set me thinking. I joined the "City of London" in Avonmouth. I had been elevated to second official and my folks came up to see the boat. Chief C B Parks Bradbury was in order and he was a significant person in his own specific manner. He composed letters and articles for The

Nautical Magazine about delivery. He was short and bold with the rosy coloring that happens to great living, and experienced difficulty with his legs. What I enjoyed about him was that he let you be on the bridge.

The boat was a liner so ran quietly adrift. She had as of late been refitted to take Sir John Ellerman, the proprietor of the organization, to South Africa. Sir John was a hermit and a world expert on rodents, or so I had been told.

We cruised for India and East Pakistan, stacking a full freight of jute for the bring journey back. We as a whole buckled down managing the stacking to acquire a decent stow, perspiring down the holds in the heat.

On appearance in the UK the boat was held up by Jack Dash and his friends for quite a long time. The London docks were protesting. This finished me off as far as the UK was concerned. What was the goal in perspiring my cojones off in terrible spots like Chalna and Chittagong to get a decent turn round on the off chance that individuals like Dash could obliterate everything. I would leave the UK and work abroad; yet first I needed to get my first mate's certificate.

It was the late spring of 1965 and I had not done a lot of study since acquiring my subsequent mate's endorsement. Junior officials in those days tried sincerely and there was not a ton of recreation time, particularly on the off chance that fascinating ports like Bangkok or Keelung were visited! I really hit the books and passed. I was a certified first mate at 22 years old. I was very content with my advancement; I needed to be ace sooner rather than later.

INDO CHINA

Through the great workplaces of Sir Julian Crossley, the executive of Barclays DCO, I got a meeting with Captain Stourmont of Indo China Steam Navigation Company Limited in London. It ended up being needless excess yet not really settled to join the organization, whose traveler transport I had seen leave Hong Kong on the "City of Poonal". Skipper Stourmont acknowledged me and I marked an agreement to serve for a very long time, later which I would be given a half year home leave. Time spent sitting tight for a boat or wiped out leave didn't count, so I may be away longer than four years. I was not stressed, I would get my ocean time for aces across the board go.

Piggy was the not exceptionally complimenting epithet of the Captain of the "Eastern Star" which I joined as third mate or rather official on appearance in

Hong Kong. He was an unapproachable person who stayed away from his officials. Russ Sanderson was the main official and we managed everything well together. The boat was stacking for Australia from barges close by. Being a Jardine transport she was secured at float No 1 in the harbor - a distinction position. She conveyed 12 travelers in incredible solace, with magnificent food and administration. Officials were relied upon to associate with the passengers.

The "Eastern Star" being on a liner run kept up with dates and her timetable required a speed of 15 bunches between ports. She was a turbine-driven liner and experienced heater issues which implied there were occasional stops adrift to fix the evaporator tubes. Water was consistently an issue and some type of proportioning was typically in actuality adrift. She was cooled which was great.

We appeared to invest a lot of energy in port around the Australian coast, with consistent gatherings in a hurry, Brisbane, our first call, was typically a short-term stop which gave time to test the neighborhood brew - later Hong Kong San Miguel ready - and eat Australian steaks. There were two calls at Sydney and the boat was secured at Darling Harbor. It was just a 15-minute taxi hurry to Bondi Beach which, I'm embarrassed to say, I won't ever visit. There were various young ladies every night for the ceaseless party. I don't know Melbourne was any more steady and Adelaide didn't satisfy its strict standing. North-bound we stacked coal at Gladstone, much to Piggy's finished and utter disgust.

"We are a traveler transport not a ridiculous collier," he seethed. It was whenever a particularly modest freight first had at any point been stacked on a Jardine Australian run

transport. We released it in Nagoya later calls at Osaka and Kobe, the strength being extremely poor having stacked it toward the end in the tween decks, the boat rolled appallingly.

From Japan we cruised for Shanghai in the hold of the Red Guard Terror, presently practically neglected. There was a ceaseless torrent of socialist publicity from amplifiers shorewards 24 hours every day. Red Guards attacked and painted mottos in our convenience and our group were panicked. They were made to stoop newborn child of their examiners in the official's cantina and two were taken off and never known about again. There were some chaotic gatherings shorewards in the Seaman's Club; and a night on Chinese style champagne gave me an unfortunate cerebral pain the following day and a furious thirst.

Back in Hong Kong I was moved toward the "Eastern Argosy" as second official with an altogether different Master. Commander Sullivan participated in every one of the gatherings. The fourth mate was a live wire and he held a pilot's permit. The boat called at Port Kembla and following a the entire night party, we contracted a plane. The fourth mate flew three of us up to a little air terminal north of Sydney, where we partook in a brew and returned once more. He even let me fly the thing.

I think there was one of the enduring strikes by which the dockers held the Australian country to emancipate when the boat was in Sydney. A few companions from Beaulieu - Commander and Mrs Borthwick and their family - were positioned in Canberra on secondment from the Royal Navy, and I flew up to go through an end of the week with them. It was my first time in Canberra, a city totally unique in relation to the remainder of Australia. Emma, their most youthful girl who was around six right now, a long time later wedded my most youthful sibling. I was his best man.

In Adelaide I was analyzed as experiencing a peptic ulcer. I had been hacking up blood and not feeling 100%. No doubt stirring up a lot of repugnance for the central official the specialist said I ought not stand a watch while the boat returned me to Melbourne and a private nursing home. The central official needed to stand a watch!

I was given an agreeable private room in the nursing home, and later many tests and conversation it was chosen not to work. The specialist let me know my style of life was not the issue, it was my demeanor to life which expected to change. I was excessively upstanding, excessively tense and assuming I didn't transform I would be dead before I was 30. It was breaking news for this driven individual. How could I approach changing my demeanor to life? All things considered, I probably succeeded or I would not be composing this more than fifty years later.

The guardians of a companion of my folks in Beaulieu lived in Melbourne. The specialist concurred I could proceed to remain with them in their enormous house in Toorak on the grounds that they utilized a cook and landscaper and I would be appropriately taken care of. Woman Bassett and her cook cared for me while I was as yet in bed until I was permitted to get up and move around the house and garden.

Lady Bassett was an author and was composing a book for which I followed a guide. Sir Walter, her significant other, was the resigned administrator of Mount Isa, a noticeable mining organization. He took me cruising in his boat, drove me around the field in his vehicle and engaged me yet no liquor obviously. I was on the cart for six months.

They possessed an end of the week house on the Mornington Peninsula at the entry to Philip Bay at the head of which is Melbourne. We went through an end of the week there and I took long strolls on the nearly abandoned ocean side on the ocean side of the promontory. Two months in the wake of being analyzed I was proclaimed fit enough to work and returned via air to Hong Kong.

On appearance in Hong Kong I joined the "Eastern Maid", a little freight transport on the India-Japan run with every one of the transitional ports, including Bangkok and Shanghai. Skipper Parrish was the marine-director, and the chief was Captain Lewis. The director of Indo China was David Newbigging and the organization was possessed by the incredible Hong, Jardine Matheson. David Newbigging later became Taipan of Jardines.

It was not long later my return before I found I had joined some unacceptable organization. The organization who claimed the traveler transport I had seen was China Navigation, possessed by In any caseterfield and Swire, but, regardless, I was in Hong Kong – a live, clamoring place.

It is hard to depict the diverse inclination between Indo China and the home organizations. It is conceivable that the staff were somewhat more courageous, having put forth an attempt to leave the UK. The ethos – assuming that is the method for depicting it – was unique. We as a whole worked for the organization and were taken care of by the organization together. In home line organizations everybody appeared to be battling 'them' in Head Office, and individuals were a fanatic for rank. Not really with Indo China where Christian names were bound to be utilized than not; inconceivable in home lines.

Life on board the "Eastern Maid" was extremely charming. Full silver assistance in the cantina. With white decorative spreads and napkins and peaked silver and porcelain – regardless of no travelers. We had wine with supper consistently. Ok Soo took care of me and the third mate as it were. He managed all the domestics,

was available to come in to work night and day for cold beverages, and in port, in the event that I went shorewards, would be close by to check whether I needed anything when I returned!

She was just a little boat with four holds, two forward and two rearward, and a solitary tween deck however she was on a liner run with dates to keep. We stacked and released for the accompanying ports: Hong Kong; Singapore; Port Swettenham; Penang; Rangoon; Calcutta; Chalna; Chittagong; Penang; Port Swettenham; Singapore; Bangkok; Hong Kong; Yokohama; Nagoya; Osaka; Kobe; Shimonoseki; Shanghai; and back to Hong Kong. The boat was rarely unfilled and it took significant expertise with respect to the main official to design the freight work so each of the four holds could be worked simultaneously, and no overstowing.

I was second mate and cared for the outlines, Sperry gyrocompass, winding the chronometer and the route. I drew the seminars on the graphs and I don't recall the skipper changing any.

I was ready for north of a year with a similar boss official, commander and third mate. The group won't ever change. Ok Soo was prepared to bring me cold San Miguel brew when I was on stations rearward close to feast times. The second mate of a Ben Line transport, who was watching us compartment in front of him in Singapore, nearly fell over the edge when Ah Soo turned up wearing his white No. 10 uniform holding my lager and glass overtop on a silver tray!

If the extraordinary and suggestive young ladies of the East are known, it isn't the case simple to have wild evenings out in India and disregard Bangladesh. When the remainder of the Straits ports – Penang – was cleared north-bound, John, the central official, would spread out his Scalextric on the boat deck and since a long time ago confounded races would result when the boat was in port. The stevedore foreman would need to sit tight for a solution to his inquiry assuming that a race was on and he came up to the boat deck. There was a reasonably found chime to ring for the obligation kid to raise cold lagers to keep us invigorated during the long warm afternoons.

***

Shanghai was very little fun. The Red Guards were going out of control, clearly speakers impacted socialist publicity 24 hours every day, and there was an air of dread noticeable all around. The team were alarmed. Youthful Red Guards strutted round the boat with rifles through our convenience and there was no way to stop them. They would frequently paint trademarks in the back streets outside our lodges and the climate was totally different from my visit on the "Eastern Star." Ashore individuals checked out us yet nobody made any unfriendly move.

The Seamen's Club, with its incredible long bar, did a flourishing business in light of the fact that there was very little else to do with the exception of burn through cash in the companionship store. They were the main two spots we were permitted to visit. There was consistently a minder with us ashore.

The terrific structures along the bund were still there, though requiring a facelift, however the traffic was just bikes. I, for one, was glad to see the back of Shanghai when we left. This was the last call we made to Shanghai. The Indo China Australian run transport "Eastern Moon" was captured, the European officials beaten with rifle handles and made to destroy the British banner. It took all Jardine's impact – which was extensive – to have the officials delivered and sent back to Hong Kong, while another set were shipped off Shanghai to cruise the boat. Some portion of the arrangement was for the boat to go round the Australian coast with the motto 'Hang Wilson' painted on the side.

After a year both the captain and chief officer went on leave and life changed. Ken Millar joined as master and our nice, peaceful existence was over. I was promoted to acting chief officer at the age of 23, which I was very satisfied about, acting could be turned into permanent! However, Ken was newly promoted and very much the new broom. He had difficulty remembering that he was the captain not the chief officer, so I found life a little difficult on board. Ashore he was a genial host and some fairly extensive parties ensued – not least in Calcutta where the European stevedore manager came on board for his glass of gin for breakfast! He would take us for extensive curry dinners in the evening.

On the south-bound Hong Kong call we were up to speed in the mobs which the Gurkhas figured out. The features for me were fleeing from poisonous gas in Kowloon, winding up in some bar, and strolling through the abandoned roads of Hong Kong later time limit. It was extremely scary to hear my own footfalls, something ordinarily unthinkable in occupied Hong Kong. I paid off a bumboat to return me to the boat, and we cruised without a pilot quickly afterwards.

The following time we brought in Hong Kong I was removed the "Eastern Maid" and joined the "Ho Sang" as boss official. This was something else entirely of life and was actually a return to a pre-war presence. The boat was an old domain boat, worked for administration in the Second World War. The skipper and officials' convenience were amidships over the cantina and officials' kitchen. The specialists and group were rearward around the motor room, and the motor was an old steam up-and-killjoy. The primary distinction about this little boat was that we conveyed our own stevedores for stacking and

releasing freight in Borneo. The complete supplement on board was 99; on the off chance that we conveyed 100 we would have been compelled to convey a doctor.

On the south-bound outing the team were permitted to convey their own freight at hand, for which advantage I, as boss official, gotten a little installment; the commander a greater one. The north-bound freight was logs. The chief was 29 and I didn't see a whole lot him besides on boat's business.

Loading south-bound, albeit apparently under my watch, was finished by the Hong Kong stevedores. It was for just a few ports so was not extremely troublesome. North-bound the bosun was the stevedore foreman and he needed me far removed! I was viewed as excessively proficient on the grounds that I examined the holds double a day. There was, obviously, an obligation official on the job at all times.

In Borneo picnicking on abandoned virgin sea shores was the thing to take care of, and the bosun would never get the boat in the water adequately quick. The main steward would make up a hamper for a grill and enough cool lager for the afternoon. Here and there visitors from aground would go along with us, and a chipper time was had by all.

Sandakan and Tawau were the principle ports, with an intermittent calls at Jesselton south-bound and Bohian Island north-bound. It was a really sensual life sprinkled with an ocean journey across the China Sea to and from Hong Kong. The food on board was great, supper at 19:30 with wine and, obviously, full silver service.

The log release was round the rear of Lantau Island, so I used to live in an inn in Hong Kong or Kowloon. Now and then I remained with Graham Sneath, then, at that point, specialist general of Hong Kong.

Jardines claimed two cruising yachts – "Bandit", a Dragon; and "Jadalinka", a 30-foot cruising boat. We were permitted to recruit them for an exceptionally unassuming charge and I exploited this advantage. I went through some glad hours cruising in the waters of Hong Kong with simply the boatman as group. The yachts were kept at the Royal Hong Kong Yacht Club, of which I was a transitory part through my enrollment of the Royal Cruising Club. I met Graham at the Yacht Club and we became companions. He claimed a Chinese garbage called "Peccavi", which he kept out in garbage cove at the RHKYC club house. We went through numerous a glad day cruising and swimming and eating and drinking.

I had not been feeling very just as I generally do and at last went to the specialist. I was analyzed as having tuberculosis. I was very broken by the news thinking it was a capital punishment and was hospitalized at the

Mathilda Hospital on Hong Kong Island. The emergency clinic was arranged on the Peak with broad perspectives disregarding the back way into Hong Kong. It was over about fourteen days before I worked up the determination to ask the specialist how long I had left to live. He giggled and said to a mature age assuming I maintained good manners and took the drug endorsed. The help was very monstrous and surprisingly later 50 years I can in any case reproduce the feeling.

I was there for a considerable length of time. Chief Parrish, the marine-director, visited me consistently, for which kindness I am unceasingly appreciative. Colin De Mowbray, a lieutenant in the Navy who lived in Lymington – and whose sibling was at school with me however was unfortunately killed in a fender bender – visited. He entertained me with accounts of his runs aground in Hong Kong, including a most interesting story of a one-legged woman. Graham turned up frequently and ultimately I got authorization from the organization and the specialist to proceed to remain with him. A wedded couple resided in, cook and house kid, so I was appropriately cared for. His level was at center level with a great view over the harbor before the airport.

I was in the long run pronounced fit enough to return to the ocean yet was not permitted any liquor and was obliged to require 64 pills per day for the following three years.

H BOATS

I joined the "Hang Sang", sister boat to the "Ho Sang", on the Borneo run. The primary expert was a grim Australian and later him a complete psycho called White. I managed everything well enough with White by overlooking him!

Not really set in stone to get the record for the most logs conveyed northbound, however this was just conceivable if enough 'sinkers' – the weighty logs – were provided right off the bat in the stacking to give soundness. The last stacking was finished by lifting a log and, assuming the boat obeyed excessively, set it back in the water and tap out. I would then work out the security, ensuring we had positive soundness going into Hong Kong. On one journey I made it with the logs stacked high at hand. The main issue happened in Hong Kong. The boat was, obviously, amazingly delicate; I should think we were fortunate on the off chance that we had zero solidness, not to mention certain. Commander Parrish ventured onto the corridor simultaneously the group raised and swung out a derrick. The boat recorded and Captain Parrish considered making the plunge. He was not satisfied and reprimanded me about being untrustworthy. He later complimented me on the measure of logs we had conveyed – a record!

The logs were released and we brought the "Hang Sang" round to the harbor for stacking. The humble H boats were not secured to No. 1 float yet further down the fairway towards Stonecutter Island. There was a hurricane cautioning out and freight work halted, the canal boats all looking for cover in the get-together misery. At the point when it was clear the hurricane planned to disregard Hong Kong I proposed to Graham Taylor, the new expert, that we ought to veer out more link to the float yet he disagreed. It is clear to the most moronic that the more limited the link the more probable it is to break in terrible conditions. The more extended the link the greater the catenary, the more it lists the doubtful it is to part in the blasts assuming the boat began to reprimand. I clarified, coaxed, convinced all without much of any result. Possibly I ought to have loosened out more link on my own volition yet it would have been immediate noncompliance. I let the expert know that it was unavoidable the link would break. He consented to allow me to moor on the ground. The breeze expanded during the night to tropical storm power and afterward dropped to nothing as the eye ignored Hong Kong.

"There you are, I let you know we would be OK," said Graham priggishly during the lull.

How inept can an individual be?

"We have been fortunate," I answered. "This is the ideal opportunity to slack out more cable

before the breeze is much more grounded from the other

way." "No, she will be OK," he countered.

"You're off-base, we are in counterbalance and we will loosen up." I contended yet it was to no avail.

The breeze expanded shortly to storm power with significantly more noteworthy force than previously. We were on the scaffold paying attention to the VHF and boats were starting to drag their anchors or break unfastened. I realized it was inevitable before we did the same.

The team were terrified and Graham requested everybody to wear their life coats, which was not actually a resolve sponsor. The breeze yelled round the antiquated extension and expanded much more to a scream. The windows of the wheelhouse shook in their attachments, the glass mismatched with tape in the event that they crushed. The boat began to reprimand or jolt at the link as the ocean got up even in the sanctuary of Hong Kong Harbor. The motors were on reserve and I recommended that we steam ahead to facilitate the pressure on the link, yet I was yelling at a scared man and it was without any result. The inescapable happened and the link snapped with a bang plainly discernible over the yelling wind. The "Hang Sang" brought off like a rocket down the harbor all the way crazy, hauling the anchor I had given up. I slithered forward with the bosun. It was totally difficult to stand up in the breeze, and, some way or another, we loosened out more link until practically every last bit of it was out. Why it didn't break when the weight came on I don't have a clue, yet it didn't. I crept back to the extension and demanded that we steam gradually ahead to help the link, which Graham consented to. We were near another boat however swinging clear.

As the night drew on so the breeze gradually directed and in the sunlight we checked out our position. The pipe was practically uncovered, the point peeled off. We had floated past about six boats and it was a finished marvel we had not hit any. We later moved back to our float, the wrecked link hanging in the water. The marine director when he came installed asked me for what reason I thought we had broken loose and I told him straight.

HOMEWARD BOUND

I was expected leave yet there was a crisis and I joined the "Eastern Ranger" as boss official for the outing up to Japan. In transit we had exceptionally awful climate avoiding another tropical storm, which didn't help my nerves. I was prepared for leave. The deployment had been decreased from four years to more than two. I had served two years and ten months – time off debilitated didn't count – and I had my ocean time in to sit for my lord's certificate.

I flew down to Hong Kong and cleaned up my undertakings, including paying Hong Kong personal duty. Skillet American Airlines was the least expensive method for flying home by means of the spots I needed to see. I traveled to New Delhi and went through the night in the extremely great Ashoka Hotel. The following day I flew Royal Nepal Airways over the mountains to Kathmandu. What a difference for me to be 4,000 feet above ocean level and no ocean! Sadly, the nation was in grieving for King Mahendra had passed on and everything was closed. Fortunately the inn bar man was vulnerable to a little honorarium and I could in any case get a beverage in the bar where I met another Englishman, David Lomax, who was doing a TV thing.

The following day I recruited a vehicle and driver and was driven on the recently made street to the Tibetan line. The view was tremendous, with profound canyons and high mountains. At the boundary there was an extension and in the center was a Chinese watchman. I escaped the vehicle and approached the extension. At the point when I moved forward on to it the watchman lifted his rifle and as I drew nearer to him, he pointed it at me. I considered honor to have been fulfilled having remained on the scaffold and eased off, the watchman bringing down his rifle when I was back out and about. I got in the vehicle with driver shaking his head! He didn't talk any English.

On my last day the climate was fine and clear. I again employed a vehicle and driver and was driven as far up the closest mountain as could really be expected. I strolled further and partook in the most terrific and sensational perspective on the Himalayas extending into the distance, the pinnacles generally sparkling white in the daylight – the rough landscape actually 'streaks upon the internal eye' – and the quiet. It caused me to feel inconsequential among such normal magnificence, however a really otherworldly experience.

The trip back to New Delhi was uneven and low cloud concealed the view. I took off in a Pan American flight bound west. Around ten minutes into the air the chief of the Boeing 707 declared, "We have an electrical issue and when we have casted off the fuel we will get back to New Delhi."

A brief time later I watched out of the window and saw blazes shooting out of the starboard inward fly. I nearly froze in shock and thought my last second had come. I squeezed the ringer for the attendant and when she showed up brought up the flares. She reasonably flew back to a phone, and soon the blazes halted. The fly had been closed down.

We arrived at New Delhi with fire motors on the runway. The travelers landed onto the runway and were driven into the air terminal structure. I was a sack of nerves – the Hang Sang storm, evading the one while heading to Pusan, and presently this. I figured I could never make it home.

I addressed a Pan American attendant and asked how I could be moved to a BOAC plane I had seen sitting on the runway. She was generally excellent, telling me not to stress, everything would have been okay and negative, I couldn't transfer.

Some hours after the fact – and most likely, a small amount of fluid reward – we as a whole got on a similar plane and it took off for Rome, the electrical issue had been rectified and I was guaranteed the flares I had seen were very ordinary when fuel was being discarded. I wondered.

Rome was the main European city I remained in for very nearly three years. I appreciated strolling the roads respecting the structures – the Colosseum, St Peter's Cathedral, the Vatican – and eating Italian food. I went to the show in the monumental Rome Opera House.

While sitting in the higher up bar of the inn I was remaining at I was called to the phone and heard my senior sibling at the opposite end asking me to return home to go to the Daffodil Ball, or whatever thing. I don't have the foggiest idea how he had found me however I cut off my Rome visit and went to the Ball.

ANATINA

It was the mid year of 1968. My senior sibling Donald worked for Herbert Despard, the originator and executive of Cannon Street Investments. He was a fellow benefactor of Slater Walker, however had set out all alone and been effective. Arthur Rob kicked the bucket while planning a delightful sketch, the plan drawings being done by Robert Clark. Herbert had her implicit wood and fitted out to be a definitive cruising machine. Donald regulated the structure and acquainted me with Herbert. He requested to cruise with them to Norway.

"Anatina" was 54 feet in length with a long fall and drew 6 feet, with wooden-laid decks, poles and competes. Down beneath, the lodge was open arrangement with white settees in the cantina and a wooden-laid lodge sole. The entire impact was light and vaporous with a sensation of room.

There was a cooler – an incredible extravagance back then – single side band radio, VHF, and the principal Decca Navigator fitted to a yacht. This was before the times of present day hardware and the machine was a major boat one on enlist from Decca and required a bunch of Decca latticed charts.

She was entirely agreeable to cruise and the diesel motor gave a cruising pace of six bunches. Herbert and Minda, his better half, consistently provided the best of food and wine. It was a brilliant multi day entry to Kristiansand on the South bank of Norway. I was the pilot. We then cruised the inner leads to Oslo and back to the island they owned situated inside the outer island of Jomfruland. The closest town was Kragero reached by speed boat.

We invested some energy at the late spring house – different visitors showing up and leaving – and afterward cruised to Marstrand in Sweden, cruising back through the internal prompts the island. Herbert was a great captain and have and the yacht ran as expected with a cheerful climate on board.

I flew home to England and set off with my mom in "Mary Helen". She was 26 feet by and large with no mod cons by any means. There was a compass, a hand lead line, and I took my sextant with me. What a differentiation to "Anatina"!

MARY HELEN

We cruised down into the Bay of Biscay only south of La Rochelle under the scaffold to Ile D'Oleron winding up the trench to Marennes. We were the principal British yacht to visit the port since the finish of the conflict and we remained for three days lease free. An angler, Maurice South took me out on his boat fishing in the Coureau d'Oleron beginning at 03:00 and by 04:00 we were drinking red wine and eating shellfish, bread and cheddar. He took me to take a gander at the Pertuis de Maumusson which my mom wished to go through. We returned about early afternoon having a decent day! I told my mom, "There were incredible breaking oceans right across the entry, and pyramids of strong water jumping into the air. A bad situation for enormous or little." We didn't leave by that entry. We got back to Lymington having visited 41 spots in 47 days. She won the Royal Cruising Club Founders Cup for this cruise.

All the traipsing around on yachts was not propelling my profession, in particular acquiring my lord's testament. The time had come to return to work. I went to South Western House in Southampton – the assessment community for experts and mates – to have my ocean time checked prior to going to class. To my total awfulness I observed I was a month short, and cruising in yachts didn't count. I checked with the central inspector Captain Freaker that a beach front journey would be adequate and joined Stephenson and Clark. I went to Newcastle and tracked down the little collier

"Amberley".

This was something different again – home exchange drifting. There was the expert, me the mate, a Pakistani second mate and various team. Be that as it may, just a large portion of the group were obviously ready the boat at any one time, albeit all on the finance. At the point when I scrutinized the way of thinking of paying individuals to accomplish no work, I was told to stay out of other people's affairs! Which I did.

The expert didn't keep a watch so it was four hours on and four hours off for the Pakistani and myself. We took a full freight of coal from Newcastle – all of 2,000 tons – and released on a waterway billet so the "Amberley" took the ground at low tide.

We steamed in balance to Rotterdam, cleaning the hangs in transit for a full freight of grain to Middlesbrough. My month was up and I gathered my packs and left, considering how in the world the organization brought in any cash. It had been an intriguing encounter yet not one I wished to rehash! The Amberley was lost in a tempest 1973. "Anatina" was significantly more fun.

MASTERS

I went to the School of Navigation at Warsash, as I had accomplished for my different testaments, and really hit the books. The South Africans were exuberant individuals so I would in general blend in with them, drinking in the Silver Fern later an evening's study.

I inhabited the school, taking my suppers in the lounge area with its brilliant view over Southampton Water. Britain was altogether different from Hong Kong and appeared to be inhabited by individuals who were not quite the same as the English in Hong Kong. Perhaps it was on the grounds that everybody worked in Hong Kong there were no hand outs.

It was the principal Christmas I spent at home since going to the ocean, which was entertaining. My first Christmas away was on the "Dara" in Bombay; "Okla" in Cochin; "Bulimba" in Chalna; "City of Oxford" adrift; "City of Worcester" in Chalna; "Eastern Star" in Sydney; "Eastern Maid" in Calcutta.

I bombed the composed assessment on my first endeavor; in spite of the fact that I breezed through the singular tests I didn't arrive at the generally 70% pass mark required. I passed on my next endeavor, and orals. I was given my 'pined for' formal notice, however they would not give me my authentication until my 26th birthday celebration, I was excessively youthful. I was very happy with myself, having accomplished a goal – my
expert's. I kept in touch with Indo China to let them know the uplifting news and they composed back to illuminate me I was excess, which pricked my

little air pocket! It was spring 1969.

MY FIRST COMMAND

I kNew about somebody needing an expert for a conveyance journey. I met the proprietor or coordinator, I don't know which, and wound up as expert of a pull and three tows. The pull was lying in Portsmouth and not in her first youth, so I selected a resigned engineer administrator through a R.N. companion as the central designer to make all the difference for her. The four pulls had been offered to Italy, the three tows to be dropped off at Naples and the towing pull at Ancona. I realized nothing about towing except for learnt quickly.

The group were a collection however somebody probably known what they were doing on the grounds that the tows were manipulated, endorsed for protection, and I set off with my first order before the age of 26! The tows were close by until outside the harbor and the pilot had landed. We streamed them effectively one behind the other and set off down divert in fine climate and across the Bay of Biscay.

"We're sinking!" the anguished voice of the main specialist yelled as he ran onto the bridge.

It was a fine bright day and I had quite recently taken the morning sight. My heart halted and I projected forward to the Court of Enquiry removing my not yet gave certificate.

I quieted Jack down enough to find that water was coming into the motor room bilges. We immediately researched and I found that the water – which was salt, so ocean water – was coming from over the obvious waterline and was not continuous.

"The siphons are containing it!" I yelled over the thunder of the motor. "Indeed," he answered, offering the go-ahead signal.

"We should go at hand and remove a look."

We went from the motor room and onto the tow deck, keeping underneath the tow wire. I investigated the side at the rough spot we had seen the water and saw a scupper opening. Water was slopping onto the deck as the pull moved in the swell, yet not emerging from the scupper opening – the line was broken. It involved minutes to plug the scupper and the structure was tight again.

There were no different episodes and I effectively dropped off the three more modest tows at Naples. We had a wonderful free run round to Ancona. Nobody addressed the VHF when I showed up external the harbor, so I steamed inside and blew the whistle. It was momentous how rapidly a pilot and various authorities turned up! I berthed her close by the quay and the new proprietor gave the boss and I an excellent lunch sitting in the sun.

ANATINA

Back in England Donald was fitting out "Anatina", and Herbert requested that I go along with them for the mid year journey. It was to be somewhat more aspiring and as guide I had some good times requesting the graphs. I like British Admiralty outlines; I like checking out them and arranging where I might want to go, regardless of whether a captivating looking bay is an appropriate dock or not.

Herbert, Donald and I set off along with different of Herbert's companions for Norway and the late spring house on the island. The climate was not generally excellent and we were happy to make Kristiansand. Different travels were made along the coast, "Anatina" being abundantly respected any place she went.

Later in the late spring we cruised across the North Sea in exceptionally terrible climate. The yacht acted well in the intense conditions. Fortunately the breeze was toward the back however it was very rough.

We brought in at a fishing port unused to yachts to fix the decca. Then on up the Firth in the rain to Inverness. The Caledonian Canal is extremely lovely, even in the downpour. We cruised from Fort William to Mallaig, and afterward into a bay behind Loch Morar where Herbert had laid a securing. He claimed Morar Estate – about 10,000 sections of land of slope – with a hotel on Loch Morar. The landscape was awesome, with the heather turning, and it was exceptionally quiet. A quick arrival make was utilized to move individuals and saves the loch to Mallaig. It was a following bequest, which was not my scene, but rather it was extraordinary to walk and fish.

My dad voyaged north and went along with us for the sail south. It was late in the year and it involved avoiding the hurricanes overall quite well. It was only the three of us ready – Donald, my dad and myself. We were storm bound in Holyhead some days, even laying out the fisherman's anchor to prevent "Anatina" from dragging.

A youngster swam out to the yacht one day and I fell head over heels! She was remaining at the Fishguard Hotel and we ate there when we could get shorewards. We left among storms and got round the Lizard before the following one hit. We dashed up the channel at ten bunches, riding on the waves, simply missing the RCC meet which we needed to go to in the Beaulieu River. "Anatina", with her long fall, was entirely agreeable in the harsh weather.

I compared habitually with my American woman companion from Fishguard, yet we didn't meet again for quite a while. Later a mid year cruising the time had come to continue ahead with my profession – the following target being to acquire order as

quickly as possible. I had no desire to be at sea for the next 35 years, but I did want a command before coming ashore. Indo China was an excellent company to work for, with good promotion, a non-contributory pension and retirement after 20 years' service. If I had not been made redundant I would have retired at 43 years of age! However, I had been made redundant – no doubt being ill twice had not helped – so I knew I had t find another company. I picked Bank Line because I thought promotion would be quick.

BANK LINE

I went for a meeting at the workplaces of Andrew Weir, the proprietor of Bank Line, and was extended to an employment opportunity as boss official on one of their new ships the "Teviotbank". I joined her in Antwerp where she was stacking urea for Chittagong.

Well, I didn't know very what's in store Nonetheless I didn't realize that individuals like Captain Howe existed, I thought they were illusions of rather bent minds. He was a boisterous mouthed martinet from the earlier century, and the main redeeming quality was that his significant other was ready. I realized I was in for inconvenience not long after strolling ready. The main official I diminished couldn't get off the boat sufficiently speedy, and Captain Howe was yelling nearly when I met him. I nearly strolled off the boat without further ado prior to marking on. However, I made an examination of the boat and enjoyed what I saw so chose to 'try it out' and attempt to discover a type of convenience with the master.

The central architect was an older man and I sympathized with him. At the point when Howe urged me excessively far I blew my top and was going to assault him outside my lodge. The boss forestalled it by putting himself between us. I'm extremely appreciative to him, for assaulting a British expert on his own boat is an intense offense for sure – particularly for a main official. Notwithstanding, it had its impact and Howe restrained himself later that incident.

We released the compost at Chittagong, where I didn't go shorewards. In stabilizer it was typical for the profound tanks to be ballasted to give the boat some draft. Notwithstanding, Howe needed the profound tanks cleaned and would not yield to common sense – either from me or the boss engineer.

We went to Trincomalee totally light, with the foot of the bow practically out of the water. The pilot came ready and denounced with Captain Howe, letting him know he would not compartment the boat until there was some counterweight in her. Essentially I was justified. We carried on to

Visakhapatnam, where we stacked a full freight of iron mineral for Japan. The specialist took me out for several great curries.

While getting the ropes out of the hold before appearance in Japan, I crushed the third finger on my right hand. It was extraordinarily difficult, with a piece of the nail ripped off. Once in port I went to the medical clinic where, watched by several grinning attendants, the specialist began to eliminate the remainder of the nail. The aggravation was very unbearable however not set in stone not to shout out before the

as yet grinning medical attendants. I requested a sedative. I got it – two infusions out of the dark nail bed, which was nearly just about as excruciating as having my finger nail eliminated without it. When the pieces were taken out, he sewed up the wreck and I got back to the boat. The finger was excruciating for a really long time and the fastens were taken out, agonizingly, in Glasgow.

After the release in Japan, we cruised with the profound tanks full for Australia, where we stacked a full freight of grain for Scotland. It was whenever I first had stacked grain in a tween decker, and the utilization of feeders was fascinating. These were wooden boxes built in the tween deck and loaded up with grain, which kept the grain tight as it settled during the journey. In the event that the grain was slack it acted rather like water and the boat could wind up with negative solidness and turn over. Howe went around like something frantic yet everybody overlooked him, the Australian stevedore is an extreme nut.

The boat called at Durban for shelters and I was happy to leave her in Glasgow. The organization offered me another new boat however I said that Howe had been sufficient and left amicably.

I went to London and remained with my American woman companion. We thought we were infatuated with each other and chose to make an outing to Bronte country. She was an author and abstract leaning. At the point when she came to remain at Thorns Beach my mom put her in the Windmill, which was a decent 100 yards from the primary house so we were in discrete rooms! My folks were somewhat careful about an American.

I acquired Edward's blue MGB sports vehicle and we headed to Howarth. The initial not many days were incredible, driving round the field in a games vehicle seeing the sights, feasting and wining by candlelight, and having intercourse. I thought this is it. She requested that I wed her and I challenged right away and afterward things changed. What had been a charming pre special night relationship transformed into a calamity. I cut off the outing and drove her back to London in stony quiet. I have not seen or known about her from that day to this. What turned out badly I actually don't have a clue, however it consumed a large chunk of the day for the enthusiastic injuries to heal.

ANATINA

The late spring was coming up, "Anatina" was prepared to sail, and I was approached to explore. I had some good times purchasing the outlines for this present summer's journey. Herbert, Donald and I set off from Lymington, west about round Land's End and up the Irish Sea to Scotland. At Mallaig we bunkered and continued north through the wonderful Western Isles past Skye to Stornoway, which we entered around evening time on the radar.

The following day we set forth out into the Atlantic, with a decent figure. A couple of days after the fact the climate changed, the gauge began falling and we realized we were in for a blow whatever the figure said. The breeze expanded and we reefed. The breeze expanded more and we took in more reefs until, at last, we brought down the mainsail totally. It was at that point hard to carry on a discussion in the cockpit with the breeze wailing in the gear, the air loaded up with spume off the ocean, and the waves starting to break.

The indicator fell much further and the breeze expanded to storm power 10. We brought down the mizzen and staysail and lay a body. It was light however the perceivability was limited by highest points of the waves being brushed off, swirling around with spume. "Anatina" lay easily around 60 degrees off, the breeze lifting to the ocean. An incidental breaking peak came ready however nothing serious.

The tempest screens were put on a show house windows. Down beneath the organic product bowl stayed on the table, which had the fiddles up. Dinners were eaten in their typical style with a glass of wine. At regular intervals or so the man on watch would examine deck to see that everything was well and there were no boats, not that we were in a precisely jam-packed piece of the ocean.

The gauge tumbled to 954 millibars, which is exceptionally low for sure for summer, and the anemometer passed over the highest point of the pole in a whirlwind force 11. Donald, when cruising with Lord Riverdale, had encountered comparable climate yet "Bluebird" was in the Gulf stream off the American coast and the oceans were a lot of more awful. They had been compelled to run before it. We surely didn't wish to run since that would have removed us from our objective and "Anatina" was riding the climate astoundingly well.

We talked about existence and one or the other on the grounds that it isn't consistently one is out in a little yacht in storm conditions north of Scotland, not a long way from the Arctic Circle!

When the breeze tumbled to about power 9 we lifted a little piece of the mizzen to
keep the bow up towards the wind.

The following day the climate adequately directed to make sail and we continued our course.

"What is that shining in the daylight to starboard?" asked Donald.

We were unable to make it out, took a gander at the graph and afterward understood that it was from the four ice sheets on the Southern central area of Iceland. It was a mixing sight. Heimaey was located ahead and we headed towards the harbor, which implied directing directly at the upward precipice and afterward, without a second to spare, changing direction to port and going through the limited entry. A few years after the fact the entry was shut by a magma stream during an emission of the spring of gushing lava whose pit lies over the town.

We were exceptionally satisfied with ourselves to have made Iceland, Herbert's white ensign causing just interest. We praised close to regular, indeed, perhaps an additional a suppress of champagne!

We climbed the dark coarseness to the cavity over the town. A couple of days after the fact we cruised on to Reykjavik. The Cod War was on however once more, despite the fact that the gunboats were in port, nobody took any notification of the white ensign, with the exception of inactive curiosity.

Herbert recruited a vehicle and we cruised all over the lunar-looking scene along un-metalled streets. Whenever we were halted by the police for speeding and vowed to be great. It was totally not the same as anything I had seen elsewhere.

Herbert returned home for Minda's birthday and Malcolm, our fourth sibling, turned up. We flew up to Akureyri burning through the majority of the trip in the cockpit, including landing. This was north of the Arctic Circle. We took a visit and swam in natural aquifers, respecting the rough scenery.

When Herbert returned we cruised to Horndafjordur, passing the new volcanic island of Surtsey which just showed up in 1963 later a volcanic ejection. We were most likely the primary British yacht to pass it. A few anglers came ready and gave us a new halibut, which was very scrumptious with red wine.

We proceeded with the staggering South shoreline of Iceland and made an entry to the Faeroe Islands. My mom visited the Faeroes when she was 17 with her dad in his un-engined yacht "Emmanuel" and distributed a record Adventures in the Faeroes.

Malcolm didn't actually like the entries, being nauseous, yet he kept his watch. Bergen was the following stop and it down-poured, in sharp difference to the

heatwave we had in Iceland. Malcolm flew home and Minda joined, alongside different visitors.

We essentially motored through the inward leads in downpour to the Sognefjord where we commended midsummer's day – a most significant day for Norwegians. Different team, now and again Donald and I, took the yacht back through the inward prompts the island. The Norwegian view in the inward leads was entrancing, initially set apart for cruising ships with ring bolts in places so they could twist the boat. The view was continually changing from tough rocks to slopes and mountains, going through merrily painted, wooden house villages.

INDO CHINA AGAIN

I flew home and rejoined Indo China Steam Navigation Company Limited. The organization had a joint endeavor manage Divlov Simmerson, a Norwegian organization, by which Indo China monitored and dealt with the boat. I don't know who the proprietor was but rather the arrangement was to open sponsorships from states to assemble ships.

I headed out by ship to Denmark, train to Copenhagen and ship to Landskrona where the "Vianna" was being constructed. She was a metal oil mass transporter of nearly 100,000 tons, a long ways from the conventional Indo China transport – however the universe of transportation was evolving. Transport building isn't my strong point albeit very interesting.

I was assigned to take over as boss official once I had gotten familiar with everything on the grounds that I had never been on a big hauler. The significant thing was to gain proficiency with the funneling framework and how to load and release oil freight. To be honest, it left me stone cold however I locked in and imagined excitement. Buller Cole was the expert and had never been on a big hauler all things considered. The central official was the just one with big hauler experience, so he needed to show every one of us. It was to his greatest advantage to ensure we adapted so he could get off and go on leave.

Landskrona was a little Swedish town, with the shipyard being the fundamental manager. There was no work at the ends of the week and the town was not actually a swinging city. In any case, Copenhagen was several hours away by ship and was absolutely swinging – I saw my first sensual show with Europeans performing! There is a ton to do, historical centers to see, the Tivoli Gardens, brilliant eateries and every one of the attractions of a wonderful capital city.

Edward, who was in the military, was positioned at Osnabruck and I went via train from Copenhagen to see him and remain in the officials' wreck. It was fun and intriguing for me. We organized to meet around early afternoon on an after Saturday at Hamburg Railway Station and had a night out on the Ripa Barn, which was 'instructive'. On the train back through Germany I took out a Times to peruse and the main other inhabitant of the carriage left. The fascinating thing going via train was the train ships between the islands. There was a standard end of the week ship outing to Travemunde in East Germany, which was enjoyable. The vast majority didn't try to get off in East Germany, the principle fascination of the ship was liquor and the offices ready. It made an exceptionally charming a few days' excursion.

The boat was at long last finished, ocean preliminaries effectively finished, and we

cruised in balance for Ain Sokhna in Egypt, a terminal fifty miles south of Suez. The Suez waterway was shut so we adjusted Africa getting mail and stories at Cape town. Stacking was finished in 24 hours, an extremely escalated time for me getting acquainted with everything, and we cruised for Rio de Janeiro again calling at Capetown for mail and stores. The sculpture of Christ with arms outstretched ruled the horizon at Rio, yet there was no an ideal opportunity to go shorewards. Ambitious Ladies of the Night turned up at the release float for the individuals who had sufficient opportunity to so enjoy. They had been flown out in helicopters.

We were off inside 24 hours of showing up, destined for the Persian Gulf in counterbalance through Capetown where the specialist drew out the mail and stores in a dispatch. We experienced unpleasant climate crossing the South Atlantic and the boat flexed alarmingly, the center of the boat going all over some feet.

You are not permitted shorewards in Ras Tanura, Saudi Arabia, regardless of whether you needed to and had sufficient opportunity. The journey to Japan was ordinary and we released at a float off Yokohama. Helpless old Lee Emery was left as boss official while I went shorewards with Captain Parrish, headed for Hong Kong and the Australian run. Prior in the journey I kept in touch with the workplace saying that big haulers were not for myself and mentioned an exchange. Some time later Lee Emery got his vengeance since he wound up with the shore work I was after.

The "Eastern Rover" 4,408 gross tons was a marginally bigger freight transport than the old "Eastern Maid" 3,603 tons and along with the "Eastern Ranger", ran a month to month full circle administration from Hong Kong to Brisbane; Sydney; Melbourne; Hobart in Tasmania; Sydney; at times Newcastle; Brisbane; Cebu and Manila in the Philippines; Kaohsiung and Keelung in Taiwan; and back to Hong Kong. The accomplishment on this run, with its tight timetable, was to load and release at the same time. For example, in Hong Kong one stacked for every one of the ports while releasing freight stacked for Hong Kong at different ports. It required extensive expertise with respect to the central official to accomplish this without over-burdening or over-conveying and was a test. An intermittent Australian strike tossed the timetable out with resulting issues for the freight work. The boat was run in the standard Jardine style and was much more fun than big haulers. I managed everything well with George Taylor, the chief, who was exceptionally friendly and had loads of companions around the Australian coast. I saw some Stawell cousins in Hobart and time elapsed very pleasantly.

All beneficial things reach a conclusion and I flew home for some leave and afterward joined the "Eastern Saga" in Antwerp. She was a dry mass transporter. Buller Cole was the expert and Don B was the main designer. I did a roadtrip with Don to see the delightful city of Brussels. We stacked a steel freight for Houston, Texas.

The "Eastern Saga" was a mass transporter of 40,000 tons, five seals served by cranes. It was one more joint endeavor this time with Wah Kwong, a Hong Kong Chinese possessed company.

In Houston I employed a vehicle, played golf and considered much as I could of the States, it being my first visit. We stacked urea in Pascagoula, Alabama, and Baton Rouge up the Mississippi, empowering us to visit New Orleans kindness of the charterers. We went the entire night in the bars paying attention to jazz and wound up in Tiffany's for a champagne breakfast.

Anchored outside Chittagong easing up transport was a healthy change yet the climate was great. The release of the free manure for Bangladesh was finished close by, yet Chittagong was not Calcutta.

We cruised in weight to Bangkok to stack a full freight of manioc for Europe. Both Buller and I had kept in touch with the workplace groaning and moaning about the new boat in spite of Don's expression, 'Assuming you can't take a joke you shouldn't come to sea!'

I got a letter from David Newbigging, the director, clarifying how the old Indo China was being joined onto the new Wah Kwong. The genuine article was that I would rather avoid the settling for the status quo, nor did Buller. The chief of Jardine Agency took us out and attempted to convince us to remain yet it was without any result. I stayed with the boat to Rotterdam, where Donald turned up with a vehicle to take me home with my gear. I quit smoking. Thus at long last finished my experience with Indo China, one of the most established British delivery organizations established in 1832 to exchange among India and China. They had probably the best trimmers of their day and, with the coming of steam, exchanged all round the China coast and up the Yangtze. Their introductions to slog transportation as the conventional liner exchanges collapsed up eventually fizzled and Indo China is no seriously being sold in 1974.

SHORE JOB

This was to be my keep going year cruising on "Anatina". Herbert, Donald and I left Lymington and had a quick entry across the Bay of Biscay. Brilliant daylight and a reasonable breeze down the Portuguese coast before long had us in Lisbon examining new sardines and drinking vinho verde the light white wine. Herbert employed a vehicle and we saw the sights and ate at the best restaurants.

During the excursion Herbert and I had talked away, ordinarily around evening time. I clarified that I had left Indo China and why, and was considering what to do. He said that he had an attorney companion who was searching for an expert sailor to join his firm. I communicated interest. Herbert called Robert Elbourne and I traveled to London for a meeting held in the City Club. I acknowledged the bid for employment and flew back to Lisbon later a decent lunch in the Club.

Herbert flew home and Edward joined Donald and me. We made a decent entry to the Azores. In transit Donald had done something to the siphon. While siphoning the bilges one day they began to fill. Nobody could comprehend that the quicker we siphoned the quicker the water came in, I truly thought we planned to sink. Nonetheless, when we quit siphoning the level continued as before. When the valve was turned round completely was well, however it gave us all truly a turn!

The Azores were exceptionally wonderful; Edward went off and Herbert returned. We motored a decent arrangement of the way to Falmouth, where we bunkered and carried on to Kristiansand. I flew home to London and a new position, and a better approach for existence with Elbourne Mitchel.

Being a lesser legitimate colleague rather than boss official – with every one of the domestics dealt with – was a major leap. I needed to coordinate washing my own garments, looking for food, and cooking. I surrendered and ate out. Furthermore I had an hour's drive every way in the underground, which I detested. I recruited a room in a mews level possessed by Gilian Green, whom I had met on "Anatina".

I preferred the work. Robert Elbourne, elated and certain, was senior accomplice and I worked for him to begin with. The firm well versed in marine work and had a wide range of intriguing sea clients.

Robert followed the floor at Lloyds for work. Stephen Mitchell was the other senior accomplice yet I never truly got to know him. Dennis Rixon was the whizz kid at taking proof on every marine matter: crashes; rescue; fires; and any kind of oceanic hazards. I got to realize him very well indeed. Beam Clarke

worked with Whitehouse Vaux in a different office and they worked for the Indonesians. Burglarize Wallis was a laid back, golf-playing articled agent; while anxious, pestered Keith Barnes did all the back up work for Rixon. Nicholas Burke had practical experience in sanction party work, while Richard Shaw did marine work.

The covered workplaces were at Three Quays on the highest level, with a view sitting above HMS Belfast. I was fortunately given an office sitting above the stream and used to watch what little waterway traffic there was, some of the time longing for the jungles when the downpour was pouring down on a colder time of year's day. There was an unmistakably daggy bar across the street where we once in a while congregated. Lunch was regularly eaten in El Corvinos, a costly underground café close by.

I got acquainted with everything by being engaged with the cases. Ultimately I wound up ostensibly working for Richard Shaw, however enjoyed a decent arrangement of my experience with Dennis Rixon – sadly, a ton of it in the pub.

The primary case I was shipped off all alone on was the rescue of the Woolwich ship by a Brathwaite and Dean pull. Private accommodation to assertion was concurred and I arranged the papers, having taken photos of the space which improved our case. Mr Braithwaite was not discontent with the result.

A significantly more troublesome case included a boatyard debate in Devon. I remained in an inn in Torquay and met our customer in his home. One more case in Devon included the rescue of a fishing boat – we represented the insurer.

I headed out up to Middlesbrough with Rob Wallis for an impact. Our customers were the Poles. Dennis Rixon was ostensibly in control yet he remained in London. In the wake of taking proof for around six hours I had a meeting with Rob and we understood that the case didn't make any sense. Instantly of understanding I understood that, for the crash to have happened by any means, our boat probably been making harsh way. We plunked down and retook all the proof. The one thing I learned was that assuming you lack reality from your customer, but awful, you have no case.

On one more case we headed out up to Felixstowe where a holder transport had thumped a compartment crane into the water. One of Richard Shaw's cases included a crash in the waterway while heading to Antwerp. I arranged the nitty gritty graph from the proof of the impact for the preliminary. It was generally fascinating to go to the court and pay attention to the proof and addressing or cross examination of the observers. Little did I figure I would wind up in the court

myself one day blamed for misrepresentation!

Elborne Mitchell represented Selco Salvage in Singapore. Robert Elborne was the accomplice in control however Dennis Rixon accomplished the work and overhauled the customer. He believed Selco to be his pet child and desirously watched his fix. Keith accomplished the jackass work. Dennis invested a significant energy in Singapore however was in London for the majority of the assertions. I used to go to some of them with him and Keith. I turned out to be exceptionally inspired by rescue, in the long run arriving at the resolution that it would be amusing to be a salvor.

Dennis Rixon was not a simple individual to work with and now and then was tremendously undesirable, so disagreeable that I would have rather not work with him. He could be beguiling when he needed to impress.

I regularly worked really hard in the workplace when Dennis was visiting the area, sending messages for him – basically to Singapore. The time contrast implied that Singapore opened similarly as London was shutting. Later 18:00 in the workplace there was ordinarily a jug of wine to make all the difference for us. A stroll across the road into the daggy bar for the last one for the street regularly implied I didn't return to the mews level until 21:00, excessively late to begin cooking. Dennis more likely than not got back in Bromley significantly later, which couldn't have been a lot of good times for his wife.

I returned home most ends of the week to Thorns Beach and was happy to escape London, however I detested the profit from Sunday night. I might have had a significantly more dynamic public activity however reserves were tight and, at 30 years old, it was embarrassing.

I cruised with various new companions on certain ends of the week in the late spring of 1973, when driving down to Hamble with a youthful advodate in his Bristol.

Donald lived in London in the colder time of year and I at times met him in the Royal Ocean Racing Club rooms in St James. One evening I met Norvella and I fell head over heels. Donald left and I ate with her in her level in Westminster. We saw a ton of one another and I requested that she wed me however she said, "You are too juvenile, return a few years' time."

About a year In the wake of joining the firm, Alan Bond, the Selco supervisor, was in London and I organized to have a meeting with him during an end of the week. Herbert Despard loaned me his Volvo. I headed to Dungeness and observed the bar where I met Mr Bond, a tall aloof man. Right up 'til the present time I don't have the foggiest idea why the bar at Dungeness was picked for the meeting since Bond was remaining in London. He drove down in a contracted Ferrari. I was appropriately met and extended to an employment opportunity as boss official on the new pull Selco had purchased in Japan. I

acknowledged. Dennis Rixon was by all account not the only justification behind needing to leave London. My compensation was derisory contrasted with that of boss official and I was living on my reserve funds, however these had gone up the spout with some awful stock trade speculations. Truth be told, I owed large chunk of change to the bank.

I more likely than not dropped out with Gilian in light of the fact that the last month I spent in London was on my Mastercard, living in an inn in Green Park, expanding my obligation to the bank. It was with blended sentiments I left London. Robert Elbourne had been excellent to me and urged me to become qualified while Dennis Rixon was dead against it. I understood later that he thought of me as a danger to his position and was happy to dispose of me.

I took off to Singapore and a totally new life.

NEW LIFE SALVAGE. SALVALIANT

I showed up in Singapore throughout the late spring of 1974 and it was hot and moist. I was set up at the Orchid Inn on the Bukit Timah Road. I showed up at the workplace out at Jurong – around 45 minutes' drive from the lodging – wearing a tie and coat. I before long understood my mistake.

No one appeared to be exceptionally inspired by me so I meandered around the shipyard for, aside from pulls and barges, Selco possessed a yard and slip. Tony Church, an ex-sailor, showed compassion for me and loaned me a vehicle for half a month to cruise all over and 'learn' Singapore. Being the showcasing man he generally wore a tie however no coat. Ultimately I was given little responsibilities to take care of including ocean preliminaries of two little pulls the yard assembled which was interesting.

Captain Peter Lankester showed up with the 'new' pull. She was an old Japanese pull driven by two motors coupled to a solitary shaft. Moving was done on one motor and to stop the propeller, the motor must be halted, huge boat style. The "Daisy," 993 gross tons, length 186 feet, and draft 15 feet, fueled by two Burmeister and Wain motors totalling 4,600 demonstrated pull giving a speed of 15 bunches. was to be totally refitted at Selco Shipyard.

Peter, being a most experienced pull ace, knew precisely what he needed done – paying little heed to discount. She was renamed "Salvaliant." The refit was to require months and I lived in the inn, going to the pull every day with Peter.

Peter Lankester was a major, weighty, brawny, extreme Dutchman with a kind nature. It was blistering in Singapore – being practically on the equator – so lunch was typically at the swimming club, joined by a couple of brews to supplant all the perspiration lost during the morning! The equivalent in the evening returning to the hotel.

Peter lived in a level on the opposite side of the city with his significant other, Unke, and their two kids, Peter and Caroline. At ends of the week I would once in a while go for barbecues.

Knobby Halls, a resigned maritime negligible official, was the architect director. Truth be told, he served as marine-director too. He was a rational competent man who finished things and was tremendously useful and strong to me. He and his significant other, Anne, resided in a level at Sembawang, the maritime base, and when I improved I used to proceed to remain for a night from the tug.

Ernie Kahlenberg, a more seasoned man, was the live wire – the dynamo of Selco –

and he appeared to fancy me asking me out for Sunday lunch and to visit his home to meet his better half, He used to show up at the workplace in a major escort driven vehicle; a humble little man sitting toward the back – his white, rather scanty, hair only apparent through the back window. He was the administrator and overseeing chief and claimed the company.

One evening I got a call from Selco's activity room. We were all on pagers when away from the workplace or pulls. A van would get me and take me to the workplace. In the activities room I was told to go with the "Salvana" and her Filipino expert, Captain Hannibal, and tow in a boat from the Malacca Straits.

The "Salvana" was the first 'enormous' Selco pull of somewhere in the range of 2,500 HP and Peter had been in order. This was my first work and I was exceptionally energized. The "Salvana" was in the shipyard and it was close to low tide so required a little pull to tow her out. We didn't need any harm to the propeller. When clear of the yard Captain Hannibal, having acquired authorization from port control, steamed west at max throttle through Western Anchorage and into the Malacca Straits. In Singapore nobody moved in the port without consent except if they needed a single direction outing to Changi prison. Some other rescue pull in Singapore would screen the VHF and realize that a Selco pull had cruised. What they would not know was whether or not it was a rescue cruising.

The ocean was quiet in the Malacca Straits – Indonesia to port, Malaysia to starboard – and it was a fine evening. There was the standard traffic in the waterways, the primary passage to Japan: loaded big haulers from the Persian Gulf; holder ships from Europe; and little fishing boats from the two sides. The pull appeared to be tiny contrasted with the boats I had been on yet her 12 bunches appeared to be a lot quicker being so near the water.

I preferred not to concede to Captain Hannibal – an extremely experienced rescue pull ace – that I had no rescue insight in spite of the fact that I had towed the minesweepers to Italy. I presume he knew in any occasion in light of the fact that there was a very decent hedge transmit in Selco, particularly among the Filipinos.

I went onto the tow deck to watch the group setting up the towing gear. The 'setback', as a boat in trouble is known in the rescue world, was secured around forty miles north of Singapore. It was around 02:00 toward the beginning of the day when we contacted her. Tasks had given me the position.

Captain Hannibal remained by the secured transport while I went across in the elastic boat. A wooden pilot stepping stool was brought down and I got energetic about a Lloyd's Open Form in my pocket. I was taken to the scaffold and met the

ace, a Korean. I offered him the structure. He realized we were coming and consented to sign. I filled it in and we both marked. I was massively satisfied, it was my first Lloyd's Form – the no fix, no compensation contract that salvors work on.

I called up the "Salvana" on the versatile VHF with Selco's private frequency.

"LOF marked. You can come close by and interface up, Captain," I talked into the radio. "Illuminate Ops."

"Roger, Cap," came the answer through the speaker. Skipper Hannibal didn't squander words.

The loss was stemming the tide, that is bow to the tide. To make the association effectively and rapidly it was fundamental for Captain Hannibal to bring the "Salvana" close by in the 69 position, that is the harsh of the pull to the bow of the loss. He needed to come close by with the tide behind him – not a simple move with a solitary screw pull – and, to stop the propeller turning, the motor must be halted. Skipper Hannibal did it very well with the group of the setback taking the lines. The "Salvana" team before long had the towing gear associated up. I educated the expert of the setback to hurl up his anchor and stayed forward with the two "Salvana" riding crew.

"Anchor is aweigh," I told Captain Hannibal on the radio. "Remove her."

"Let go above and beyond," I trained the riding crew.

When the lines were pulled in the "Salvana" manoeuvered clear of the loss, going to starboard and steaming ahead to initiate the tow. At the point when I saw the towing gear was all together I went to the extension and stayed there with the expert. The riding group lubed the fairlead at customary spans to secure the tow wire. The boat followed the pull very well.

At the pilot station Captain Hannibal moored the "Salvana" while the Immigration and Customs conventions were finished and with a pilot ready, gotten the anchor and continued the brief distance in to Western Anchorage.

I was on the forecastle of the setback when the towing gear was slipped and the anchor let go. The expert marked the end letter and I got back to the "Salvana" in the elastic boat. The sun appeared to be sparkling especially brightly.

Captain Hannibal took the "Salvana" back to the yard where – exceptionally satisfied with myself – I took the LOF to Ops, just to be informed that Chris Herbert had

concurred an agreement tow. So much for my first LOF and rescue reward. What's more I had kept such great notes as well!

The "Salvaliant", ex "Daisy", was secured close by the yard; a wide range of shipyard gear at hand – pipe, pieces of metal, all the typical confusion of a boat under refit. Peter got the word that there was a boat ashore on Nipa Shoal and the "Salvaliant" was needed.

"Hoffre Domma!" he shouted. "How would they anticipate that we should move this load of trash away, take a gander at all the garbage on deck."

But inside the hour the "Salvaliant" was in progress to Nipa Shoal. The Shoal is right inside Indonesian waters with a light kept up with by the Indonesians, which implied it was out as regularly as it was lit. Nipa Shoal was dedicated 'Selco treasure island' due to the quantity of boats Selco salved there.

The team and I worked like frantic things to get the towing deck and stuff prepared. We were practically prepared when we arrived at Nipa, about an hour's steaming from the yard. I sadly seriously curved my lower leg on one of the lines on the tow deck so lashed it up and wore a couple of boots. It was three months before I could take the wrap off, however it didn't stop me working – it was excessively invigorating. Peter just advised me to be more cautious in future and gave me a cold beer.

The "Frederich Engels", an advanced East German freight boat of exactly 11,000 gross tons, was practically helpless on the reef. She was in weight and had gone on solid land at maximum speed accepted to have been 22 bunches.

Peter secured the "Salvaliant" nearby and sent me across in the elastic boat to discover what was happening. I observed Captain Hancox, the rescue ace, with the skipper of the boat. Commander Hancox was a slender, gloomy person who was for truly composing – filling his journal in slick dark print. He talked in a one tone Australian voice. Peter could have done without him which was the reason I had been sent across. Commander Hancox let me know that the LOF was marked and the "Salvaliant" ought to be associated as fast as possible.

I was thrilled and was back on the "Salvaliant" as fast as could be expected. Great versatile radios were costly and weighty back then and Selco just had a set number. We were almost certain our primary adversaries tuned in to our private recurrence thus, until a rescue contract was marked, the radios were utilized as little as possible.

"Hoffre Domma!" shouted Peter on the extension of the pull, opening a virus jar of brew and passing me one.

It was blistering and the sun was sparkling brilliantly. He continued to disclose how he expected to associate. I was to sound round the harsh of the setback, which was as yet in the water. He would secure the "Salvaliant" as close as could be expected, send away a courier connected to a securing line joined to the towing stuff, and I would hurl it in ready the grounded transport utilizing the capstan. The pelican snare – an immense, fast delivery snare – and its wire strap would be taken across to the setback in the elastic boat and I would hurl it up at hand utilizing the boat's capstan toward the back. I would make it quick cycle one bunch of bitts and back it up to one more arrangement of bitts. At the point when the eye of the towing gear was at hand it would be associated with the pelican hook.

This was totally done inside an hour or so and the "Salvaliant" was associated. The team functioned admirably under the bosun Javier Patani. The towing gear was paid out. It comprised of a 60 foot wire strap of 8 inch perimeter wire associated with a 50 foot twofold nylon cot, the nylon being 12 inch outline. This was associated with the primary tow wire, which was 2,000 feet of 6 inch outline wire on an electrically determined drum which empowered it to be hurled in or loosened out as required.

The anchor on the "Salvaliant" was hurled up and Peter moved the pull toward the back of the loss while the principle tow wire was paid out. He then re-moored to anticipate Captain Hancox's instructions.

I was sent back ready the "Frederich Engels" to see Captain Hancox. He was extremely educational, let me know the fuel and counterbalance circumstance and the consequences of the jumping survey.

"Even later all the fuel, water and counterweight have been removed, my estimations recommend the ground response is as yet more than 2,000 tons. We should cut her up."

He droned in his standard droning and Australian inflection with a vacant genuine face. It was some time before I understood it should be a joke, generally strange for him I learned over time.

"It will be high water in an hour and we will have a go with the "Salvaliant" to show willing, yet it will be a finished exercise in futility. Keep the rescue affiliation assessor cheerful," he proceeded, "advise Peter to hurl up his anchor and begin towing. I will stay in contact on the Selco network."

I got back to the pull and gave him Captain Hancox's instructions.

"Hoffre Domma!" detonated Peter, giving me a cool lager as he flipped open one for himself. "What does that blockhead think he is doing, that thing won't fall off in 100 years!"

The anchor was hurled up and Peter showed and showed me his ability as a pull man, clarifying all that he did. There was a slight cross current so he needed to point the pull with the tow line out on one side to keep the pull on course. He turned the pull every method for getting the vibe of her since she was significantly greater than the "Salvana", and at that point we were just on half power.

"I would rather not converse with that bonehead, so you man the radio," Peter taught me.

I educated Captain Hancox regarding the circumstance and he advised me to move toward full power. The moving situation on the monkey island was at this point to be fitted, so Peter yelled the motor developments he needed to me from on top of the extension where he could see the tow wire.

I rang down to the motor room and advised them to fire up the subsequent motor. At the point when the motor was gripped onto the shaft, the flood of force could be viewed as the tow wire nearly emerged from the water. Peter clarified that the ability was to have sufficient tow wire out so it didn't break when full power was applied, however not all that much so it hauled along the base and harmed itself on the coral.

When the motors were on full power I informed Captain Hancox on the radio.

"Toss her with regards to a little," I handed-off to Peter.

He descended onto the extension and yelled rudder directions from the scaffold wing. The wheel was put hard a starboard and the pull went to starboard into the ebb and flow, behaving as she moved sideways through the water. The tow wire emerged from the water as the heaviness of the pull was added to the motor power. Then, when close to shallow water, the wheel was put hard a port, the tug turned, heeled and started moving to port sideways through the water, with the current. Peter turned around a long time before the shallows on this side so the current didn't clear the pull onto the reef too. The ocean was smooth in any case, all things considered, the pull obeyed such a lot of that water went onto the tow deck each time.

"The tide has begun to fall on my marker on the reef, and there is no indication of any development," Captain Hancox's voice came over the radio. "Stop towing and anchor for the evening," he instructed.

Peter heard the radio, put the motor message to half speed, and rang down to advise the architects to go on one motor. Without further ado thereafter I let go above and beyond paid out sufficient chain so the "Salvaliant" lay to the tide with the

tow wire over the side.

"We will keep anchor watches," said Peter, "in the event that she begins to drag soon we are on the reef ourselves. Advise the specialists to keep the motors on standby."

I headed toward the loss and went to a gathering between the expert of the boat and the different shore individuals who turned up – with or without the Indonesians' consent – including the rescue affiliation assessor. Skipper Hancox clarified that a fortification flatboat would be nearby in the first part of the day to remove every one of the dugouts. The weight and new water would be siphoned out and ground tackle would be laid.

Early next morning the fortification flatboat showed up, towed by a Selco pull. It was put close by the "Frederick Engels" rearward where there was water. Ground tackle was laid by Dave Warner and the "Salvista," the Selco securing and rescue vessel, the weight and new water were siphoned out and everything was prepared for one more endeavor on the evening's tide. The capacity to swing the "Salvaliant" about was restricted by the ground tackle and the endeavor fizzled, without really any indication of movement.

Salvage, as I was to learn, is an estimated science. By estimation we needed more power with the "Salvaliant" and the ground tackle for the boat to refloat. Nonetheless, on the following evening, comparably the "Salvaliant" had moved toward full power, off she came. The ground tackle was slipped and, when clear of the reef, the "Salvaliant" was slipped. A plunging review was made while the bosun gathered our strap and pelican hook.

Shortly thereafter Captain Hancox excused us. Peter took the pull to Western Anchorage to clear Immigration and Customs and back to the yard. It had been an intriguing encounter, incredible fun, and we would get a reward for sure. I was not discontent with my choice to join Selco.

The refit was at last finished and the first towing position was a flatboat to

Songklha in Thailand. Bumpy Halls accompanied us to ensure every one of the fixes and upgrades worked. I ensured we had a decent supply of pop water for him. In the wake of conveying the flatboat we stayed in port for a couple of days. The night life isn't quite so fluctuated as Bangkok!

Back in Singapore Knobby proclaimed himself happy with the pull and we went on rescue station in Eastern Anchorage. It was not well before we were requested to Loyang, where we got two team boats for Brunei. The tow was in fine climate and they were securely delivered.

Communication with Ops was by radio, and an ordinary timetable was

kept up with by the radio official. Operations was monitored 24 hours per day. At the point when the radio official was not on the job there was a speaker turned on right up the alley, with the radio went on to the calling recurrence. The VHF was constantly turned on to channel 16, the pain recurrence. It turned out to be natural to consistently have one ear tuning in, for in the rescue world minutes count. It is generally expected the primary pull who arrives at a the loss job.

While moored off Brunei we got directions to continue to a position north and tow an apparatus. This ended up being a most requesting position for us, being a solitary screw pull, and we were in extensive struggle with the device pusher on the three-legged lift rig "Chris Seger". Peter needed to attempt to hold the pull across the current to consent to his directions while he got secures, and the device pusher would not consent to any of our suggestions.

Eventually we got going and with most extreme (all things considered, almost so) power we towed the apparatus at a normal speed of over two bunches. The apparatus was at long last situated and secured and the "Salvaliant" was excused. We returned the protection assessor to Brunei, utilizing him with our "Salvaliant" exceptional – which was an especially deadly gin-based concoction.

We were respecting the dusk when the radio official gave a message to Peter. He gave me the message while heading to the motor room telephone.

"Two motors greatest power," he requested into the mouthpiece.

'Drop assessor. Continue most extreme speed Bombay Reef' read the message.

It was marked Bond, a man of not many words.

There was a boat holding up at Anchorage to remove the assessor and Peter turned the pull and traveled north along the coast. Bombay Reef was in the South China Sea South of Hong Kong in Chinese regional waters, yet there was a gigantic space of unsurveyed reefs among us and the reef. It was important to steam north to clear the region, and afterward west out across the China Sea. The climate approved of a low swell, to which the "Salvaliant" plunged her bow as she roared along at 15 knots.

Once out in the South China Sea, the North East storm was blowing and the pull rolled vigorously when the course was changed toward the west. Four days subsequent to dropping the assessor we came up on the "Nienberg" in the evening, similarly as the sun was setting in our eyes, her outline dark against the red sky. She was ashore on the windward side of the reef, with waves breaking around her harsh. The remaining parts of a disaster area nearby – the kettle standing quiet and alone – an obvious token of what might happen to the "Nienberg," somewhere in the range of 11,000 gross tons, assuming we didn't get her off.

It was a dismal and genuine Peter, all good humor gone, who said, "This will be troublesome and perilous, one mix-up and we are on the reef ourselves. It's getting dim, it's absolutely impossible that we can make an association now and it looks too sad to even think about going across in the zed boat. We'll need to stand by till morning."

Peter talked on the VHF radio to the expert of the setback and told him there was nothing we could do until the morning. There was an enormous socialist Chinese vessel toward the west, quiet and watching. The reef displayed on the radar and Peter steamed the pull round toward the south side into the lee, where we spent an agreeable, however for me restless, evening steaming all over. I was too worried envisioning a wide range of revulsions for the following day – a line round the propeller or the motors halted and we float vulnerably onto the reef. This was remote ocean sea rescue and I was happy I was with a particularly experienced and educated master.

Peter and I were both on the scaffold a long time before light, alongside our Filipino officials and bosun. The group were all out at hand as we steamed back to the "Nienberg", pitching intensely once clear of the lee and afterward rolling once we traveled west. It was getting light now yet it was a grim and solemn day break with weighty cloud and a dark sea.

Off the loss Peter dropped back harsh first to the reef, pitching into the North East rainstorm, while my eyes were stuck to the screen of the reverberation sounder. I yelled out the profundities to Peter who was at the monkey island control position. Following an hour or so we had a very smart thought of the profundities toward the back of the "Nienberg". Peter boiled down to the bridge.

"We'll make a stop to hold her head into wind and ocean, utilize the rocket weapon to shoot a line across and supplicate," he said.

He addressed the expert of the loss, intriguing on him the indispensable need of hurling the tow line across as fast as conceivable once they had the courier. We realized they had power from the lights the boat had shown the night before.

The anchor was given up close to the edge of the reef and Peter moved harsh first towards the loss where the team were coating the rails rearward. With the greater part of the chain out, the harsh of the pull was in shallow water around one link from the harsh of the "Nienberg". We were unable to draw any nearer without steering into the rocks ourselves. The pull was pitching into the oceans, which were all the while breaking around the harsh of the grounded transport. It began to drizzle.

Peter utilized the motor to facilitate the load on the link. Jesus Armosilla, the second official, took the Schermuly rocket and line box onto the tow deck, where the tow gear was generally fit to be paid out. I was extremely anxious in spite of the fact that, obviously, I attempted to seem certain about front of the team. I had never utilized a rocket firearm in my life previously. The crate and line were conveniently spread out on top of the toward the back hold. I remained on the bring forth to acquire a little stature and steadying myself against the pitch and roll of the pull, I got the firearm, focused on the scaffold and terminated. The extension and convenience were rearward. There was a boisterous bang and the line went shooting not yet decided towards the loss. We as a whole watched it with teased breath and a cheer went up as we saw it land close to the pipe. Energetic hands got it and the courier wound on the bring forth wound out over the side, trailed by a long polypropylene line.

I looked up at the stone like figure remaining by the message on the monkey island and Peter offered me a go-ahead sign. The polyprop line drifted and it was soon ready the "Nienberg". They put it on the capstan and the line came out of the water as they heaved the towing gear across – wire pendant first, then the stretcher and finally the main tow wire – the joining shackles slipping over the greased towing gunnel. The tow deck was continually submerged as the pull rolled and pitched, however the towline was between the cart pins – two versatile bollards on the towing gunnel – and the propeller was clear.

There was one more cheer as the group on the setback demonstrated that they had gotten the towing gear. I went ahead with the bosun and began to hurl up the anchor, Jesus loosened out the fundamental tow wire to Peter's bearing. It was indispensable to keep the tow line sensibly close so it didn't get round the propeller. When the anchor was aweigh Peter steamed ahead, loosen out the tow wire until around 1,000 feet was out.

"Secure the winch!" he yelled down to Jesus, who recognized with a flood of his hand.

"Ring down for two motors," he said to me having gotten back to the bridge.

Once power was expanded the cart pins were brought down so the tow wire could run free and swing across the tow deck, empowering the pull to be moved. The "Salvaliant" was in a most problematic situation on the windward side of the reef, presently associated with the loss. On the off chance that we couldn't stem the current – or anything turned out badly – the pull would be on the reef in minutes, the waves breaking over her. It would mean passing to a large number of us. Steady watchfulness was required.

Peter addressed the expert of the "Nienberg" on the VHF radio and told him we would have a re-drifting endeavor. The motors were expanded to full power and Peter flung the pull from port to starboard, transporting substantial oceans on the tow deck. The loss utilized her primary motor yet announced no development. Following an hour or so the re-drifting endeavor was paused and power was decreased on the tug.

'10:30 associated. Refloating endeavor made. Fizzled.' The concise message Peter shipped off the office.

' "Gooney bird" while heading to help,' returned a sign from the office.

"All assistance appreciatively got," commented Peter. "She's pretty vigorously on solid land and we will be fortunate to get her off."

The Chinese boat was as yet quiet, watching and pausing, her shape vague in the shower and misery, similar to the heater on the reef a steady token of what could happen.

In the early evening a vessel was noticed coming from the east.

"Incorrect way from Singapore assuming it's the "Gooney bird"," commented Peter.

We all looked as the secret boat came nearer and one of our group said, "It's the "Virginia City"."

"That is the last thing we need here," protested Peter.

The "Virginia City" had a place with the Filipino rescue organization from Manilla. I turned her upward in the Register and saw that she had been worked in 1944 – north of thirty years prior – was diesel electric and American built.

Jesus addressed the "Virginia City" in Tagolic on the VHF.

"Cap, they say they have LOF and need to associate," detailed Jesus. "Let him know he can do what he prefers yet stay away from us," said Peter.

After the re-drifting endeavor Peter had moved the pull up toward the west of the "Nienberg" so that the "Salvaliant" was up current. This implied the "Virginia City" would need to interface down ebb and flow of us hence, in the event that anything turned out badly, they would be cleared away from the "Salvaliant" rather than on to her.

The "Virginia City" was contributing and moving the ocean and swell, similar to the "Salvaliant", however the pull was nailed somewhere near the tow wire and we were very agreeable. I felt frustrated about the expert of the "Virginia City", attempt as he would he was unable to make an association. The pull was greater than the "Salvaliant" yet extremely delayed to move and the towing point was excessively far toward the back. At last he inquired as to whether he could associate with our bow. I thought Peter was going to explode.

"Hoffre Domma. Does he need to put us on the reef? He will pull us round; our towing gear isn't sufficient for two pulls." He was breathing intensely as he opened a container of brew, giving one to me.

"Let me think. Turn that ridiculous radio off," he snarled. He tossed the vacant brew can into the ocean. "Alright, Ian, rig the pelican snare on our port bow and ensure that you can get at it to sneak through a crisis. We'll make him quick to the pelican snare and when associated I need a man with a mallet remaining by 24 hours per day. That is a major, old 'store of scrap' and I would rather not lose my pull as a result of him."

"Jesus, advise him to come and interface on our port bow and assuming he contacts us I will shoot him."

Jesus chuckled and talked into the microphone.

The "Virginia City" steamed over towards us. The bosun had his men prepared with hurling lines and when the pull steamed gradually past, water pouring off her tow deck as she rolled, they tossed them at the pull. One of them was gotten and made quick to the courier. The "Salvaliant" men quickly heaved it on board, then put it round the windlass drum. The eye of the towing gear was soon ready through the forward fairlead and associated with the pelican snare. The "Virginia City" streamed her stuff going directly out.

"Jesus, tell the "Virginia City" to go to port and keep up current of us, and afterward we will have a re-drifting attempt."

It failed.

Night fell. It was exceptionally dull with an intensely cloudy sky. The lights on the "Nienberg" shined brilliantly toward the back, and ahead the dimmer lights of the Filipino pull along with the lights of the Chinese vessel drifting nearby. An AB was at the bow with a mallet, remaining by the pelican hook.

We steamed the entire evening, checking our situation on the setback to ensure we were not cleared down current. Peter sent me off to bed at midnight.

Some time later I arose to a huge thunder.

"He's maneuvering us onto the reef, slip slip."

I hurried out of my lodge and onto the foredeck. The AB with the sledge gave the pelican snare ring a huge hit, it slid free, the snare opened and the "Virginia City" tow wire vanished out of the fairlead. I looked toward the back and saw the "Nienberg" up to port.

Jesus, I thought, we are on the reef! I surged up to the scaffold, my heart palpitating in dread, and took a course which affirmed my most noticeably terrible considerations – we had been hauled directly down nearly onto the reef.

I went into the wheelhouse and found Peter in the driver's seat with it hard to

port. I could hear the snap of the gyro compass as the heading changed. The "Salvaliant" was mauling her way off the reef. The "Virginia City" steamed off into the night.

"Disposed of the jerk," was all Peter said as he got his container of beer.

And that is all I at any point discovered. When the pull was back up current and standing firm on her situation, Peter said, "All yours, I'm to bed." And he strolled off the bridge.

***

I watched the day break toward the east of the "Nienberg", her lights blurring in the social event light, the kettle of the disaster area turning out to be more unmistakable. I was presently used to the movement of the pull, we had been towing for just about 24 hours. The breeze was less and the ocean appeared to have gone down a bit. I concentrated on the harsh of the setback through the enormous, incredible optics on the extension wing. Just an intermittent ocean was breaking round the harsh yet nothing amidships. I looked for quite a while and started to figure it very well may be feasible to get across with a skilful zed boat driver. The "Salvaliant" was furnished with a new, hard-lined, elastic zed boat with a 50 drive outboard.

After an early breakfast I called Peter and told him of what I had noticed. He looked his typical self and said, "to have a go, then, at that point, OK. However, be cautious, assuming you miss the point you'll be a gonner on the reef."

I called for volunteers and the zed boat was dispatched. The loss was cautioned. Peter advised them to put a freight net over the side and a pilot stepping stool. I drove the boat with two group, and remained off the harsh to watch.

The whole team of the "Nienberg" were coating the rails. I went in at maximum speed later a wave broke round the harsh, gathered together head to the ocean at the pilot stepping stool amidships, and with the team clutching the freight net, scaled the stepping stool with the painter. When I gave the painter to a "Nienberg" group part I yelled down for the two team to follow me. When they were out of the boat I took the painter forward and secured the boat in the nearly quiet water round the bow.

Elmo, one of the team who was a jumper, had carried a sounding line with him. I advised him to explore round the boat while I went to see the master.

The "Nienberg" was completely loaded so had no balance. She was because of fortification in Singapore so was coming up short on fuel and new water. There could have been no other reply, we would need to discard the freight if we somehow managed to get her off. I went onto the scaffold and conversed with Peter on the VHF. He concurred and said he

would tell the workplace. While on the extension I saw a boat coming from the Chinese boat and they effectively came alongside.

Elmo concocted the sounding arrangement and with the drafts I had gotten from the expert, it affirmed that the boat was vigorously ashore and a ton of freight would need to be discarded. I returned to the expert's lodge to observe three Chinese inside, one of whom was clearly a mediator and one I speculated was the commissar. They were let the expert know that they planned to lay ground tackle. I was startled. Nonetheless, as long as it didn't meddle with the "Salvaliant", it could cause no damage. But how they were going to do it with their great, big ship I did not know.

I returned to the "Salvaliant" in the zed boat. Whenever having done it, it didn't appear so awful and the ocean had gone down additional. On board I examined the circumstance with Peter and concentrated on the freight plan I brought back. On the off chance that we could get at the zinc in the lower holds we could ease up her very quickly.

Peter got a message consenting to the discard and simultaneously, a climate forecast.

"Hoffre Domma! he shouted. "There's a hurricane coming thusly, might be four days. That is all we need."

This gave an additional earnestness to the circumstance. It was suspicious if the boat could endure a storm, and we would need to leave before it showed up if we somehow managed to endure ourselves.

I returned to the "Nienberg" with about six team, along with different unit, and the zed boat driven by a jumper got back to bring more. The expert consented to the discard later I showed him a duplicate of the message from Selco, and he knew about the typhoon.

Jettison began inside the hour and a test of skill and endurance started. The boat's group helped and a boat diverted up from the "Tiburon" with more men. I drove a winch and the boat woke up as freight was lifted out of the holds with the derricks, swung across the deck and tossed over the side. The Chinese initiated work to lay the ground tackle.

Work proceeded with the entire evening, and the following day too – the "Nienberg" providing us with food and drink. The zed boat was lifted at hand, out of the way.

On the fourth evening the "Gooney bird" turned up. We dispatched the "Salvaliant" zed boat and helped with making the association by towing the courier across. They brought back some extreme, beefy Germans to assist with the jettison.

In the evening the climate began to break down and the ocean and swell expanded. The storm was traveling thusly and was two or three days away.

The following morning the climate had decayed such a lot of that it was difficult to utilize the zed boat, oceans were breaking round the harsh of the loss and clearing at the edges of the boat. We were caught ready. The hurricane was under two days away.

I talked about with Peter over the radio what we ought to do, aside from proceed the discard as fast as possible.

"It is conceivable she might appear to be the swell moves in from the tropical storm. We are likely inclination it now," he said, "in the event that she won't fall off when I need to leave, you should counterbalance her down, secure everything and implore. You are caught on board."

"All comprehended," I said. "We've discarded just about 1,000 tons now and when remaining on the harsh, there are clear indications of development as the oceans hit the stern."

"That is a decent sign. We will triumph ultimately a last endeavor at 16:00." He marked off.

I talked with the Germans from the "Gooney bird" and the Filipinos from the "Virginia City" and let them know the arrangement. I talked with the expert and asked him how the Chinese planned to slip their ground tackle wire. There did not appear to be a plan, so I asked him to have cutting gear standing by nearby.

At 16:00 I left the casting off and went to the extension. The "Salvaliant" was towing toward the west and the "Gooney bird" down current toward the east. The Chinese ground tackle wire was even further down current. The two pulls expanded to full power, I could see the bubbling water round their sterns from the propellers. The tow wires were bar tight. As one the two pulls began sheering to port and afterward to starboard, behaving as they moved sideways through the ocean, water falling off their tow decks. The "Nienberg" motor was put full toward the back. On the third swing to port there was positive development, the "Nienberg" swung a couple of degrees and halted. The ground tackle was holding her.

"Ian." I heard my name over the radio. "Cut the ground tackle wire."

The "Salvaliant" welder was among the cast off party however I told him to reserve at the ground tackle when I left the hold. I pursued down to the deck and advised him to cut the wire. He lit the cutting stuff and put it on the wire. It was bar tight, murmuring with the strain. I remained behind him to loan moral help. Assuming you remain at the purpose in separating, the wrecked wire won't hit you.

It took boldness to cut that wire. Some Chinese was prattling endlessly however I took no notice.

Suddenly there was a firearm going off. The wire separated and one end vanished over the side, remove a portion of the rail with it, the other more limited end flung itself in reverse inboard hitting a winch. The welder and I were clear remaining at the place of breakage. The "Nienberg" began swinging quickly to port, the harsh towards the towing pulls, and afterward there was an enormous bang and we were nearly lost our feet. She was moving. She halted and again there was a bang, and afterward she began beating and moving astern.

I hustled back onto the extension. The shivering and beating halted, she was afloat.

"Stop the motor," I requested, and the message was put to stop.

The "Nienberg" was moving in the swell as she swung broadside onto the swell. The discarding halted and the groups were cheering.

"Ian, let go of the "Gooney bird" first and afterward me," taught Peter over the radio, "and afterward steam round toward the south side of the reef."

The "Salvaliant" team were at that point at the towing associations when I returned rearward. We let exceed all expectations without trouble and I returned onto the bridge.

"I will guide you round to the opposite side of the reef," I told the master.

"Slow ahead," I requested. "Hard a port," I trained the man in the driver's seat, and strolled to the radar. It was practically dim however as on the "Salvaliant", the reef displayed on the radar.

The two pulls were recuperating their towing gear, their brilliant deck lights enlightening their tow decks. The "Nienberg" was rolling vigorously in the ocean and swell; the portals were open, free stuff moved around at hand, yet it was not some time before I adjusted south and afterward west into the lee of the reef.

There were common congrats in general, even the Chinese grinned. The boat's group and rescue team shut the seals and brought down the derricks. We were generally quick to steam south as fast as could really be expected, out of the way of the typhoon.

The woodworker detailed there was no spillage in the holds or tanks. The boat was sound. The central designer announced the motors to be in great order.

It was around 21:00 when I at long last came to the "Salvaliant" with the end letter. I sat on the scaffold with a lager and was out of nowhere immersed by sleepiness. I'd had no rest for over two days and quite a bit of that time I had been discarding cargo.

We watched the "Nienberg" get going and followed her on two motors to keep up and get south as fast as possible.

The following morning the "Nienberg" was far away toward the south and we were well clear of the storm. Peter dialed back to prudent speed.

Several days after the fact we got a message to continue to a situation off the East Malaysian Coast among the reefs in the unsurveyed region. The climate was fine and we continued at full speed.

We showed up during the morning to track down the rescue vessel "Salviper" close by and the rescue team releasing elastic bundles onto a flatboat. Chief Hancox was in control yet subsequent to assisting with releasing for a day, we got guidelines to continue to Singapore.

***

In Singapore we went on rescue reserve in Eastern Anchorage. This was the exhausting piece of rescue – trusting that something will occur. You don't have the foggiest idea when it will happen. Assuming that I went aground I had a pager if accessible and if not, I needed to telephone Ops and let them know where I was. So assuming that I went to two bars and a café, each time I moved I needed to telephone in. Assuming there was a crisis they would telephone and I would return to the pull as fast as could really be expected, ordinarily inside the hour. There were in every case a lot of bumboats at Clifford Pier. It was something very similar for the team and just a predetermined number were permitted shorewards at any one time.

On load up, the Selco channel and VHF channel 16 were observed constantly. Peter remained at home most evenings however he could be gotten with the zed boat inside twenty minutes.

Eastern Anchorage was intriguing according to a transportation perspective due to the assortment of delivery moored there.

I met Mr Kahlenberg a couple of times in the workplace and he was particularly satisfied about the "Nienberg", which was a generally excellent rescue. He was in every case well disposed, yet in every case very busy.

On Christmas Eve I got a message over the Selco organization to continue to Mr Kahlenberg's home. At the point when I arrived at the shore I needed to telephone Ops to discover where it was so I could tell the driver. All things being equal it was hard to track down in the dark.

I strolled up the drive once the guard let me in and was perspiring when I showed up at the entryway. A servant let me in to the cooled house and I tracked down Mr K as he was all the more tenderly known, or EEK which were his

initials, sitting in a huge easy chair in the wooden-amazed drawing-room. There were bunches of Christmas improvements, with a huge Christmas tree in the corner.

"Great evening, Captain Tew," welcomed Mr

K. Advancement finally, I thought.

"Plunk down and have a beverage. We observe Christmas Eve rather than Christmas Day."

The servant presented to me a lager. I was behaving as well as possible; there could have been no different visitors and not every person will have a beverage with the executive in his house.

A short, strong moderately aged woman came into the room and Mr K presented his better half, Hilda, as I stood up and shook hands. She plunked down and was quiet as Mr K and I visited about salvage.

About ten minutes after the fact an energetic, sharp looking young woman went into the room and I was acquainted with Marie Louise, the Kahlenberg's little girl.

Without further ado subsequently we as a whole went into supper at a wonderfully set table with blossoms and candles. It was the conventional dish goose with loads of wine. It ended up being a sprightly evening, even more so on the grounds that it was so unforeseen; brief sitting on the pull, the following in the administrator's Christmas-designed house eating cook goose with his family!

There was no rescue, so I spent Christmas Day at Alan Bond's open house, and got to know significantly more Selco work force: Chris Herbert – trimmed as regular with radios and contraptions – an extremely huge man for sure, joined by his accomplice; Knobby Halls and Anne; Dave Warner and his better half and youngsters; David Hancox and his Japanese spouse, Akiko; Peter and Unke with Peter and Caroline; Daniel Boon, the staff man, somebody to keep in with assuming I needed a specific group; Ismael Bin Dollah, responsible for Ops, a most significant man. Mr K turned up all alone. There were different other non-Selco individuals, specifically the rescue affiliation boss assessor and other shoreside individuals engaged with pulls and barges and salvage.

I went through the following a half year with Peter however there was not another "Nienberg", in spite of the fact that we actually played out a couple of rescue occupations and a couple of bogus alerts. There was nothing more awful than having a crisis just to observe the opposition showed up first, or the boat was at this point not in distress.

We towed a Greek freight transport in weight from the center of the Malacca Straits, yet it was an agreement work so no reward. We helped with extinguishing a fire on a boat in Eastern Anchorage, yet the Port fire pull was there too – and

our rivals – and the fire was out rapidly, so very little energy. One night there was a crash in the Singapore Straits off Eastern Anchorage. I had the anchor aweigh as Peter jumped on board from the zed boat and he took her at maximum speed in obscurity through the Anchorage and out into the Straits.

He went straight close by the consuming stacked big hauler and we lit battling the fire which was seething forward, the blazes jumping out from the forecastle. The "Salvaliant" was made quick on the starboard shoulder. Two rescue team worked the fire screens over the monkey island, playing planes of water over the forecastle. I was on the deck of the big hauler, with the remainder of our team playing fire hoses from the pull at the angrily consuming fire. I was exceptionally cognizant we were remaining on top of stacked tanks, an intermittent smell of raw petroleum giving added criticalness to our putting out fires efforts.

At one phase there was a colossal bang, the team all ran toward the back and I fell on the deck thinking there had been a blast. The way to the paint room had blown open and flares jumped out. Whenever I had gathered my brains together I stood up, motioned to my group to get the hoses, and advance on the flares. We before long put it out and following four hours, the fire in the forecastle was extinguished.

The messman kept us very much provided with cold beverages – Peter sneaking in several chilly lagers for me – for it was a hot, tropical night separated from the hotness of the fire. Similarly as we put the fire out the "Salviper" turned up, the boat she was going to sank. We were not exceptionally satisfied with Captain Hancox muscling in on our rescue later the fire was out and partaking in the rescue bonus.

Dave Hancox, the morose Australian, was a Walter Mitty type character. He envisioned he had gotten things done, and truly trusted it, when, indeed, they were fantasies of his rich creative mind. It was extremely challenging to tell truth from fiction. For example, he said that the fire on the sunk boat had been so extreme it had liquefied his sweet spot windows, Be that as it may the "Salviper" windows were flawless. He said the "Salviper" had been encircled by consuming oil however there were no singe blemishes on the immaculate paint or consumed elastic on the elastic bumpers. He constantly recounted accounts of how he battled in the Vietnam War; all things considered, he had been there however on a rescue work not battling. However, when you sifted through the fiction, Dave was a truly proficient salvor and overall aided me a lot.

An enormous big hauler steered into the rocks in the shoals off one Fathom Bank at the

access to the Malacca Straits. This was a significant rescue on Lloyd's Open Form and a large portion of the Selco armada turned up. Part of the unrefined petroleum freight was to be released before she could be refloated.

Captain Hancox was accountable for the rescue and he was in charge of the rescue vessel "Salviper". We held on with the "Salvaliant" associated with the loss prepared to tow later the ground tackle was laid. A little pull and barge showed up, stacked with gear and bumpers required for the easing up activity. The group boat "Salvital" showed up with a collection of assessors and proprietors' representatives.

I used another tug and our zed boat, with a portable echo sounder to find a way out through the banks once the tanker was refloated. I felt like a wayfarer of old and was satisfied with the outcome. I directed the easing up big hauler and put her close by the grounded transport, which was should we say animating not having moved anything bigger than a rescue pull. It was an acceptable first for myself and I was appreciative to Captain Hancox for giving me the responsibility.

After a couple of days the big hauler was effectively refloated and the eased up freight reloaded. I steered the salved vessel through the channel I had found, once again into the Straits and south to Singapore.

A completely loaded Indian big hauler, the "Lal Bahadur Shastri", steered into the rocks on Helen Mar Reef on the Indonesian side of the Singapore Straits. This was another LOF rescue with ground tackle being laid by the "Salvista". Skipper Hancox was in control, the "Salviper" offering help. The "Salvital" drew out The Straits Times each day.

The "Salvaliant" was associated and various little pulls turned up with staff and hardware. I directed the easing up transport close by and took her off again when stacked – difficult in the solid cross current however helped by Selco tugs.

During these rescue activities I kept great notes, so had the option to give proof to Dennis Rixon when he came out. This was in some cases a trial on the off chance that he was feeling awful and he reminded constantly me I was given the occupation on his proposal. Mr K relied upon him by and large in the legitimate work, so I needed to endure Dennis. Then again he could be beguiling and we had some extremely charming suppers together, and

Sunday snacks with EEK.

Dennis was a really young looking, thick, stocky man with a perpetual asset of jokes which he amused the collected organization, or it very well may be just me, over

various lagers. At the point when diabetes was analyzed he was much more troublesome and touchy, particularly when he was on the cart for a little while. Nonetheless, it significantly helped my vocation for my proof to turn up at assertions in London and my name became known among the authorities and QCs associated with the rescue world.

The "Showa Maru" was one of the greatest Lloyd's Open Form rescue tasks of its day. This Japanese big hauler steered into the rocks in the Singapore Straits on the Indonesian side en route to Japan stacked with 250,000 tons of raw petroleum, penetrating her tanks and contaminating the Straits. Individuals diverted up from London and Tokyo to prompt on the contamination, however the best thing in these conditions to restrict contamination is to treatment the boat, which the present hippies appear to forget.

Captain Hancox was in control and I turned into his collaborator, living on the "Showa Maru" for quite a long time. When ground tackle was laid from each of the four corners of the boat the "Salvaliant" was excused. I remained, being Captain Hancox's colleague, living with one of the new Motorolas Chris Herbert purchased which worked inside the boat. I could speak with Ops, or any of the pulls, or Dave Hancox 24 hours every day any place I was located.

The boat was opened up along her base and a portion of the raw petroleum was lost, yet when a water base was set up the spillage halted. It was important to ease up her to refloat.

A little Shell big hauler was contracted to ease up the "Showa Maru" while she was ashore and transport the raw petroleum to a bigger big hauler for transport on to Japan. Yokohama bumpers, immense drifting elastic bumpers, were utilized for the big haulers to lie close by both the "Showa Maru" and the bigger big hauler moored off. Selco pulls were utilized to aid the berthing operations.

The funneling framework on the loss was harmed during the establishing so unique using pressurized water driven sub siphons were flown in from the States, alongside their Coast Guard working groups. These were utilized to siphon the raw petroleum out of the tanks 'over the top' and into the boat's complex, where it was released into the easing up big hauler. Selco Salvage groups helped the United States Coast Guard groups, kept watch on the ground tackle, the securing lines between the boats, the bumpers and the numerous other endless positions that were needed to be done.

Captain Hancox and his counselors – advisors from London – determined the release arrangement so the harmed body didn't separate. I invested a great deal of energy with him, gained some significant experience, and managed the rescue crews.

She was effectively refloated with the "Salvaliant" and helping pulls, and moored. A full release was required with the goal that the boat could be dry moored, and this was done at anchor. At last, the "Salvaliant", looking tiny from the scaffold of the now unfilled "Showa Maru", towed her to off the dry dock where she was secured and the end letter was signed.

It was late around evening time when I came shorewards in the "Salvital" with the Japanese proprietors' agent and Captain Hancox. We were met in the generally abandoned office by Mr K who gave us an excited greeting and congrats. Dave, as morose as could be expected, denied EEK's solicitation to his home and went off. The Japanese agent and I went with Mr K to his home, where neither Hilda nor Marie Louise were extremely satisfied to see us at 1:00 in the morning!

Nothing reluctant, Ernie set to and we had fried eggs and tinned shellfish, washed down with champagne as a celebratory dinner. All things considered, Selco had accomplished a world overthrow in the rescue world and the Japanese were happy to have their boat back securely salved. It is consistent with say that Selco raked in some serious cash and I got a huge rescue reward thus, all things considered, everybody was happy.

SALVIKING MY FIRST COMMAND

I was advanced expert of the new Selco-fabricated rescue and securing vessel "Salviking". Chief finally at 32 years old! There could be no other inclination on the planet than being expert of your own boat, or if nothing else that is the manner in which I felt. It was my boat and my group and I was extremely pleased with my first order. I had a team of right around thirty, it differed a piece contingent upon what work we were performing.

Tony Church was acting expert on ocean preliminaries which were not yet finished, so whenever I first took her out was on preliminaries. I really wanted a pull to tow her out of the base yet before long became accustomed to taking care of this level lined boat, with her horns for securing work standing out ahead. The scaffold was toward the back and the functioning deck extended ahead, with the gigantic rescue securing winch underneath the wheelhouse and the 30 ton derrick simply forward. Her length was 200 feet and pillar 20 feet and her nearly shallow draft was 10 feet. The preliminaries were effectively finished and I went out with Tony for a couple beers.

I didn't realize anything about securing work and the main occupation with the "Salviking" was to upgrade the Port Dickson securing and floats. Fortunately Charles Deeney had joined Selco and he was a specialist, so he went along responsible for the securing work.

The short journey round to Port Dickson in the Malacca Straits was made without episode, the jumpers traveling via land. The chains were lifted, examined and relaid. I observed the work inconceivably exhausting and passed on it to Charles, moving the "Salviking" at whatever point required.

Once the securing position was finished, I got a message to continue north up the Malacca Straits 'on spec'. Tragically, the 'spec' didn't need support, so I traveled south back to Singapore. In transit the climate exploded, as it can in the Malacca Straits, to about power 7. With the unpolished bows the ocean came on deck which, under typical conditions, would not have made a difference – running off through the scuppers. Sadly, water got underneath in the hold which decreased the freeboard, making more water come ready. I turned and ran before the wind with the sea astern until it moderated, then continued back to Singapore.

It worked out that the elastic pressing, which ought to have made the bring forth watertight, was missing. The bring forth was arranged in, and was flush with, the functioning deck so any water coming over the bow went straight down the side of the incubate. I got a letter from Mr Bond accusing me for this and was enraged – the vessel having quite recently been overviewed by NKK, the Japanese characterization society – and passed by Captain Hancox, who was acting administrator accountable for the "Salviking".

When I went to protest with Bond he essentially said, "You are the expert, it's your obligation to check the vessel is stable. Try not to attempt to fault other people."

The primary rescue activity I performed with the "Salviking" was at Batam in Indonesia, directly across the Straits from Singapore. Dave Warner, with his red hair and forever burned by the sun face, with four jumpers went with us. I secured the boat with the horns forward over the indented pull and the jumpers put wire straps round her, being mindful so as to divide wires at the edges so the depressed art was not 'cheesed'. She weighed around seventy tons and the "Salviking" 's bow was practically submerged when the rescue securing winch was placed in twofold stuff and the lift started. At the point when the pull was at the surface, versatile electric siphons were put ready and the water siphoned out. As the level fell in the motor room so the hardware was saved from the impacts of salt water.

Fernando Legaspi, moderately aged and little, was my central designer and he knew basically everything about the "Salviking" motors since he modified them. Arturo Briosi was my main official, an all around prepared rescue man from the "Salviper", stocky and solid. Pepe, tall and proficient, additionally ex "Salviper", was the bosun. John, an Indian, dim and wise, was my radio official. The welder, nicknamed Ikan, was a virtuoso at fixing things. There were three super durable jumpers with their unit; four fitters in the motor room; six capable sailors at hand; two deck officials; and two specialists. With everything taken into account, an all around monitored rescue vessel.

After our pull raising position, I continued back to Singapore to get ready for a line pulling position in Indonesia. I was not that sharp since this kind of work didn't actually intrigue me however Peter was in charge of the "Salvaliant" and Selco, around then, didn't have any more enormous pulls. So I held my peace.

The amount of equipment for this pipe pull was immense and included over a mile of wire with which to pull the pipe; the sledge on which the edge of the pipe would be made fast; drums to assist the pipe to float; bottles of oxy acetyline; boxes of welding rods; beer; soft drinks and tinned food for six months; and a full freezer. At the point when everything was ready, including the 15 ton "Charlie Brown" work boat, the "Salviking" was over-burden, yet I chose to disregard notwithstanding Bond's letter!

I withdrawn right off the bat in the New Year 1975 headed for Balik Papan. The speediest course was out past Horsburgh Lighthouse at the entry to the Singapore Straits and across vast ocean toward the Southern finish of Indonesian Borneo. I wished I had exceeded everyone's expectations by means of the Bangka Straits.

Half daily past Horsburgh Light it exploded new and in the evening, blew a full storm. The vigorously loaded "Salviking" toiled, transporting substantial oceans across the deck and rolled. I slowed down to the minimum speed possible to keep steerage way and hove to but she still seemed to be almost permanently under water and even when I put her bow to sea, she rolled.

It was a dull cloudy night without any stars apparent, simply white ponies overwhelming the boat. I was unmistakably worried with the conduct of the rescue vessel and it didn't help when a few drums loosened up and were in the end lost over the edge. There was a lot of water on the foredeck for anyone to go out. I had been adrift in much more regrettable climate: "Anatina" off Iceland; "Eastern Maid" in the China Sea; "Eastern Ranger" off Korea; yet I had until recently never been uneasy with regards to the boat. I honestly figured we may be overpowered however, obviously, didn't voice my apprehensions to anybody and kept up a bright disposition the entire evening, supported by cups of coffee.

It didn't look much better in light and I remained hove to. About early afternoon the climate directed, and by evening the "Salviking" was back on prudent speed.

Indonesia was bad, and assuming one is to work there you need to acknowledge that reality and pay off. On the off chance that you don't nothing occurs and you can't begin, not to mention total, an agreement. Normally this was took into consideration when bidding.

In Balik Papan, which was a one-peered toward place, the "Salviking" was held up for the 'freight' to be checked. The individual who should have 'organized' this didn't turn up so the right palm was not been lubed. At last we were cleared in and the license to remain and work in Indonesia gave. Our agreement was with Pertamina so you would have thought there would be no issues yet, as I said, Indonesia was bad. Be that as it may, having got 'in' to Indonesia the following issue was to be permitted to leave Balik Papan and at last, following a couple of more squandered days, I was given the 'freedom'. In the case of nothing else, the climate was fine yet warm and surprisingly the club appeared very fun.

I steamed up the coast north-bound in fine climate, a periodic nation create being the main traffic, the coast shrouded in thick, green wilderness. It was warm and tacky outside, yet the scaffold was cooled so I didn't improve my sun tan.

There was nothing at Sangatta, in a real don't sense anything – it was organizes on the outline. Mr Panigada, Paddy for short, was setting up a headquarters to live, and beams on which to weld the lines. I moored the "Salviking" seaward where there was no shelter.

We were there for quite some time. There were deferrals and more postponements however ultimately the line was pulled, with the "Salviking" secured a mile seaward. The line was in areas. As each segment was welded, the welds tried and reviewed, we would pull that part and afterward trust that the following segment will be welded on. The stunt was not to permit the line to sink into the mud, in any case it took a ton of pulling to unstick it, particularly when right around a mile was on the base. We wrapped up with the line one foot out from its arranged position.

Charles Deeney went up to do the securing and seven months in the wake of leaving Balik Papan, we returned. It appeared to be an incredible clamoring, sparkling city later the greater part a year at Sangatta.

Our inconveniences were just barely starting on the grounds that the Indonesians would not release us. Clearly the right palms were not lubed and time appeared to be of no item. The apparent justification for not giving us a leeway was that we were not leaving with the equivalent 'freight' we had shown up with. Indeed, that was not shocking in light of the fact that we had eaten the food and the vast majority of the deck freight framed the line and securing framework at Sangatta!

John, the radio official, given me a message one Friday morning.

'Acquire freedom and continue greatest speed to facilitates north of Balik Papan.' Signed Bond.

More difficult than one might expect in Indonesia which is a Moslem country. I found the agent, loaded the car with cold beer and made the rounds of all the officials to obtain a clearance to sail for a vessel in distress. The authorities were not extremely inspired by the misery, just the amount we were ready to pay! We got the leeway before the day's over exclusively by ensuring to return and significant pay-offs. "Charlie Brown" was abandoned and I cruised in the evening similarly as it was getting dull. It had been a drawn out day and there was very little lager left in the car!

I returned in five days. Our Filipino rivals were given the job.

The following two or three weeks were enjoyed salving a few scows with Charlie Brown, which was very fun.

***

One evening, prior to going shorewards to the dance club, John said there was a

call for me on the radio from UK. I was generally amazed. My dad had passed on. It was a bolt thoroughly out of nowhere and I was tragic and sorry I had not seen him for quite a long time. We had managed everything sufficiently well and he had forever been there for me.

I made an impression on Singapore requesting a consolation so I could go to the memorial service. I flew from Balik Papan to Djakarta and thereupon to Singapore, giving over the "Salviking" in the bar of the Orchid Inn. I got the 22:00 trip to Heathrow, where I employed a vehicle and drove home. It is weird the endeavors made to respect the dead, yet can't put forth the attempt to visit the living. The burial service was at Stoke Fleming, taken by his Godson, John Giles, child of Jack Giles. Father's dad was vicar at St Peters between 1913 to 1915 when he passed on from a riding mishap. Father was covered in the family grave with his folks, which has a brilliant view sitting above Start Bay. The daylight shined on the ocean from which he had drawn his living, being a maritime designer, and his pleasure – little boat cruising. The post burial service party was held at Gunfield Boathouse in Dartmouth, with its all encompassing perspective up harbor towards the Naval College, which rules the harbour.

At this time, Donald was a chief with Bristol and West Building Society, the occupation with Herbert having collapsed with the breakdown of the securities exchange – "Anatina" and the bequest in Scotland being sold.

Edward was a significant with the Royal Engineers, Malcolm was a flight lieutenant, and James was a lieutenant in the Navy.

SALVALIANT IN COMMAND

I flew back to Singapore and took order of the "Salvaliant", Peter having assumed responsibility for the new huge Selco pull "Salvanquish". The pull was brimming with old appearances among the team: bosun – intense, trustworthy Javier Patani; cook – messy, dull Conrad Diotay; jumpers – extreme, large Paquito Delos Rey and attractive Elmo Ramos; welder – Ikan from the Salviking. Jesus Armosilla was as yet the central official and Edgar Selorio was the second. Moderately aged Fernando was as yet the main architect, and the greater part of the motor room group were something very similar. The pull had nearly turned into a family.

The "Salvaliant" was outfitted with just a solitary drum tow winch, which implied it was hard to tow more than one boat immediately. The pull was contracted to tow the Royal Fleet Auxiliary big hauler "Green Ranger" to Hong Kong and the ex Strick Line transport "Foochow" to Canton, both going for scrap. The North East storm was blowing unequivocally as indicated by the climate gauges I got. We manipulated the tows in Western Anchorage. The "Salvaliant" was close by the "Foochow" in the 69 position and when the rescue affiliation assessor was happy with the arrangements, Dave Hancox turned up on the "Salviper" with an old kettle as supply and an enormous blower. There was no power on the tow so the anchor was hurled up utilizing air rather than steam. I towed the "Foochow" out of Anchorage and streamed the tow, keeping it short for the section through Singapore main strait.

Meanwhile, Dave cruised off with the heater and blower to lift the anchor of the "Green Ranger", which was being towed with the "Salvanquish," Peter in order. Off Eastern Anchorage Peter got up to speed and brought the "Salvanquish" close by the "Salvaliant" – our elastic tire bumpers adequate in the smooth waters of the Strait. The "Foochow" was on the fundamental tow wire which was loosened out permitting space for the "Green Ranger," which was on the proper wire. The proper wire was disregarded to the "Salvaliant" and made quick. I presently had two tows and sped up. When Peter saw that everything was well he wished me karma over the radio, blew three impacts on the whistle and continued back to Singapore. Both the tows followed quite well and by 12 PM we were passing Horsburgh Light and out into the South China Sea.

Although it was longer, the Palawan Passage course – suggested by the rescue affiliation – called for continuing up the shoreline of Borneo, East

Malaysia and the Philippines, then crossing the South China Sea with the weather on the beam to Hong Kong. I say 'suggested', which is the authority word, yet assuming I didn't follow this course the tow would be uninsured, so it is more similar to a guidance. Nonetheless, this is the Admiralty suggested course for low controlled vessels and I concurred with it.

The tow continued well until I began crossing the South China Sea with the climate simply forward of the shaft. When clear of the lee of the Philippines, the ocean and swell got up and the breeze expanded until it was blowing a storm. The pull rolled intensely and was generally awkward. The towing gunnel was consistently lubed to ensure the tow wires. Progress was slow yet the "Salvaliant "extended 600 tons of fuel so that was no problem.

On a dull night south of Scarborough Reef the motor fires up abruptly expanded somewhat more than the standard change with the pitch and roll of the pull. I left onto the scaffold wing and looked toward the back. I just had one tow, the "Green Ranger" had gone. My heart sank. I strolled back onto the scaffold and checked out the radar screen; there she was, the distance gradually increasing.

The bosun went onto the extension trickling wet. "Wire broken, Cap," he said, "all gone." So nothing was looming over the side.

'Green Ranger broken hapless. North-east storm. Coordinates....' Signed Tew.

That was the message I sent when I called the radio official. I plunked down to figure what to do. I could simply leave the tow, which was the simple thing to do, and convey a navigational admonition. Even having lost a tow, the "Salvaliant" was not making a lot of progress and it was rough.

I advised Jesus to ring down and tell the motor space to diminish gradually to half speed. I watched the "Foochow" through the optics, her framework only apparent in obscurity and the red sidelight.

The "Salvaliant" was nearly halted in the water and we were lying serenely, however the "Green Ranger" was floating away very rapidly.

I at last decided. I would stand by the "Green Ranger" and wait for the weather to moderate, then try and pick her up and reconnect the tow. I would not send a navigational admonition, which would bring out rival rescue pulls who might attempt to get her and take her off me. I advised the central official to caution the bosun I planned to turn and steam downwind, following the "Green Ranger" until we could get her again.

"Alright, Cap," he acknowledged.

The turn went good, albeit the pull rolled frightfully, and with the pull going gradually, the "Foochow" followed – floating shaft onto the wind.

We held up four days, gradually floating back towards Singapore. The climate at long last directed enough to make an endeavor conceivable to get the tow. A fishing boat showed up and went towards the "Green Ranger" about a large portion of a pretty far. I blew the whistle and sped up. They proceeded and went close by the floating boat. I was next to myself with rage, this was my boat and nobody planned to remove her from me.

I kept on blowing the whistle, my group were all at hand presently yelling and waving at the fishing boat. They failed to acknowledge and one group began to jump on board utilizing the crisis towing wire. I hurried down into my lodge, grabbed the rifle out of my closet. I opened the safe and snatched the pistol and all the ammo and got back to the extension. We were close now and one man was ready for one more after him up the wire.

"Anybody know how to utilize these things?" I asked.

Ricky, the radio official, took the rifle and stacked it while Jesus did likewise with the revolver.

"Point it at them and shoot," I requested Ricky.

Suddenly there was a rodent a-tat like an automatic weapon going off and projectiles showered onto the "Green Ranger". I took the gun off Jesus and discharged several shots yet it was superfluous. The two men on the "Green Ranger" shot once again into their boat, which took off at rapid back towards Manila. Ricky had the rifle on programmed rather than single shot, yet it had the ideal impact. The group were all outshining and snickering with glee.

The following issue to address was the manner by which to get the "Green Ranger" while as yet towing the "Foochow". I was unable to go toward the back on the motor or I would have the tow line round the propeller, and I was unable to stop for a really long time or the pull may float over the "Foochow" tow line. I in the end arrived at the resolution that the best way to do it was to put the boats on various tacks. The "Green Ranger" was heading about south-east so if I turned the "Foochow" so she was heading north-west there would be time to pick up the drifting ship before the "Foochow" turned on her tow wire and came drifting back to collide with us. This is the thing that I did and the group were fabulous at getting the crisis tow wire and harness manipulated at the edge of the "Green Ranger" and associating it to another decent tow wire.

" "Green Ranger" reconnected." I gave Ricky the message to ship off Singapore as the pull and tows got speed.

I plunked down to partake in a brew, all around satisfied with myself and the crew.

I later composed an article for the Nautical Institute Magazine portraying the get and guaranteed it as a world first and nobody to date has questioned it.

Off Hong Kong I conveyed the "Green Ranger" to the scrapyard pulls and proceeded onto the entry of the Pearl River. A pilot boarded, alongside a commissar, and it was very clear that the pilot didn't realize anything about towing. A pull was made quick on one or the other side of the "Foochow" and, rather than the pleasant tranquil tow she had been – following compliantly behind the pull – she turned into something wild sheering from side to side.

The pilot was jabbering directions into the radio and I understood we were not going to get up the stream like this. It was very wide at the entry however it turned out to be logically smaller the further up one continued. I chose to assume responsibility. I taught the pilot to advise the two pulls to stop their motors. Quickly the "Foochow" began to maintain good manners. The pilot appeared to be most surprised.

Once things were settled I brought the pilot and commissar down to the extra lodge, which contained an ice chest loaded with brew, and proposed they may jump at the chance to unwind and I would call them when I needed help.

I had the Admiralty diagram of the waterway and followed the floats up to Canton, the tow acting entirely following the pull. I called the pilot not long prior to arriving at the city and asked him where we should drop off the tow. He looked like he had lived it up with the substance of the refrigerator! The tide was making and he said we needed to moor, so I turned the "Foochow" head to tide, sent the zed boat across with a rescue team and they let go above and beyond. Loads of individuals turned up yet I got my conveyance letter marked and detached the tow. I went close by the tow to gather all our hardware and spend the night.

The following morning our freedom and a pilot turned up and I continued down the stream, the pilot exploring! I dropped him off at the entry of the Pearl River and steamed in the back manner to Hong Kong, past the distant islands. I took up rescue station in the harbor, with the perspective on Hong Kong Island and the Peak apparent on fine days. The "Foochow" was the biggest boat around then ever to have been towed dead up the Pearl stream, a smaller than usual world first.

The green painted Star Ferries, employing to Kowloon side, and the dark Yaumati vehicle ships, hurrying to the islands, made a nonstop wash – increased by an intermittent boat cruising by. White painted fly foils run on Boeing air motors, hydro foils and customary ships, hurried to Macau. The harbor was somewhat more modest from my Indo China days for there had been a great deal of infilling on the Hong Kong side, so the tide ran a little stronger.

Our representatives were Everett Steamship Corporation and the head men were English. I turned out to be especially agreeable with John Davison, who had been in British India Steamship Navigation Co Ltd. I initially met him in Calcutta when I was cadet and he was a subsequent official. He was hitched to a Chinese woman and had a child. We delighted in numerous a pleasant lunch or dinner.

Marie Louise, Ernie's little girl, was the Selco delegate in Hong Kong and she worked in an office in Everetts. We additionally had a couple friendly snacks and meals together, now and again alone and at times with individuals associated with the rescue world.

Hong Kong was a flourishing, clamoring, occupied spot. Everybody wore suits to work and you were unable to get into the best places except if you were appropriately dressed, so I had two or three suits made.

Salvage station is inconceivably exhausting yet I had a pager and organized a couple for the group so we could get shorewards. I additionally had a worldwide phone put on the scaffold so we could be in moment correspondence with Singapore. My time was tremendously invigorated by Marie Louise and the Everett people.

The most noticeably awful harasser on the "Chindwara" was a man called Thorn and in conversation with John it worked out that he was in Hong Kong as an assessor. He had lost a boat on Pratas Reef, among Taiwan and Hong Kong, in awful climate and was currently shorewards. John thoroughly understood the "Chindwara" and figured it would be a smart thought assuming that we met and let the phantoms of the past go. I was not entirely certain yet John guaranteed me he was not a miscreant, which was not my recollection.

John organized a noon meeting in the basement bar under the Connaught Center, which was the workplace watering opening. Lunch reached out to an evening drink and supper and the apparitions were, to be sure, let go – alongside a shocking headache the following day. He was not genuinely horrendous all things considered and let me know how they had all been put through hell on the "Chindwara" and the harassing was stopped.

Marie Louise gotten an agreement for us to tow a traveler transport which was lying at the scrapyard to Manila. I took the pull over to Junk Bay and made my underlying review. She was an ex Silver Line transport – my outdated companion, Johnathen Priest, was with them – and it was shocking strolling through the unfilled, quiet, abandoned boat. I felt assuming that I had an enchanted wand I could unexpectedly make her wake up; everything was set up, all it required was individuals and power.

The pull was moored in the sound and I got back to bring her close by the reprieved transport. While moving toward I was remaining at the moving situation on the monkey island and put the message from half ahead to slow toward the back. In addition to the fact that nothing happened, the motor fires up expanded. I put the message to full toward the back. I was going directly toward the white frame of the traveler transport. The motor, rather than going back and forth toward the back, expanded fires up to full ahead. I was presently steaming at full ahead with the message at full toward the back and, acknowledging something wasn't right, put the steerage hard over to starboard. I gave the crisis twofold ring toward the back on the message however settled the score more fires up ahead.

I yelled at Jesus to telephone down to the motor room and get the motor toward the back speedy before we crashed into our tow-to-be. The "Salvaliant" gradually began to turn, and with my heart in my mouth, she scratched past the boat at max throttle with crawls to extra and back out into the sound. I put the message to stop and the motor stopped.

Shaking with dread and gibbering with rage, I let the pull float while I caused a ruckus at the main specialist. Poor Fernando had never seen me so furious and I trust never to blow my top like that again. In the end I quieted down enough to apologize, for despite the fact that Fernando committed the underlying error I intensified it. When I understood there was an incorrect way motor development I ought to have put the message to stop. The messman presented to me a cool brew and we attempted again and went close by with no problem.

It was an unpleasant outing down to Manila however the tow went quite well. We didn't spend some time before getting back to Hong Kong for Christmas and really celebrating. My progression cousin, David Wynne Davis, was positioned in Hong Kong with the military and I took him out to supper in the Eagle's Nest at the Hilton Hotel, with its view over Hong Kong. He welcomed me to a Beating Retreat, which was nostalgic and impactful with the sun setting over China. I additionally took him for supper at the highest point of the Hilton, which was great yet costly – not unexpected from an inn classed as truly outstanding in the world.

I was planning to go to Midnight Mass at the basilica however my pager went off and I passed up a major opportunity, and it was not so much as a salvage!

The "Salvaliant" went about as an 'anchor' for a flatboat while the towing pull went into dry harbor in January 1976. It was cold and I was happy when that exhausting position was finished and I got directions via telephone from Singapore to continue to Brunei at efficient speed. For quite a while I needed to arrive on Scarborough Reef, which was coming, having passed it ordinarily on the 'H' boats.

I continued at maximum speed from Hong Kong and visited the reef, the jumpers looking over an appropriate spot to secure in the lee.

We spent a most charming six hours in brilliant daylight swimming and swimming on the reef. I sat on the extension in the sunset eating new crawfish got by the jumpers, washed down with a decent white wine.

I proceeded at affordable speed, showing up at the "Runna" at the time given in my unique ETA from Hong Kong, nobody any the more shrewd of our little reprieve and recreation!

The "Runna" was a stacked log transporter with a motor issue. She was to be towed dead boat with next to no team ready, and my rescue group arranged her for towing and manipulated the towing gear. We lifted the anchor ourselves and got going with next to no help. The journey up the Palawan Passage went very well in fine climate; the "Runna", being stacked, yawed about a little however nothing to stress about.

North of the Philippines and south of Taiwan the climate was still fine and I went across in the zed boat to assess the tow. Everything was all together however moving over the deck freight of logs I slipped and separated my shoulder. It was distress. I had separated it once before in Hong Kong when descending the pilot stepping stool of our tow to Manila and must be brought down. It had required 30 minutes of agonizing control by Ikan to get it back in and I didn't go to the specialist. I attempted to get it back in myself yet was ineffective. I was loaded up with dreams of being marooned on the tow for I was unable to get once again into the zed boat. On this event the rescue team with me came to my guide and on top of the logs – with much torment and heaps of yelling – figured out how to get it back in. I was extremely diminished to move back ready the tug.

We experienced mess climate up the shore of Taiwan and on to Japan but – the "Salvaliant" being a major, weighty pull – there were no issues when the "Runna" yawed out aside or the other or remained out on the pillar.

It was cold in Japan when we delivered the tow to a small port in the inland sea and the "Salvaliant" had no heating only air-conditioning! No one spoke any English so I was glad our Japanese Selco representative turned up and we were able to get cold weather gear and some heaters.

The "Chenai Jayam" was a completely loaded 50,000 ton mass transporter and she separated in the scope of Hong Kong. I ran free at maximum speed in harsh after climate to her area, and it was still unpleasant when we associated the tow. The mass transporter was somewhat enormous for the "Salvaliant", particularly in the harsh climate. The "Chenai Jayam" would in general yaw out to the shaft and stay

there, so progress was slow, yet I was not stressed – thinking it was a rescue.

I was outraged when I got a message illuminating me that it was an agreement tow, and I sent some stroppy messages to Singapore about salvage.

'Have you enough fuel to arrive at Japan?' Signed
Bond. 'Indeed.' Signed Tew.
Later, when the sluggish advancement was
seen, 'Would you be able to arrive at
Japan?' Signed Bond. 'Indeed.' Signed
Tew.

The climate turned out to be more regrettable with a full hurricane blowing as we moved toward Japan with substantial oceans. The oceans were enormous that the tow was practically far away on occasion and I took some great photos. One I later offered to Nautical Publishing who distributed it in their book This is Heavy Weather Sailing.

We finally arrived at Shimonoseki where the "Chenai Jayam" moored and we went into port. I was still exceptionally irritated with the workplace for fixing an agreement tow rather than a rescue tow, on the grounds that neither the group nor myself got a reward for agreements and I felt emphatically that we ought to for hazardous and troublesome pick-ups adrift – and told them so in messages.

Mr Koyanagi, the more youthful Selco agent in Tokyo, was there to meet the pull. He took me to a legal official public – or the Japanese same – and with much bowing and scratching, duplicates of my log showing the unpleasant climate were notarised. The legal official was an elderly person in conventional dress, and entering his office resembled returning in time.

I got a message from the Indian proprietors of the "Chenai Jayam" that their agent on board the boat off Kobe had a reward for me and the team assuming I wanted to proceed to get it. I got the Japanese quick train Shinkansen, usually known as the Bullet, and went to Kobe. I was met by their representative and taken out to the boat and given $5,000 as a little something extra for the team. I felt more than legitimized in my stroppy messages to Selco, and I had until recently never known about proprietors giving a money reward. My group were more than cheerful when I showed up back ready the "Salvaliant" and gave them their bonus.

Half a month after the fact we ran free back to Hong Kong and I had a decent groan at Marie Louise about rewards which, most likely, went straight back to her dad, which was the intention!

We held some fairly fluid curry snacks on board the pull in the harbor, the wine being served in great cut glass. They probably been fruitful in light of the fact that individuals returned a subsequent time, and regularly lunch didn't complete until

16:00 in the afternoon!

**

I was conveyed on spec for a boat with a motor breakdown, however she got rolling once more. In any case, rather than getting back to Hong Kong, I was told to continue to Singapore for dry docking.

William Crafter, or Bill to his companions, was introduced in brief office close to Mr K. Why EEK utilized this man I didn't find until some other time, and it absolutely was not so much for his ability. He was a resigned significant who, he said, had been on the staff of General, presently Field Marshal, Carver.

Major Crafter was a major man with a somewhat high impacted voice and he didn't know anything about pulls and surprisingly less with regards to rescue. He was obviously higher ranking than Alan Bond and near Mr K. His name had showed up on a portion of the answers to my stroppy messages. My groaning more likely than not had its impact in light of the fact that there was discussion of giving the team a reward, so I needed to compose a reminder clarifying I had effectively gathered one from the owners.

I think Crafter chose to humble me since he and Bond examined the pull close by in the yard. Bond, who was not given to composing reminders, composed an exceptionally shirty one to me whining about the condition of the pull, and specifically some oil areolas which were not working. I composed back expressing that Mr K had told me not to squander paint on the grounds that the pull was going into dry dock on her re-visitation of Singapore. I called attention to that the areolas he grumbled about were been welded up on his, Mr Bond's directions, and for that reason they didn't work. I replicated Bond's update and my answer to Mr K and that was the finish of the matter!

Singapore Port Authority would just issue a port leeway substantial for 24 hours and afterward it must be recharged. They dismissed the case for giving a rescue pull an open port leeway – which was the conspicuous thing to do – and assuming too many port clearances were given without being utilized they protested. Commonplace civil servants keeping guidelines. I proposed to Mr Bond that when the pull was prepared we ought to get a port freedom and sail, remaining external port cutoff points. We would then beat the opposition who were inside port restricts; the bet was which side of Singapore to stand by!

The refit was finished and the pull was completely put away for quite some time, including wine and beer.

I cruised and moored outside port cutoff points on the Western side of Singapore, in fact in Malaysian waters.

'Continue rescue speed to....' the given directions were north of Sumatra

'... what's more help "Sealift Mediterranean".' Signed Bond.

It was not some time before we were running at a little more than fifteen bunches up the quiet Malacca Straits in splendid daylight hoping to be responsible for the salvage.

It was the point at which we showed up I found another worker of Selco was at that point nearby and was the assigned rescue ace. I sent an exceptionally terse message quite back and got one back from EEK.

'Continue ahead with the rescue and will examine on your return.'

The "Sealift Mediterranean" was what could be compared to the British RFA, and the public authority were not satisfied that one of their boats – a stacked big hauler – had torn open her base on a graphed rock and was contaminating the ocean north of Indonesia. Just speedy activity by the expert of a Selco pull working in the area had forestalled the boat sinking. A full release of the freight was made to an easing up big hauler. Selco jumpers fixed the immense slash in the base, from the forepeak to 2 feet forward of the motor room. They worked encompassed by sharks. We avoided potential risk with junk, unloading it with a little pull no less than five miles from the casualty.

The senior Americans used to come on board the "Salvaliant" for rewards, which were not accessible on the dry American boat, and to watch a periodic suggestive film. I found I was nicknamed The Duke by the Americans!

When the fixing was done I towed the "Sealift Mediterranean" to Singapore. The 'rescue ace' remained on board my pull for the time being and the following morning I found that the refrigerator in the extra lodge, which had been brimming with brew, was unfilled. The rescue expert couldn't be awoken. I was not satisfied, I was incensed.

I had my gathering with Mr K, who apologized for the circumstance and said it was power of conditions and not to stress – different freedoms would happen. I educated him regarding the unfilled ice chest and maybe there was an issue. The man didn't keep going long. He didn't show up at the workplace for four days and Knobby Halls thought that he is in his level passed out encompassed by void containers. He was flown back to the UK.

***

Selco Shipyard constructed nine freight boats for Iran and they were to be towed as three tows three high. "Salvaliant" was assigned to tow them and, later conversation, it was consented to tow them one behind the other. The flatboats were stacked in the yard – the lashings welded – and they were towed out to the

"Salvaliant" in Western Anchorage.

I put two of them close by in the 69 position and one toward the back.

Streaming the tow was interesting yet effectively closed, and the long tow to the Persian Gulf initiated. The climate was fine and the journey ordinary. The most fascinating piece was up the shore of India from Cape Comorin to Trivandrum, which I passed near and composed an article 'A Day on the Coast of India' which was distributed in the Nautical Magazine.

At the entry to the stream for Bandar Mashur, the Iranian port on the east side of the top of the Persian Gulf, there were a great deal of boats at anchor. We held up with the freight ships unstable toward the back, anticipating a significant delay. A portion of the boats had been hanging tight for a long time. There was a sure measure of boat visiting, the climate being fine.

About seven days after the fact I got a message in the
evening. 'Pilot boarding a.m.'

This was uplifting news and the group buckled down preparing the tow. We put one tow on one side and one tow on the other, and the third tow toward the back in light of the fact that it was impractical to tow up waterway with every one of the freight boats toward the back – we would have been excessively long. As it was we were a huge 'transport' 400 feet in length and 140 feet beam!

The following morning the pilot boat came over and the pilot said, "What speed can you make?"

"Goodness, around eight bunches," I replied.

"That is OK. Follow me, I am taking that boat up." He highlighted a stacked freight transport. "I will tune in out on channel 16." And with that he departed.

"Jesus, hurl up the anchor," I said, and, to Fernando, "Reserve engines."

I got going and gone to the fairway float, the team actually looking at the freight boats. The boat the pilot boarded overwhelmed me and I sped up, the pull guiding typically adjusted by the flatboats either side.

The Admiralty graph showed the waterway was floated the whole way to Bandar Mahshahr and the encompassing banks were level swamps. The boat with the pilot was pulling ahead, doing around fifteen bunches. I called up on the VHF yet there was no reply, and inside the hour he had vanished and I was all alone! It was quite far up the waterway yet, having begun, I was not turning around so proceeded. The tide was ebbing so my advancement was delayed over the land and as the water fell, so a greater amount of the banks were uncovered. It was level and featureless and I was extremely subject to the buoys.

At sunset I moored along the edge of the channel yet spent an uncomfortable night
in light of the fact that the pull hauled. The following morning I showed up at

the port and conveyed the barges.

Three days after the fact I accepted my leeway and the specialist said that as I had come up the stream without a pilot I could go down the waterway without one also. Mostly down I moored and removed the raft to a flatboat up a spring I had seen on the upriver trip. It was on solid land however by dint of towing with the raft, I returned it above water and towed it once again to the pull and associated up. I made an impression on Selco illuminating them I had salved a canal boat and how might they like me to manage it. I forged ahead down the river.

'Anchor the canal boat and continue Dubai for shelters,' the guidelines returned, which is the thing that we did – leaving a light on it. I was exceptionally satisfied with myself and crew.

I left Dubai for the Straits of Hormuz. In transit I passed a green wreck float with the word 'Dara' composed on it and halted the "Salvaliant" to offer my appreciation to the 238 dead. It evoked numerous recollections of the debacle, not least my time in the water, the body, the envisioned shark, and the consuming hellfire on B deck.

I forged ahead to Colombo where I went close by the Yugoslav freight transport "Volosko", which had motor issues and required towing to Singapore. The "Salvaliant" likewise endured motor issues and the cooling had gotten together on the pull also. It was hot in the port so I resigned to the Oberoi Hotel, while the central architect and motor group fixed the motor. The Oberoi is a staggering lodging with a tremendous chamber, the rooms running off the encompassing balconies.

Seven days after the fact – with the Yugoslavs jumping all over with the deferral – we were prepared. The trouble was to get the "Volosko" out of the restricted entry. Later conversations with the expert specialist (harbor ace in different ports) and Razzle Dazzle, the senior pilot, who had been fourth official on the "Dara", I chose to tow her out with the "Salvaliant" on an exceptionally short tow with the two harbor pulls either side. Everything worked out positively, with Razzle on the "Volosko", and I towed her out of Colombo and on to Singapore. She yawed pretty much everywhere, being balanced, yet despite the fact that she was now and again out on the bar, the pull acted quite well and I had the option to direct at all times.

Nobody said anything regarding my visit in the Oberoi and the organization took care of the bill through the pull portage bill.

I gave proof to Dennis Rixon who was living in a suite in the Goodwood

Park Hotel, one of the most costly and most pleasant lodgings in Singapore. The food was awesome and the brew costly. Notwithstanding, there was a period limit on my visit in Singapore and he continued ahead with the work –

the helpless secretary staying at work past 40 hours. There was a chipper Sunday lunch with Mr K in the Hilton.

I ran free up to the Gulf, bunkered in Dubai and went close by the "Majma Two", which had been secured on the Dubai Petroleum oil field for quite some time. Along with "Majma One", these big haulers were the capacity ships which held the rough siphoned up from the oil field.

The motor room and convenience had been cut off so they were totally square toward the back. The rescue affiliation assessor demanded that we tow the boats with 25,000 tons of balance which appeared to be very ludicrous. It would dial back the tow impressively and to my brain not make it any more secure. Peter on the "Salvanquish" concurred thus reinforced in Singapore. As a wellbeing precautionary measure if there should arise an occurrence of breaks – for the boats were old, which was the reason they were going to Singapore for refit – we put convenient siphons on deck.

Eventually we got going and when the oil field was carefully hidden, I sent my rescue team across to the "Majma" and advised them to siphon out the balance. Peter did likewise with his and we sped up by a few bunches. The "Salvanquish" was an impressively more remarkable pull than the "Salvaliant" and towed the "Majma One" significantly quicker. Peter was soon days in front of me and got round Sri Lanka before the storm truly broke.

One of the motors on the "Salvaliant" was wiped out. We manipulated a sail on the fundamental pole using hatch covers, which both sped up a bit and steadied the pull in the pillar climate. My group protested saying in the event that anybody saw us they would be embarrassed however livened up when they understood the sail truly made a difference. Assuming you are just completing four bunches, an increment of a large portion of a bunch makes a major difference.

Eventually the starboard motor turned out to be wiped out that it must be paused and must be utilized in a crisis – the square was broken. Speed was down to more than two bunches or so and clearly I planned to require help.

The South West rainstorm had broken with its solid breezes and downpour. That was fine for Peter currently round Sri Lanka, it gave him a reasonable wind.

'Continue Amani Island and help "Pacifico Everrett".'

The originator of the message appeared to have failed to remember that I was towing a 40,000 ton stockpiling big hauler and had motor issues! It was the prior days satellite guides or GPS and I had not gotten sun sights for a really long time, I

posted lookouts up the mast and on the monkey island and we found the island in heavy rain. It was a relief. It was much too deep to anchor, so I steamed up and down in the lee of the low palm-treed island.

The setback was on the opposite side of the island, the windward side and the best way to contact her was with the elastic zed boat across the tidal pond. The issue was getting into the tidal pond. We found the entry was at the northern finish of the island however the oceans were breaking across it. I took the zed boat away with the two jumpers and the fitter Eusebio leaving my pull and tow accountable for the main official Edgar. We held on off the reef entrance and watched and an example arose when there were no breaking waves. In the wake of giving and acquiring understanding from the three team with me we chose to try it out. Picking the right second I sped up and made for the entry and as we entered a wave ascended behind us and appeared to pursue us in, breaking simply behind the elastic boat. We would have been dead in the event that it had overwhelmed us and tossed us onto the reef.

Laughing with help we made it over the tidal pond with Elmo the jumper remaining in the bow coordinating, showing me where the coral heads were. We made it securely to where the "Pacifico Everett" was ashore high and practically dry on the reef with waves breaking over her. I moored our boat and we swam towards the edge of the reef and the side of the boat. I slipped and wound up being cleared towards the harsh of the boat where the waves were breaking and I realized I would be cleared into the surf and certain terrible demise. Romeo Eusebio saw what was occurring and some way or another grasped my arm and pulled me to my feet saving me. We at last ascended installed through a pilot ladder.

After my investigation and the report of the jumpers who sounded round and Eusebio who sounded the tanks I realized she was done it was absolutely impossible that we could ointment her. The Pacifico Everrett was scrap.

We advanced back across the tidal pond and acknowledged we were unable to get out through the consistently breaking channel oceans. We went shorewards and conveyed the boat across the island meeting certain individuals who proposed to help us. I asked them what their identity was and they said "we are pariahs" and to my timeless disgrace I dropped the boat and with my three team we ran into the water. The pariahs fell with regards to snickering and let us know they were not irresistible and we would not find a single thing from them. Saying 'sorry' we returned and together conveyed the boat to a protected dispatch place and crossed the reef back to the "Salvaliant" towing the tremendous "Majma."

It was with impressive help I climbed locally available, showered, sank a chilly lager and formed my message to Singapore. In answer to my question concerning the untouchables the message basically said "don't contact." They were sending Peter with the "Salvanquish," which had arrived at Singapore securely to help. Different ideas were made for rescue however none were practical.

***

The "Salvanquish" properly showed up certain days after the fact along with the P and I club assessor who announced the boat a complete misfortune. With arrangement from nearby head who was visiting the island we handled the group of the loss and they were carried out to the "Salvaliant" in an island paddling boat. We took them to Cochin subsequent to surrendering the tow to the "Salvanquish" Peter tossing a void jar of lager over the side as he pulled away.

We were three weeks in Cochin. Bumpy Halls was very welcome when he turned up – extremely strong and a friendly sidekick. He figured out how to weld up the motor and withdrew with the debilitated AB back to Singapore.

I lived in the Malabar Hotel, which was on the island in the harbor, and the specialist came for drinks consistently. It was generally exceptionally Indian and honorable, and the lodging was an out thing of the 1930s.

I visited the place of worship focus of the most seasoned Jewish people group in India – diminishing in numbers – and the grave of Vasco de Gama.

All our cholera immunisations were outdated and the wellbeing specialists demanded that we as a whole be infused. The female specialist turned up with an antiquated needle and needle and surprisingly more older style thoughts of cleanliness. At the point when I recommended that the needle may be cleaned, she told me not to be particular; and when I criticized at the utilization of a similar needle for everybody she let me know no infusions, no declaration, no port freedom. I submitted.

***

I cruised out into the South West storm with directions to continue to the Somali coast. It was harsh and the "Salvaliant" pitched intensely, transporting oceans, and rolled. One of the jumpers was so nauseous I however he planned to pass on me. He was unable to hold down anything and turned out to be seriously got dried out. In the end he was sneaking all through cognizance. At the point when we arrived at the coast and the ocean quieted down he wonderfully recuperated, inside a few hours he was eating and back to normal.

I saw as the "General King" secured off the shore around fifty miles north of Mogadishu. The north-bound current was running at around seven bunches and

I considered how I planned to tow this stacked boat against the current to the port. The sun was sparkling, which was welcome later the downpour adrift during the intersection from India.

There was an enormous measure of rescue insight among the group, particularly the bosun and Paquito, the jumper, and the officials. Later conversation I secured in front of the boat and dropped back, putting the harsh close by the anchor link – ever aware of my weak propeller. The bosun shackled a strap round the chain and the fundamental tow wire to the strop.

I steamed ahead, getting our anchor. I needed to steam at seven bunches through the water just to stay fixed over the land, and the subsequent motor was gripped in before the anchor was done. Speed was gradually expanded, the strap ran down the anchor chain of the "All inclusive King" until it caught on the anchor and when enough power had been put on, the anchor took off the base and I had the tow taken care of at seven bunches through the water. With full power we just made just shy of eight bunches and required right around two days to arrive at Mogadishu.

The port was not yet open, albeit constructed, so the tow must be moored in the stream in the solid current. When in place I dialed back, loosen out the tow wire; the anchor went on the base, mooring the "Widespread King". The anchor of the "Salvaliant" was given up and I dropped back close by the link. The tow wire was hurled up the tight chain and the strap returned up to the outer layer of the water where it was unshackled.

The "Salvaliant" was releasing like a sifter through the harsh organ. There was a dredger in the port and I connected with the expert inquiring as to whether there was sufficient water for me to come in. At the point when he answered in the certifiable I requested that he assist me with getting consent to come in, he clearly realized the harbor ace. Authorization was allowed, the harbor ace came ready and drank all my Mateus Rose wine with me while the jumpers repacked the harsh gland.

The harbor ace was a lively individual. He told me not to go external the port except if I was in a taxi on the off chance that I esteemed my life; the Filipinos would be protected enough. The specialist, who was the specialist for the "Widespread King", was not actually inspired by us.

I passed by taxi to the best inn and spent numerous hours attempting to get past on the phone to Singapore. I in the long run conversed with Alan Bond and he concurred, when I had got my end letter marked, I ought to continue to Mombasa for fixes. There was nothing in Mogadishu aside from dust, heat and

rather flimsy individuals. When the Mateus Rose ran out the harbor ace said we needed to go yet fortunately I had the end letter by then.

Mombasa was a much needed development, in spite of the fact that it had gone downhill since autonomy. I had a disagreement with a Kenyan traditions man about the lager and wine in my refrigerator – utilized for engaging – and it accepted hush money to keep me in the clear! He took steps to have me beaten to a pulp.

Knobby turned up again and cared for the fixes and dry docking. I was utilizing a lodging for sending messages to Singapore until I understood it was claimed by the Italian salvor Murri Frere. I changed hotels!

I approached and befriended Peter Philips, who claimed another rescue organization, I figured the association may be valuable to Selco. Peter was truly neighborly and possessed a delightful house on the central area disregarding the rear of Mombasa.

I recruited a dinghy and cruised in Mombasa harbor. Bumpy and I remained in the Oceanic Hotel ignoring the entry to Mombasa.

Shortly later Knobby left to return to Singapore, I got guidelines to cruise for Saldanha Bay in South Africa. I had not been feeling very well in Mombasa and was practically nauseous when we cleared the reef at the entry and hit the sea swell.

Europa Island, in the Madagascar Channel, has no port and its only inhabitants are a few meteorologists and seagulls. I was instructed to look for a fishing boat that had run aground, and steamed round the island to find her. She was high and dry above the surf line on the windward side, great rollers beating down on the reef and throwing spray high into the air. My crew were apprehensive at being so close and so was I if truth be told.

I moored on the reef in the lee of the island, with the harsh kept clear by the seaward wind. I was feeling unmistakably undesirable so sent Edgar off with a rescue team to advance overland to the fishing boat.

They made some wonderful memories with the cordial meteorologists, who drove them across the island on a farm vehicle. The birdlife was really thick that some were squashed by the wheels.

Edgar revealed they boarded the fishing boat however she was a discount. A dining experience of seagulls' eggs was eaten, the anchor was hurled up and I continued coming – the team, who had reveled in the rich eggs, lost them when the sea expand was felt.

"I'm an European Englishman." I closed on my appearance message to the specialists, Ellerman Lines in South Africa. Such countless individuals in new ports came

on board reasoning that Captain Tew from Singapore should be Chinese or Asian. I didn't need any disarray in politically-sanctioned racial segregation South Africa.

***

ILL

I cleared in at Capetown. The specialist came on board to clergyman to the 70% of the group who had gotten 'something' from their excellent, silk-cleaned, Somali sweethearts. When leaving the port I was debilitated over the pilot's feet; he was not extremely intrigued. I was feeling particularly sick and considered going to the specialist. Be that as it may, in Saldanha Bay, which was north of Capetown, I felt somewhat better and began planning for the long tow to the Persian Gulf. The "Salvaliant" was contracted to tow a dredge.

I was feeling sick again and working up determination to take a brief trip and see the specialist, when somebody turned up and let me know that a boat was in a tough situation south of the Cape of Good Hope. It was cold and horrid climate yet I livened up at the possibility of rescue and made arrangements to leave. I called Singapore and Alan Bond concurred I should leave on spec and he would examine the talk. It would be an upset for Selco to play out a rescue on the shoreline of South Africa.

I steamed out of the harbor and ran down the rough coast past Capetown. There was, to be sure, a boat in a difficult situation, yet so was I. I was feeling exceptionally sick and I quit eating, not ready to hold anything down.

Once south of the Cape, the "Salvaliant" was practically in the Roaring Forties
– the Westerlies that scope round the world causing tremendous oceans in terrible climate. Tasmania, off the Australian coast, was the following stop toward the east; and Tierra Del Fuego, in South America, toward the west.

The "Ville de Mahebourg" was, without a rudder, heading towards Antarctica, holding her bow up into the climate. I hustled south at most extreme speed – the old young lady running in the virus water at more than fifteen bunches – plunging and moving over the expands, or so it appeared to me. 500 miles off the Cape of Good Hope, profound into the Southern Ocean – the sky cloudy, the ocean dark – I came up on the "Ville de Mahebourg" gradually clearing a path towards the South Pole.

"Do you concur Lloyd's Open Form?" I asked the expert on the VHF.

"Oui, yes," returned the reply.

That was adequate. I had an agreement, I had a LOF in the Southern Ocean. I was cheerful, a Selco first; Mr K would be satisfied, even Mr Bond would be satisfied and I would have one up on Captain Hancox! I just needed to be fruitful. I was feeling so sick I could scarcely stand up, and had not eaten since leaving Saldanha Bay.

The expert of the loss would have rather not stop because of a paranoid fear of rolling too vigorously when he swung pillar onto the gigantic swell, however I let him know he would need to when I associated. I let him know I would be however speedy as could really be expected and it seemed to be dependent upon him to hurl in the towing gear fast.

I climbed intensely up onto the monkey island and advised Edgar to concoct a seat and remain with me; Loreto, the subsequent mate, should man the radio. I felt debilitated and lightheaded yet still up in the air to interface and tow the "Ville de Mahebourg" to safety.

The pull was transporting substantial oceans on the tow deck. Extreme, trustworthy Javier Patani, the bosun, and wild Paquito Delos Reyes, the jumper, were holding on the later incubate – with the group taking a gander at me and afterward the rolling and pitching loss. It was getting dim, the sky was heavy and bleak and I needed to hurry up. I chose to face a challenge, I realized I could rely upon my group and I speculated I could rely upon the French; it was whether I kept going out sitting in my seat, supported against the development of the tug.

I crossed the bow of the now floating boat and a hurling line crashed onto the tow deck. In an instant it was made quick to the polypropylene line and with the French hurling like psychos, it flew out over the side and up onto the "Ville de Mahebourg". I gave a kick ahead on the motor – turning the pull corresponding to the setback – the propeller away from the line. The wire pendant slid over the very much lubed gunwale, trailed by the cot. The pull was extremely near the boat and the wire pendant vanished through the fairlead on the forecastle of the casualty.

Shortly a while later the French flagged they had made quick. There were cheers from my pull and the tow and I steamed ahead, paying out the tow wire to nearly its most extreme length. I wanted the catenary in the weighty swell.

I sped up, turned north and when the French let me know they had upheld the bitts on which we were towing, I expanded to greatest power. The "Ville de Mahebourg" went out on one side and remained there. We made great speed.

I catnapped in the commander's seat on the scaffold, feeling extremely sick without a doubt. The association had removed it from me and I was experiencing issues holding down any fluids, so was becoming got dried out and now and again hallucinating.

I livened up somewhat four days some other time when I saw Table Mountain, the level plateau

above Capetown, ruling the city covered by cloud. It was cold and begun to rain when the pilot and pulls came out. I demanded staying associated and towed the setback on short tow to the billet, helped by the harbor pulls. When the group detached and recuperated the towing gear – their wet climate gear trickling with water – I tediously hopped on board the "Ville de Mahebourg". The skipper marked my end letter, offered me reward, which I rejected, and I got back to the pull nearly toward the finish of my tether.

I cruised in no time a while later for Saldanha Bay and let Edgar assume responsibility, resigning to my bunk. I figured out how to be on the extension entering Saldanha Bay and, once close by, I took a taxi to the nearby inn and hit the hay. The specialist was called and he analyzed jaundice and needed to place me in medical clinic there and afterward. I rejected until an alleviation turned up. I called Alan Bond in Singapore and let him know I was debilitated and kindly send a relief.

Edgar turned up for guidelines, coming into my room. The spouse of the proprietor said that he was unable to remain, he would need to remain in the passageway since he was dark. I blew my top, yelled at her to call the police; Edgar was remaining and he merited 100 individuals like her. She resigned hurt yet I had not any more rubbish. Different team went up to hope everything works out for me and let me know how much fun they were having in South Africa.

Ebullient, extraordinary, garrulous Hughie Murray diverted up from Singapore. He was a resigned leader from the Navy and mentally unstable; somewhat like a wild beast on the loose. He finished things, was astute yet trample on toes. I was incredibly happy to see his huge figure and left in a rescue vehicle to medical clinic in Capetown. After two months I flew back to England.

"What were the mobs like, I was stressed?" my mom inquired.

"What riots, Mum?"

Amazing how the Press contort the news.

I put in a few months in England recovering however my mom doesn't profess to be a decent medical caretaker. Assuming you are wiped out head to sleep, on the off chance that not then you are well! I remained at Thorns Beach, which is a superb spot to convalesce with the always changing perspective out of the window. Since we had the freehold – which I had paid for – there was a changelessness which, when it had been leasehold, was absent. There was nobody 'day it must be given back'.

The main cloud not too far off was the waterfront disintegration, and consistently every year a little piece a greater amount of the bank along the ocean side was washed away. My rescue life appeared to be totally remote from the harmony and calm at Thorns and the

birdlife at low water.

I gave my "Ville de Mahebourg" proof to Dennis Rixon in London. Robert

Elbourne, as enthusiastic as could be expected, and every one individuals I had worked with were satisfied to see me. Richard Shaw had passed on to set up his own firm. The daggy bar across the street was no more excellent and Corvinos had not changed.

SINGAPORE

Singapore was just about as hot and tacky as ever when I showed up back, and I remained in the Orchid Inn. The "Salvaliant" was not back from the bay and her long tow. I went out with Mr K a couple of times however was stringently 'on the cart' later my jaundice.

The "Citta di Savona" had an impact in Singapore Eastern Anchorage one evening and was emptying unrefined into the harbor Selco rescue vessel "Salvista" revealed. I was in the workplace and quickly went over the street and boarded the quick team boat "Salvital." after an hour I was locally available the loss however the expert wouldn't sign my LOF. I at long last convinced him and set to work. Selco jumpers were soon on location, loads of little pulls, the 'Selco oil barge, the "Salvital", the "Salvirile" and an oil blast. The Singapore Port Authority were there with their fire pulls, dispatches with assessors, and old Uncle Tom Cobley what not! In the midst of all the movement the expert said his proprietors trained him he was not to sign the LOF but rather it was at that point locally available the "Salvista." However he appeared to be very glad to allow us to continue ahead with the rescue, happy I was currently answerable for salving his ship.

The overall bedlam straightened out, the jumpers stopped the hole, freight was moved to one more tank to diminish the degree of oil to underneath the harm and

– by light – everything was taken care of. The commander offered me a lager and I contemplated internally on the off chance that I am sufficiently fit to perform rescue tasks I am adequately fit to have a brew. He marked my end letter and I left very much satisfied with myself. A marked Lloyds Open Form inside Singapore port cutoff points and endorsed by me.

Selco kept generally excellent associations in Djakarta, which were fundamental to work in degenerate Indonesia. I flew down to Djakarta, the level land confused with channels entirely noticeable from the air, and a hot nightlife suggestive of Holland and Amsterdam.

Mr Soekardono met me at the air terminal and took me to his office, where plans were made for me to go out to the boat ashore on a reef around fifty miles from Tanjong Priok. Pulls and barges were in transit from Singapore. I figured it a smart thought to take one of his office staff with me as a translator, and he demonstrated exceptionally valuable managing the Indonesian expert and the different authorities who turned up. He and I went out on a sanctioned pull later a decent dinner.

The Selco armada showed up. I laid ground tackle, released sufficient freight to refloat, and took the boat to Tanjong Priok where the freight was reloaded from the Selco barges. It was considerably more sweltering and stickier than Singapore!

Selco bought a wore out traveler transport that was on solid land off Port Klang for scrap. Alan Bond advised me to proceed to bring her down to Singapore – the "Salvanquish" was in transit from Madagascar. The "Salvirile" with Juanito Ventua, the ex-boss official of the "Salviper", in order was close by. It ended up being somewhat more troublesome than it sounded. The ex "Cambodge" was intensely on solid land, with a 15 degree list and halfway flooded.

I lived aground in hot and hot Port Klang, going out every day with the jumpers in a sanctioned dispatch. The boat was fixed and the water siphoned out. Juanito was a decent salvor, an amazing coordinator, that I was nearly superfluous.

One Sunday William Crafter showed up on the scene to take a gander at the boat. I was unable to accept my eyes when this ghost showed up wearing white pants and white shoes – white shoes to visit a rescue procedure on a dead, worn out, posting traveler ship!

I took him out in the dispatch and he painstakingly moved on board the pull, declining a virus drink in the skipper's lodge with Juanito. I proposed he may check out the Selco-claimed traveler transport however he took one glance at the passage board, taken a gander at his unblemished white shoes, checked out the slick deck on the traveler transport and declined. I took him shorewards and asked why for heaven's sake Mr K utilized this resigned armed force major.

After the scene of the areolas I had kept in touch with Edward, who was a significant with the Royal Engineers, and requested that he discover more with regards to Major Crafter. It turned out he had been in the commissariat and, a long way from resigning, he had left the military as opposed to confronting a court military for having his finger in the till. White shoes, I ask you!

The "Salvanquish" showed up with an extremely odd expert. All things considered, I was unable to grumble, he did what I told him to. We refloated the boat and sitting in the crow's home on the foremast of the "Cambodge" with a few cold lagers, I guided her out through the tight channel, with the "Salvanquish" towing and the "Salvirile" toward the back. We just came to the Malacca Straits before dim, and I remained on the tow to Singapore.

It was creepy on the worn out traveler transport as she quietly traveled through the dark water totally dim, the phantoms of work force en route to French Indo China (later Vietnam) effortlessly envisioned, worried maybe on the outward journey, euphoric on the back home. All completed later the fall of

Saigon to the socialists, engineered by a French instructed man.

I secured her right external Singapore port limits.

UNIQUE MARINER

I was back in charge of the "Salvaliant" which was close by the ex "Cambodge" and the rescue group were eliminating the motor stores, or those that Knobby needed. I was not very intrigued and it was incredibly hot and sleek down in the motor room and shaft tunnel.

I was on the extension of the "Salvaliant" inactively partaking in the natural air and watching out for anything untoward, as any great salvor ought to. I saw somewhere out there a boat, which gave off an impression of being halted or at anchor in Indonesian waters. Somewhat surprising, maybe a motor issue I thought. It was a fine day and I kept on watching the world's transportation entering or leaving the Malacca Straits.

Some time later the boat I had seen was still there and most certainly halted. I took a heading from the wing gyro repeater and laid it off on the graph. Indeed, directly through Selco treasure island Nipa Shoal.

My heart beat quicker, and the adrenalin began to stream as I yelled, "Activity stations, we are leaving!"

My team thought I had gone distraught until I yelled, "Boat aground!"

The motors were turned over in record time, the rescue group releasing the stores dropped what they were conveying, yelled to the men underneath and came running on board.

"Cut the lines," I requested from the monkey island control position, ringing twofold full ahead on the telegraph.

The "Salvaliant" took off like a singed feline, the water rising under the harsh scratching down the side of the "Cambodge", and in a real sense fled miles to Nipa Shoal. I don't have a clue what Fernando did to the motors, however the old pull had never been so quick in her life.

"Swing out the zed boat prepared for dispatching," I told Edgar, "and afterward reserve here with me."

Off the grounded transport I halted, gave over to Edgar and went rapidly to the zed boat. I had kept up with radio quietness, not having any desire to alarm the competition.

Paquito drove the zed boat and along with two or three rescue group, we sped over to the "Interesting Mariner", whose name I could see on the harsh. There was a pilot stepping stool over the side, so I got ready, Lloyd's Form in my pocket, and advised the man on deck to take me to his captain.

I was gotten by the Taiwanese skipper and his main official in the

chief's lodge. Later a couple of merriments I proposed to refloat him on Lloyd's Open Form, which I showed him. He concurred and we signed.

I was thrilled and incandescently happy as I returned to the pull, and the group gave a cheer when I waved the LOF. I sent the salvage crew back to the casualty with the pelican hook and told Ops I was salving a ship on LOF and was about to connect and please organise Indonesian permits.

The anchor was being weighed when I got a message over the Motorola radio from my second official who was on the loss standing by to interface. The expert needed to see me promptly and we were not to associate. My heart sank, what had turned out badly? I went over in the zed boat.

The expert needed the Lloyds Form back. He was unable to have it back. Another pull was coming to tow him off. I contended that I was there first and all prepared to interface. He offered me US$500 – tea cash – assuming I would give him the structure back. I was stunned and offended to be offered a pay off and told him so. He advised me to reclaim any stuff we had put on board his boat. I had no choice except for to consent to the directions of the expert and hesitantly provided the request and withdrew. My Lloyds Form was still until the expert 'ended' the agreement which he had not done, just requested it back. I got back to the pull generally displeased and informed Ops.

And so the "Salvaliant" entered the English law books and I wound up before the Admiralty judge Henry Brandon, presently Lord Brandon.

The learned appointed authority said, "This is a most fascinating case. In the event that I find against Captain Tew he is at legitimate fault for misrepresentation, maybe criminal extortion; assuming I find against the expert of the "Novel Mariner" he has simply made a mistake."

Food for figured, I could wind up in jail!

It is an overwhelming encounter to be an observer in court, particularly when blamed for accomplishing something I had not done. The expert of the "Extraordinary Mariner" expressed after swearing to tell the truth, upheld by his main official, that I had come on board his boat and said, "I'm from the specialists, sign here." He had been expecting a pull sent by the specialist, whom he had flagged that he was aground.

I denied I said any such thing. I was in the observer box for six hours, a large portion of it being interrogated by David Steele QC, a since quite a while ago nosed, scornful Old Etonian. He began asking me inquiries of detail which I was unable to recollect, so I went to the adjudicator and said, "Your Honor, assuming I could have my log book I could address that inquiry." "i'm not sure why Captain Tew can't have his log book," said the learned judge.

I was made up. I got my log and some other archive I requested and responded to all Mr Steele's inquiries satisfactorily.

The adjudicator found for Selco. The case is the point of reference on the main inquiry of the power of an expert to sign a Lloyd's Form. (He can.)

Selco guaranteed pay as a seized salvor and won that case as well, being paid what might have been paid assuming the rescue had been effectively completed by me.

BARGE PASTEE COLOMBO

I traveled to Bahrain and took order of the "Salvanquish". She was altogether different from the "Salvaliant" being single engined and all the more impressive, in this way more simple to move. There were issues turning over the motor yet it typically pursued a couple of attempts. Compacted air was needed to turn and turn over the motor and like the "Salvaliant" huge boat style, assuming that you needed the propeller to stop, the motor must be halted. When the motor was running it kept going.

I left Bahrain headed for Singapore running free. I needed to stop on entry off Muscat, where the "Dara" ought to have been the point at which the bomb went off, for motor fixes. Later the fixes were done the boss had a ton of trouble restarting the motor. I informed the workplace and was requested to Bombay. Bumpy turned up and we went to see the harbor ace and got consent to enter the docks so the motor could be immobilized for fixes. Multi week after the fact, with the motor obviously working, I left – destined for Singapore and rescue reserve. It had been a charming stay in Bombay, living in the Taj Mahal Hotel and doing a couple of touring tours.

The climate was foul being the south west rainstorm, downpour, wind, stickiness however the team all livened up when we were requested to Colombo and help the "Salvigilant" with the rescue of the flatboat "Pastee."

Aitken Spence were our representatives in Colombo and the "Salvanquish" was taken care of by Michael Mack and Nimal Maralande. We were given a decent compartment close to the city and Michael, who had taken me to see the Master Attendant whom I had met over the "Volosko" tow. He sorted out for an open-dated port leeway and authorization to cruise without a pilot in a crisis, if we paid for him.

The " "Salvigilant" came close by us and the expert came locally available to give me his report and a serious adventure it had been. He attempted to tow her off three weeks already and found himself mixed up with issue with the towing line around his propellors, moored on a lee shore with his harsh simply clear of the breakers on the reef. Jumpers sent by the specialist figured out how to clear one propellor and he got back to Colombo and had not been out since.

The canal boat "Pastee", stacked with sawn wood, was ashore off Bambalapitiya rail line station and I went to examine the jumpers and expert of the "Salvigilant." She appeared to be salvable so I told Singapore and they ordered me to do so. The South West storm was breaking, it had

broken further north, so speed was of the substance if we somehow managed to be effective. I committed an error, she was significantly harder ashore than I suspected and the jumpers couldn't get at the openings in the base to fix. I moved the "Salvanquish" to a stunningly better billet in the port and later a ton of gatherings and assurances to the traditions, released all the rescue gear from the pull and shipped it up to the rail line station.

The canal boat was on solid land on rocks near the shore, which was a bank around 6 feet high. A couple of yards inland was a 20 feet high divider ensuring the rail line station. Behind the divider were the stages and rail route lines. I got consent to cross the rail route lines with my stuff from the rail line specialists, which was finished with Michael's assistance.

We settled in behind the divider on the bank, with the enormous blower to drive the pneumatic machines and siphon air into the flatboat, the generator to run the electric submarines siphons and different pieces and pieces. It was hot and sticky and a swell was running in, making the canal boat move about on the rocks.

When everything was prepared, siphons ready, air siphoned into the open tanks, the "Salvigilant" came round to tow off the flatboat. The expert secured her off, the jumpers made the towing association, there was a decent swell running, and I taught him to start towing. He got the anchor and swung the pull from one side to another at full power. Aside from a couple of crushing doesn't clamor anything occurred. The "Pastee" ought to have fallen off however she didn't and we finished up she should be pierced on a stone. The "Salvigilant" got back to Colombo.

After conversation with my rescue team and Edgar, Michael took me to a designing works where I had a stand made. With the gear from the "Salvanquish" we manipulated up a breeches float situation to release the freight of sawn lumber. There was an odd inclination in Colombo, a feeling of premonition, a disquiet I had not experienced previously; somewhat like ceaselessly investigating your shoulder on a dim night for the non-existent stalker – dread. The canal boat and our exercises were drawing in a ton of interest and wood was a significant ware in Sri Lanka.

The group and officials from the two pulls and myself began to release the lumber and truck it away to a stockroom however it was slow work. A periodic board was lost, floating aground on the Colombo side of the rail line station where a group had assembled. They enthusiastically plundered the timber.

This continued for a couple of days with the group getting the boards lost over the edge expanding to around 400. Through Michael I was

utilizing a pack of Sri Lankans to aid the discharge.

***

The mind-set in Colombo had become tense, something planned to occur. One morning there were yells and shouts behind the divider and afterward the cadenced crash of tissue being hit very much like beating a steak.

Early in the early evening I saw the commotion had halted yet I was in a tough situation myself. A considerable amount of lumber had been washed off the canal boat and the group on the Colombo side of the rail route station were turning out to be extremely striking and had progressed nearly to our camp. My Filipinos and Sri Lankans, totalling a little more than 100, were turning out to be progressively disturbed. I was remaining on the bank, the two groups either side of me, the flatboat to offshore and the divider despite my good faith. Abruptly a stone zoomed past my head from the plundering group. One more flew back from my posse. I was in the center. I took a gander at the thieves and saw in their faces something I had not seen previously – a desire – the face on a fighter.

One of my Filipino jumpers ran up and said, "Return, Cap, it's undependable," and ran back to our side.

But I realized I was unable to move. Stones were going by me in expanding numbers and I understood I was in hot water. It was the start of a battle. The marauders progressed, my pack progressed. I realized that when blood was drawn there would be a full scale revolt – the eyes in the essences of the two sides had a coated look, blood lust.

I was unable to run myself, regardless of whether I needed to, with the divider on one side and the ocean on the other. On the off chance that I moved back to my side it would be a sign of shortcoming and the plunderers would assault. I felt very quiet yet unquestionably tense. I realized my life remained in a critical state and it was by my own behavior in the event that I lived or died.

I was wearing white cotton working gloves. I put my hands noticeable all around and, confronting the plundering posse, I yelled, "Stop! Stop I say." And then, at that point, half turned and yelled to my side, "Bring the police."

"Stop! Stop I say." I kept on confronting the raiders with my hands noticeable all around like a traffic superintendent halting the traffic.

My side quit tossing stones and afterward marvelously the plunderers halted. The police showed up and the marauders scattered and evaporated like a phantom, leaving on the stage the remaining parts of a man they had pounded into the ground with iron bars – the clamor I had heard in the morning.

"That is it," I said to Edgar, "we are forsaking. Gather up the gear."

I resigned to the neighborhood lodging for a quieting drink or two and rang Michael Mack. He sent down the truck with a crane and we cleared the site before dim. That evening the mobs began and once again the following not many days hundreds were killed. I moved to the Oberoi Hotel with an exceptional time limitation pass.

The mobs were over in ten days.

A boat stacked with concrete sank in the harbor and I took the "Salvanquish" close by expecting to treatment her, however I didn't have an agreement. I encountered a difficult situation moving the pull, the motor turn over issue had reoccurred.

My divers found the leak, patched it, and I started to pump out, lifting her off the bottom. A message from Selco told me not to raise her since we actually didn't have an agreement. So I topped off the profound tank and set her back into the mud.

I was living in the Intercontinental, having moved from the Oberoi to be nearer to the port. Every so often later a Smit pull steamed into the harbor, came close by the setback and Reiner Castle boarded. He was their rescue ace from Singapore. He informed me they had the agreement to treatment the submerged boat. I didn't trust him, told him in this way, and said to not do anything until I returned.

I hurried aground and called Singapore from the inn. Mr K advised me to surrender to Smits. I was brilliant with rage. London was open and I rang Ray Clarke to get the P&I club number. I rang Graham Edmiston, who had been one of Daiquiri's group on the "Fastnet", and let him know I was unable to trust what had occurred. He said their Hong Kong office were taking care of the case and he would discover. He rang back later and let me know he was heartbroken, he was unable to turn around the choice however he would hold an enquiry.

I returned ready and gave over to Reiner, advising my group to recuperate our stuff. There were significantly more issues with the "Salvanquish" motor and I showed up back in the inn in an extremely troubling mind-set – inconsistent pull, disappointment with the "Pastee" and presently the deficiency of my rescue to Smits.

Alan Bond advised me to take the pull back to Singapore for fixes on the off chance that I could get the motor to turn over. I secured the pull on the 'T' of the wharf inverse the entry to the port close to the dry dock, with light lines, the bow heading for the entry. Assuming that the motor turned over I would steam straight out of the harbor and not stop until Singapore.

The Master Attendant concurred it was a crisis so didn't require a pilot, if we paid for him. It was morning time and a fine day in the South West rainstorm. There was a weighty swell outside the breakwaters.

After 20 endeavors the main designer ran out of packed air and we delayed until the jugs were all completely energized. He came up onto the monkey island and said he figured we should make fixes in Colombo. I convinced him to have another go and later one more 25 endeavors, my nerve broke also. I twisted the pull back close by the wharf and flagged Singapore. Bumpy traveled to Colombo and we dry docked the pull in the dock close by. Bumpy at last settled the beginning problem.

STATESMAN / SALVANGUARD

I was home on leave and spent it cruising with my mom in "Mary Helen" through the Dutch trenches, inside the German Frisian up the Elbe, through the Kiel Canal into the Baltic thus to Denmark for the World 420 Championships where James my most youthful sibling cruised for England. My mom was leader of the 420 affiliation. There was just a single way through the channels with the yacht's decent pole and the railroad span in Amsterdam beginning to close on us. The scaffold is just open for ten minutes at 12 PM and we were late a result of the motor. We approached Peter Lankester who was expert of another pull, the "Cheerful Hunter", and he took us out to his home close to Utrecht.

We were 35 days in the channels and it came down on all of them! My mom reviewed the voyage for the RCC Journal and it was distributed in Roving Commissions.

Selco, or all the more effectively Mr K, bought the "Legislator" from United Towing. In spite of the fact that I didn't know it at that point, Knobby prescribed me to Bond as the best individual to assume control over the pull, I generally thought it was completely on my own benefits! Simply demonstrates what an old buddy Knobby has been throughout the long term. I was back in England and went up to Hull with him for the takeover.

It was a fascinating business. The pull of Icelandic Cod War distinction was laid up so we needed to begin without any preparation. We employed a United Towing boss specialist who knew the pull to give us the general tour and show Legaspi, who was to be the main architect. Roger Sario, ex "Salviper", was to be boss officer.

There was a strike in Hull and we were terrified we would have been held up in the docks. Bumpy and I got a scratch group together, which incorporated my sibling Donald, and we cruised the pull to Southampton. It felt unusual to be in charge of a 'super' pull in the North Sea steaming south with the shore of England to starboard, across the Thames estuary and into the English Channel, in through Spithead thus to Southampton. The excursion went well however no rescue, much to everybody's disappointment!

The "Salvanguard" – as Selco dedicated the pull – was refitted and a great deal of rescue gear put ready, generally purchased through Frank of Interworld who possessed the business in Alton, Hampshire. He was a resigned maritime trivial official who knew boats and it was a joy to manage him. Wire over radio was fitted and I think we were the main business pull to be so fitted. It implied we

could send and get messages without any other individual observing them. There was just one radio broadcast Berne in Switzerland which we could utilize. It ended up being a genuine aid. It was a completely fitted out rescue super pull that left Southampton under Selco tones, the Singapore banner flying gladly from the gaff on the aftermast.

We partook in a decent entry to Port Said however with no energy. In Port Said our 'private' specialist was Port Said Navigation and Shipping and I met the enthusiastic, lively, dedicated Sayeed Hassan, who was a definitive Egyptian Mr Fixit. He finished things in a nation where mañana and 'tomorrow' are a method of life.

It was a uninteresting, inconvenience free section through the Suez Canal and I looked ravenously at the piece ships moored in the Bitter Lakes – the caught boats of the conflict with Israel.

It was hot with a reasonable breeze down the Gulf of Suez, the desolate desert on one side and slopes on the other. Albeit several hundred miles south of the Mediterranean, the environment was very surprising from the northern winter. I visited an old wreck on solid land mostly down on the Egyptian shore, yet she was unsalvable and had been there a long time.

A little boat was halted close to the base finish of the inlet. I plotted the radar bearing and distance and observed she was on solid land on a reef.

"Activity stations!" I yelled to stir the team from their evening slowness. "Transport on solid land," I declared on the inside tannoy system.

The zed boat was made prepared and I lay off near and went across. The "Female horse" was a Turkish napkin stacked with canned merchandise headed for Aden. The skipper was quite satisfied to sign my Lloyd's Form and embraced and kissed me on the two cheeks. I telexed Selco with the great news.

The jumpers' review demonstrated that she was vigorously ashore, which affirmed she steered into the rocks at maximum speed. I should have been cautious with my huge pull, it was no utilization associating up and ripping the liner off assuming she abandoned a large portion of her base on the reef. I expected to cast off a portion of the freight and told Singapore. Sadly, the draft of the pull was too profound to even consider permitting me to go close by, any other way I would have utilized the pull as a canal boat. There was no other option except for to toss the canned products on to the reef.

'Cast off as little freight as conceivable to safeguard esteems.' Signed EEK read the wire; the administrator as consistently the businessman.

The following day We associated up the pull and handily refloated the "Female horse". The expert marked my end letter and again gave me an embrace and kisses. We

both continued south.

***

The following day, in the Red Sea, I heard on the VHF channel 16:

" "Salvanguard"! "Salvanguard"! Help, help, I am being attacked!"

I considered what in heaven's name had occurred. The climate was sensibly great so I steamed up to the now halted "Horse" and went across in the zed boat with my burliest group furnished with blades and crowbars. The group were, to be sure, occupied with a battle yet halted when we showed up over the rail. My group kept near me when I went on the extension to observe the expert, who was profuse in his much obliged. He said they had run out of food and could I supply him with any. Furthermore would I guide him to Aden, his compass was not very good.

"No issue by any means on the off chance that you sign here," I said, proffering another LOF.

He endorsed with energetic promptness so I had a subsequent Lloyd's Form on the equivalent ship!

We sent across some food and I left two of my team with a Selco radio for the journey to Aden. Not long after telexing Singapore with the fresh insight about my subsequent Lloyd's Form, I got a message to continue to Jeddah and leave the "Female horse" outside port limits.

After bunkering I progressed forward to Aden with the "Horse" following and there were no more occurrences. Outside port cutoff points I removed my team and moored while the "Female horse" entered. Quickly thereafter I was called up by the Port Control and told to enter the port myself. Aden was socialist and inconvenience and I had no goal of going in.

"Get the anchor, Roger," I trained the central official, and called down to the motor space to begin every one of the four engines.

"I'm outside port cutoff points and don't have any desire to enter Aden," I answered to Port Control.

"It doesn't make any difference, you have entered regional waters and you should clear in." The voice told me.

"I'm grieved, I should talk with my proprietors," I said.

"It doesn't make any difference, you should clear in. You have entered regional waters." "I will hit you up when I have directions from my proprietors," I said.

The anchor was rapidly aweigh and with four motors on full power, the "Salvanguard" vanished into the great beyond, with the voice actually advising me to come in. I later found from a guest to Aden from Djibouti that the "Salvanguard" was 'posted' for non-installment of port duty and pilot fees.

Djibouti, the capital of the autonomous state Territoire des Afars and Issas, was hot, dusty and poor except if you were French. It is arranged at the base finish of the Red Sea, rather than turning left for Aden you go straight on.

The Foreign Legion has a huge base, the French Navy kept an impressive presence and the French Army were in home. Albeit the Prime Minister was a Djiboutian, as were the pastors, a ton of the government employees were French.

There were a few trees in the super square Place Menelik in any case the spot was desolate and the further inland I went, the more lunar the scene became, helping me to remember a hot Iceland. The general tone on the ground is brown and the sky an unfeeling blue. In the early evening the town is dead, everybody takes a rest. There are more bars – generally the honky tonk sort – per working than elsewhere I know in the world.

Our representatives, Gellatly Hankey, were the Lloyd's representatives and the head man was an enormous, chubby man called John, who kept most unpredictable hours. Nonetheless, that didn't make any difference in light of the fact that the transportation side was effectively run and I figured out how to get an open-dated port clearance.

Svitzer, the Danish rescue organization, were situated nearby for north of fifty years at Aden however presently they were in Djibouti and Gellatly were their representatives too. There was significant contention and they detested the new Singapore intruder being on rescue station too. The pulls were of a comparable speed and whoever moved away first would regularly arrive at the loss first. There were two or three runs where the pulls dashed in a dead heat up the Red Sea yet no salvage.

Early in the New Year I got a message to continue to Assab in Ethiopia and afterward on up to Massawa. It was not satisfactory assuming Massawa was in the possession of the public authority or the Eritrean agitators, henceforth the need to call at Assab first and clear into Ethiopian waters. I was not feeling well overall, experiencing an evidently hindered stomach, yet I cruised at max throttle leaving the Danes guessing!

In Assab I got consent to continue to the "Worldwide Mariner", ashore north of Massawa. The town had fallen and was presently in government hands, yet the Eritrean renegades actually controlled the coast inverse the "Worldwide Mariner". Nonetheless, they evidently possessed no boats or sends thus I ought to be adequately protected. The Ethiopian Navy did ordinary watches. I should just move along the coast in sunshine any other way the naval force may shoot at the tug.

Although it was unquestionably hot outside, the convenience and scaffold of the "Salvanguard" were cooled. I was feeling good and cruised early

toward the beginning of the day for the "Worldwide Mariner", continuing at maximum speed to show up there before dim. The shoreline was precipitous, fruitless and cruel – no spot for the feeble – and the route was convoluted through the reefs.

The "Worldwide Mariner" was deserted by her Greek group and had that apparition transport feeling I was becoming used to. I moored the "Salvanguard" nearby and made my overview, while the jumpers made theirs.

The loss was hard ashore and two of the gas tanks were available to the ocean. She was completely weighed down with sacked grain – an unconditional gift from the Common Market to the destitute Ethiopians. There was very little fuel or new water ready. The climate was fine and pelicans were swimming nearby. We were totally all alone here, the infertile piles of Eritrean revolutionary held region noticeable under the hot, cruel sun.

I spread out the anchors of the setback with the "Salvanguard" – no simple undertaking with the huge pull. We laid ground tackle utilizing the squares and wires purchased from Frank at Interworld and the extra anchor from the boat. The jumpers couldn't get at the openings in the base. We welded on valves and spaces so we could blow air into the tanks and victory the water.

Fernando and his group figured out how to begin the generator of the loss, which gave capacity to the windlass and winches. When everything was prepared the rescue team on the "Worldwide Mariner" blew the tanks and hurled up close the chain link with the windlass and the ground tackle with the winches. I streamed the associated towing gear and towed at full power, tossing the large pull about from one side to another to side making her heel with water coming over the tow deck. It was without much of any result, the "Worldwide Mariner" would not move. I saw the pelicans had proceeded to ponder why.

***

The following day terrible climate set in, which kicked up a significant ocean. I made one more endeavor to refloat yet, once more, there was no indication of development. Selco currently put into activity their preparation, and despatched a sanctioned pull and barge from Jeddah across the Red Sea. The pelicans returned, alongside fine climate, when the pull and barge arrived.

I set the rescue team to work releasing the packed away grain onto the canal boat. I drove a winch and once in a while, to show willing, worked in the inconceivably hot hold. The men were dismal, and when I went on deck mid one morning to drive my winch I saw – painted in enormous letters on the extension front – 'Slave driver. We are not slaves.'

Roger Sario, who was a lot of a pioneer, went on leave in Djibouti and

the fat second mate was advanced boss official. He was not going to make some serious waves. Overall the group were typically really excited on a rescue and I asked him what was going on with the difficulty. He let me know the team were worn out and needed an extra reward for releasing freight. We had been buckling down for a considerable length of time. I asked him for what good reason he had not uttered a word before, why delay until not really unobtrusive messages were painted. He just shrugged his shoulders. I had nobody to talk with, being the commander, yet still up in the air to refloat the "Worldwide Mariner", no matter what. I consented to pay a reward for releasing freight and diminish the hours worked from 18 to 12. I telexed Singapore.

That evening an Ethiopian Navy gunboat came close by and the commandant, a lieutenant, came on board to ask how we were getting on. I would generally rather avoid the furnished watchmen he posted on the setback and said as much. He let me know they would be gone toward the beginning of the day and got back to his ship.

I was shaken alert by an unsettled AB who told me there was inconvenience on the setback. I surged ready and observed the Ethiopian Navy had torn open the reinforced alcohol store. A ton of them were plastered, including the outfitted gatekeepers. I flipped out with rage, realizing the Greek proprietors would blame the salvors for plundering. I additionally conveyed an adequate number of difficulties of my own without plastered Ethiopian equipped mariners running amok.

I shut the bond storage entryway, yelled at the mariners to get off my boat, and returned to the pull and onto the gunboat. I pushed past the equipped mariner who was pointing his rifle at me and yelled at him to take me to his commander. He was so shocked at this seething, yelling, humiliated Englishman that he agreed and took me to the skipper's lodge. I burst in and woke the lieutenant, requesting him to take his plastered men off my boat and take his gunboat somewhere else before I griped to his central leadership. He immediately got dressed and returned with me to the "Worldwide Mariner" and saw the messed up latch on the bond storage, the unfilled jugs and his intoxicated mariners wandering around with their rifles. The gunboat was gone inside 30 minutes. There was no more issue with my crew.

Seven days after the fact we refloated the "Worldwide Mariner" and reloaded the freight from the flatboat. The pull and barge returned to Jeddah and I towed the "Worldwide Mariner" to Massawa. The port authorities would not allow me to get her. I was bewildered. Ethiopia should be starving and I had 10,000 tons of free grain on my tow wire.

I moored the setback outside the port, left a riding team on board and

entered the following day. The port was vacant with the exception of a Russian arrival make and the killed head's yacht. I went close by the abandoned wharf and the couple of individuals I could see were not very fat.

The specialist, an anxious individual, drove me round in one of the main vehicles in the spot. The shops were vacant, and on the opposite side of the harbor – the north side – it had been leveled in the battling. The Russian arrival create was stacking cases for Aden, ammo I discovered later.

There was one lodging open with one seminar on the menu – spaghetti – and priceless little to go with it aside from gin, no wine just gin.

I was displayed over the old sovereign's yacht, and the shower where he was supposed to have been choked. Edward, my sibling, a long time prior was in Ethiopia and assembled an extension for an outcast state and Emperor Haille Selasse actually gave him a medal.

I was in Massawa for a considerable length of time. Each evening I took the pull out close by the "Worldwide Mariner", and each day returned into the harbor. I befriended the profound voiced harbor ace who said I was free to get the "Worldwide Mariner" however it was not his decision.

There were a large number of gatherings with authorities, some of whom were not there the following day for the following round of conversations. Clearly they were dispensed with, and there was a lot taking shots around evening time. In spite of the fact that we were set to be locked up or if nothing else the pull was, I and my team were permitted to go shorewards and had a good sense of reassurance. I used to lunch at the lodging on spaghetti and gin while my group went aground in the nights and contacts were delighted in with the neighborhood flimsy young ladies, there were no fat ones. I found the supply of restroom paper installed turned out to be seriously reduced, none being accessible ashore.

I proposed to eliminate a depressed wreck close by the wharf, which I did – towing it clear of the wharf and channel. I proposed to acquire the "Worldwide Mariner" and put her close by the wharf myself and I would ensure Selco pay for any harm I made to the wharf. I proposed to take a party out to the Dhalick islands where the Russians had a base. Indeed there was a party installed and I was beginning to leave when a protected vehicle turned up pointing its weapon at the extension requesting me to remain. It was an extremely scared party who left the boat. I proposed to do anything assuming that they would allow me to get the ship.

Meanwhile, the free grain began to go spoiled; and in the mean time, individuals starved. It was made very obvious to me that assuming I attempted to make a run for it the Russians would be sent later me to bomb the tug.

Eventually, out of nowhere, I was given a port leeway and told I could go. I got the riding team on the "Worldwide Mariner" and went. We were requested to get back to Singapore. I found later that the loss stayed outside the port for a long time and the grain totally decayed. A dismal illustration of man's cruelty to man even your own people.

In Singapore Knobby fitted a crane instead of the derrick for the hold toward the back, which upset working the pull. Quickly subsequently I was without running at most extreme accelerate the South China Sea for a boat on solid land in the hazardous space of unsurveyed reefs. The climate was terrible, it was cloudy, and I was unable to get sights. My heart was in my mouth when we entered the unsurveyed region with posts posted up the pole and on the monkey island. I advised the radio official to attempt to get a radio direction of the loss to help me and at last, subsequent to running over reef water, came up to the "Safina E Najam".

It was harsh, cloudy and pouring. So unpleasant truth be told we were unable to utilize the zed boat, so needed to grope our direction to the loss with the pull. Profoundly risky work.

Eventually we got a courier across, however the loss team were lazy in hurling in the towing gear and the pull went on solid land. It was the absolute most horrendous shock to feel the pull hit the base and it almost thumped me off my feet.

I went toward the back to attempt to get her off yet got the nylon cot wrapped round the starboard propeller. In addition to the fact that i was on solid land, I was immobilized myself and needing help. The area was miles from anyplace, outside helicopter range, so nobody could be saved. I believed I had let myself and all the more significantly my team down yet put on a good show when I went down onto the later deck, the pull beating and shivering as she hit the base. The daring jumpers went over into the harsh ocean and figured out how to clear the propeller. I went toward the back and she fell off. I made one more endeavor to associate from a marginally unique course, and this time the team of the "Safina E Najam" were more fruitful and we were associated. I loosened out a ton of wire so the pull was in profound water, sadly the tow wire lay on top or around coral.

I towed for three days and did all that I could imagine with the pull at full power. The climate was foul, with downpour and wind, and it was impractical to get any of my rescue team ready. Waves broke on the two sides of the loss clearing up to the deck level. A tropical storm cautioning was given by

Hong Kong radio which added extra direness to the circumstance. The expert told me there was water in the forward holds, and I was starting to give up on refloating her. Then on the third evening, just as it was getting dark, the "Salvanguard" was towing at full power right on the quarter of the "Safina E Najam" and she started to swing. It was the principal development there had been. I kept turning further to port and the casualty swung more to starboard then stopped. I put the rudder hard over to starboard, the pull behaved and moved sideways through the water past right toward the back of the boat and out onto the other quarter. The setback began to swing back and afterward was above water, moving in the difficult situations. I dialed back and towed her harsh first, yawing fiercely to the safe house of a reef toward the north.

The expert informed me over the radio how the water in the forward holds was rising, and I started to think I had refloated her just for the boat to sink on me. The reef, obviously, was dim and it was currently the center of a dull, cloudy, wet evening and I needed to feel my direction in to protect on the radar.

Edgar Selorio, my ex boss official, shown up with the "Salvanquish" and went straight close by the "Safgina E Najam" and began to siphon. The water began to fall in the holds and I realized we were headed to progress. The following day the jumpers made a review however a portion of the harm was excessively incredible for them to patch.

Edgar stacked his blower, generator and siphons on board the loss, along with a rescue group to run them. Edgar's team detached my towing stuff and

I put the "Salvanguard" close by in the 69 position and reconnected to her bow. The "Safina" was 10 feet by the head thus, when I began to tow, she yawed out aside and fortunately remained there. The tow was uninteresting, if harsh regardless, and the siphons contained the water. The tropical storm passed well toward the north of us.

I sent a navigational admonition to Singapore radio mentioning all boats to keep clear. Off Horsburgh Light, without any attempt at being subtle, a boat passed between the pull and the tow. I was extremely enticed to accelerate instead of dialing back and take his propeller off with the towline, however I limited myself and behaved.

I towed the "Safina" into Eastern Anchorage and later she was moored, left Edgar in control with the "Salvanquish" alongside.

The pull was bunkered and put away, and I was going to head out for Labuan when a Norwegian big hauler steered into the rocks in Philip Channel.

Hughie Murray was placed accountable for the rescue, much to my repugnance since I was senior. It was an easing up work and I guided the little lightening

big hauler close by the loss and afterward close by another bigger big hauler running a van service.

On the third outing around evening time I messed up going close by the moored, halfway stacked, big hauler. Alan Bond was at hand and he yelled for me to hold the little big hauler close by while they made us quick. I had gone close by excessively far toward the back and crushed piece of my big hauler's convenience under the quarter of the other big hauler and almost crushed the main specialist, as well. In spite of the fact that why the main designer was in his bunk when the boat was being moved I don't have the foggiest idea. The following day the "Salvanguard" was associated and I towed the big hauler off harsh first, barely missing a shoal.

There was little harm to the Norwegian boat so it was chosen to reload her right external Western Anchorage and I was the assigned pilot.

The prior night I was to play out the pilotage I was called out in the center of the night to a debilitated AB. I joined in and thought that he is nestled into the fetal position. At the point when I attempted to fix him I saw his guts were hanging out. Jesus, I thought, and hurried up onto my scaffold where I called Ops and advised them to get "Salvital" fast, in the interim fix me into a specialist. The specialist advised me to push in the guts admirably well and tie the injury up with a towel. Nobody would help until I blew up and afterward the subsequent official consented to help. There had been a blade battle and nobody needed to be involved. He and I did as the specialist taught yet it was truly challenging and we were unable to push in all the vile innards so tied it up decently well. We put him on board the "Salvital" and he was hurried to hospital.

During my pilotage I got a message that the AB was alive, having been on the surgical table for four hours, and would recuperate.

When the pilotage was effectively finished I took the pull at greatest speed to Labuan Bay. I towed a VLCC back to Singapore from the lay up safe haven in Labuan Bay, the interest being in the size of the tow. Not many boats of this size had been towed before however the "Salvanguard", with her spotless free towing gunwale, performed well overall and there were no problems.

I gotten back to Labuan and towed a gas transporter, likewise to Singapore, for refit in the wake of being laid up in the recession.

LLOYDSMAN / SALVISCOUNT

Selco bought what had been the greatest pull on the planet when she was fabricated – the United Towing's "Lloydsman". I traveled to Rotterdam with Knobby for an acquaintance excursion to Hull, where we were because of dominate. She was huge, 265 feet in length and high out of the water, particularly if not all around bunkered. Completely bunkered, with north of 1,500 tons of fuel, she drew 28 feet – a similar draft as a stacked tanker. This was not such a lot of a pull, more a little ship.

She was single screwed, with two motors coupled to a solitary shaft through a flywheel that weighed 54 tons. The expert, an old Pangbournian in spite of the fact that I had not known him, cautioned us that assuming she went ashore she would fall over because of her submerged shape, which was removed toward the back. Sure enough the pull went ashore, holding back to enter the lock in Hull, and fell over to a 15 degree list.

Captain Gaston welcomed us in his noisy voice. "I'm taking you both out somewhere else and remember to tell Mr Kahlenberg, whom you groaned to that we never gave you lunch when you brought the "Legislator"." (Now "Salvanguard") Which was valid. They never gotten us a beverage, not to mention lunch!

There was no strike so we remained on the East coast and dry docked her in Middlesbrough at Smith's dock. That was an enlightening knowledge with regards to why the UK was falling behind the remainder of the world. The UK appeared to be in one more century contrasted with Singapore. The men turned up for work and did nothing until the foreman showed up an hour after the fact and they were hampered on the grounds that the administrators and white caught laborers didn't show up for one more hour. The men knocked off work for lunch around early afternoon for an hour yet with no container.

The foremen ate in their own container. The chiefs knocked off at 13:00 for gin and tonics and a silver help lunch with wine at 13:30, showing up back in the workplaces loaded at around 14:30. Everybody returned home at 16:30. It couldn't endure and Smiths dock shut down soon after we departed.

I took the now dedicated "Salviscount" to Southampton to get the rescue gear from Frank of Interworld. We bunkered close by the compartment, inverse where the QE2 berthed and most tragically there was a spill and a little amount of fuel went in the water. The law is very clear – placing oil in the water is a wrongdoing, there are no special conditions. There was cleanser on board however insufficient. I called the specialist and told him to get

some more down speedy, and taught the group to clean up at hand. When I had been accounted for and the police turned up, everything was perfect and clean. Nonetheless, contamination is approached so in a serious way that a police overseer was shipped off address me on what a devious kid I had been! I was the expert along these lines I was at fault, despite the fact that it was the central architect's issue, or conceivably shoreside for siphoning excessively fast. The pull was intended to run on diesel oil, however it was restrictively costly so Knobby changed her over to weighty fuel, which would make her cutthroat in the towing market. The main issue was the colder time of year was coming on and it was important to warm the fuel.

We did ocean preliminaries in the Solent with different visitors ready, including my mom. We accomplished a speed of 18 bunches over the deliberate mile, making an enormous wash a lot in such a way as to really irritate a few group out for a sail.

When everything was prepared, I took up rescue station off Yarmouth, Isle of Wight, in the Solent taking into account Thorns Beach my mom's home. We were moored there for quite a while with no karma. I took the zed boat to Thorns to see my mom, and for the group to cut a Christmas tree.

I bought my mom's flatboat "Molette" and cruised her back to the "Salviscount". My firefly was designated "Mole" and painted dark, as was "Molette". My mom bought a more up to date flatboat and referred to her as "Moletta".

I, or rather the pilot, returned the pull to Southampton for stores. One evening I got a call from Alan Schofield of Samuel Stewart, the rescue intermediaries, who let me know that we had an agreement on a liner, the "Movement", moored off Clovelly, North Cornwall.

It was blowing a full hurricane and when I required a pilot they let me know it was storm power 10 in the channel. The pilot would not take me out through the Needles Channel, saying it was excessively risky in any event, for my strong tug.

We went out through Spithead and whenever I had dropped him off in the pilot boat, I sped up. When clear of the Isle of Wight it was extremely quite harsh, blowing south-west power 9 to 10, and the "Salviscount" was delivering oceans directly over the wheelhouse. It was an extremely dull, cloudy evening and I passed outside the race off Portland Bill.

The climate directed to intense 8 the following day adjusting Land's End, and there was a reasonable breeze up the North Cornish coast – showing up off Clovelly into the evening. The raft was remaining by the "Movement", which was not a lot bigger than the "Salviscount" but rather basically she was loaded.

The child of Captain Gaston was my effusive boss official and Roger Sario was boss official. I secured in front of the liner and dropped back,

utilizing the motor as vital. It was blowing exceptionally hard however we made the association and I towed her to off Cardiff, where a harbor pull got her. It was a Selco initial, a rescue in European waters, and a decent hit in the eye for the European salvors – particularly Smits and Wjsmuller, the lords of the rescue world.

I had a free hand to take up station where I felt like, so went to Milford Haven; however would rather avoid it so took up station off Falmouth. Fox's were the proficient specialists for ourselves and all the Eastern Bloc plant fishing ships, both in and outside Falmouth. The UK fishing boats, stacked to the gunwales with mackerel, offered their catch to the industrial facility ships. I made my number with the coastguards.

One wild night the Rumanian manufacturing plant transport, "Oltet", hauled her anchor and hit the "Salviscount" on the starboard bow. I was not satisfied. I had been on the extension the entire evening utilizing the fundamental motor to keep up with position to forestall the pull dragging.

Shortly a while later I heard a pain message and required a pilot. "You can't be serious." was the answer so I cruised without. It was blowing storm power 10, and I steamed out at max throttle to keep up with steerage on a wing and a petition since I was unable to see a portion of the floats. I some way or another felt the "hand of God" was with me. My team were incredible notwithstanding never having encountered winter climate like it.

Outside it was extremely harsh for sure once we were outside the lee of the land. A pull towing a flatboat was in hardships. The flatboat was untied and I went for the canal boat, while Wjsmuller went for the tug.

The following morning I tracked down the flatboat and inquired as to whether they could send a helicopter so I could lift a man on board the floating flatboat. It was blowing excessively hard, helicopters were all grounded.

The crisis conversation starter was caught in the hanging, broken towing gear and despite the fact that I went as close as I challenged, the group couldn't get it. The movement of the pull was savage in the substantial oceans. I could not do anything until the climate directed, yet it didn't direct before the flatboat steered into the rocks off Fowey. I moored off.

The pilot boat came out and the pilot did a con work on me and – as Dennis Rixon later called attention to – I ought to have known better. The pilot said I required his administrations in light of the fact that the pull was in port cutoff points, so I acknowledged. The pilot boat returned into Fowey and came out with void lager barrels, which we tied onto the tow wire. The canal boat was ashore so that there

was no lee side. It was fundamental to get somebody onto the canal boat or we were unable to make an association. Rene, the zed boat driver, said he could do it. The oceans were breaking over the flatboat, however every so often there would be a respite. He said he could place somebody on the barge in the breaks. In the event that he missed the point then there would be a casualty. It was cool, the finish of December and still harsh. Behind the flatboat were rocks. My heart was in my mouth when he took off with Gaston and remained by right external the breakers. Unexpectedly he shot in close by, Gaston mixed up a hanging line, and as a breaker went twisting in, the zed boat shot out – jumping over the wave before it broke. He had done it.

After a ton of exertion and help from Eurosalve, an organization connected by Selco, who got men onto the flatboat from the precipices over, the tow wire was associated drifted down on the lager barrels brought out by the pilot boat. I got the anchor and begun towing moving toward full power when the lager barrels joined to tow wire lifted out of the water. At high water the canal boat, Intermac 600 and her flawless freight, was effectively refloated and I towed her to Falmouth putting her close by at Falmouth moors. It was an excellent rescue in practically a definitive of awful climate and my Filipino group acted wonderfully. I moored in the harbour.

The following day it snowed and my group were excited, never having seen snow. My mom turned up for a couple of days having passed through the snow spontaneously! Dennis Rixon showed up to take proof and was extremely abnormal and touchy, requiring ten days to do what ought to have taken two. His diabetes was not helped by all the wine and lager consumed.

We had been on the UK coast for a half year at this point and my Filipino team being knowledgeable perused the papers, tragically unreasonably many "Every day Mirrors" and so forth with communist babble detailing. They were entirely tired of the cold and downpour. In 90 days we persevered through 45 hurricanes. I called Alan Bond in Singapore and let him know I thought we better move the pull to Spain or Portugal before inconvenience started.

A message showed up in the blink of an eye thereafter training me to continue to Toulon in the South of France. Simply past Gibraltar, Rene the incredible boat driver, taken steps to kill me and right up 'til today I don't have a clue why. He flew back to Singapore from Toulon.

The specialists were definitely disliking the Pielstick motors when they were both associated with the shaft. One would be languid and accomplish no work, while the other one stayed at work past 40 hours – the adjusting gear was not functioning

appropriately. Bumpy flew down toward the South of France and fixed it, while we arranged the drill transport we were contracted to tow to Singapore. I partook in several dinners shorewards in the costly, yet great, restaurants.

I began the tow in fine fettle however at that point things began to turn out badly and, when I arrived at Port Said, not exclusively were the motors not adjusting, one motor didn't work by any means. Sayeed Hassan, our private specialist, turned up ready and when I let him know what had occurred, he said stay silent or the Canal Authorities probably won't let us through or force extra pulls at tremendous cost. The expert of any boat going through the channel needs to fill in and sign a structure that, in addition to other things, expresses the motors are all ready. To adulterate the data is a genuine offense. I didn't fancy an Egyptian prison, then again I needed to get Selco's new super pull to Singapore with her tow. I, thusly, adulterated the structure, expressing that the two motors were working agreeably. The channel travel, towing the drill transport, was finished without occurrence yet it was a strained travel for me.

Pielstick specialists were hanging tight for us in Djibouti, where we secured for four days. The drill transport chief was getting tired of the postponement, and I didn't help by cruising my dark flatboat "Molette" in the evenings. I guarantee it to be the main time ever a Beaulieu flatboat has at any point been cruised in Djibouti.

The cooling on the "Salviscount" got together also and the convenience was unimaginably hot. Being intended for cooling, the port openings couldn't be opened. Tempers started to be on an extremely short breaker. It was cooler when we were again under way, with the specialists staying on board.

A couple of days subsequent to leaving Djibouti I got a wire teaching me to get and tow a fishing boat which had separated. I chose to delay until I arrived at the loss before I informed the drill transport captain.

It was a significant Japanese fishing boat with a full catch, yet she was just a fourth of the size of the "Salviscount." The drill transport ace was generally helpful and we immediately associated up the Japanese boat and showed up in Singapore with two tows!

I was happy to be back in Singapore however not exceptionally satisfied when Ops let me know that Major Crafter was coming out on the organization yacht with visitors to investigate Selco's most recent securing. It was a Sunday, the trash had not been gathered by the port decline boat, the cooling actually didn't work, and the pull was not in a condition for a review. "Salvalentina" came close by and the ocean side dressed party came on board.

Remarks like, "Goodness, doesn't the cooling work?" And, "Isn't it hot in here?" didn't charm them to me.

And when Crafter whined about eggshell in the trash, I said, "Don't you read the wires any more?"

To which he answered, "Gracious, no, I am in the town office. These are investors who have advanced Selco cash, and they needed to see our most recent asset."

I provided him with a speedy resume of the journey and he said, "You would be wise to join the party however say nothing to the bankers."

So I had a day out on the yacht, which was fun – swimming, liquor and sun, yet no sex!

SALVAGE MASTER

"Salviscount" was the last pull I was forever in charge of and I gave her over to Edgar Selorio, my ex boss official, and came aground. I was advanced rescue expert and marine-administrator, and lived in the Orchard Hotel, at the highest point of trendy Orchard Road.

Knobby and I went with the pull, towing a flatboat with a tremendous six-story high desalination plant as freight destined for the Middle east. In the Malacca Straits the pull experienced a power outage and the tow surpassed the pull, missing a crash by inches. Many silver hairs were added to my generally dim head! Edgar was ace yet he had no more issues effectively conveying his tow. Bumpy and I went shorewards off Penang and got back to Singapore.

There were impressive changes in the workplace. Alan Bond was caring for the piece transport project with Crafter, who had been taken out to the town office and was far removed. Hancox was currently running Selco, Mr K at any point present behind the scenes. I should be marine-director however I was not actually intrigued; rescue was my interest.

The "President Eisenhower" steered into the rocks inverse the light at the

Southern finish of the Malacca Straits on the Malaysian side. I figured I would be the rescue ace yet Captain Hancox chose to do it, leaving me in the office.

I headed to the setback's Singapore director's home on a Sunday and we marked the LOF, tragically figuring out how to sign in some unacceptable spot. I endorsed as the proprietor and the director endorsed as the salvor.

Hancox was in his amazing state of ecstasy with pulls and barges and a crane barge to coordinate. The "President Eisenhower" steered into the rocks at max throttle and her bow was 18 feet into the mud. She was a huge compartment transport and an impressive number were released onto a Selco barge before the "Salvanguard," and other grouped Selco pulls, pulled her off intact. I was not extremely satisfied to have been left aground on the grounds that I passed up a decent rescue bonus.

I saw a considerable amount of Mr K and at times went out for a beverage.

Something had changed in Selco – presently an exceptionally fruitful elite salvor. A portion of the fun was gone, individuals were more tense and I think, despite the fact that he said nothing, he understood Dave Hancox was a preferable salvor over he was director. A decent administrator puts together himself so he doesn't nod off at his work area at 12 PM and is found there the following morning, rescue activities excepted. I traveled to Japan in my job as marine-director to assume control over another pull EEK had purchased. She required a ton of work, having been laid up for years, and an architect advisor cared for the motor room.

She was in a little yard on the inland ocean close to Hiroshima and nobody talked any English, yet it was an intriguing a month and a half. I was happy when it was finished and the pull cruised from Japan, brilliant in her new Selco tones. She was subsequently hit by an Exocet during the Iran-Iraq war and sank with impressive death toll. On one more event I took over one more pull EEK had bought – the "Salviva".

The "Brilliant Vega" was a vehicle transporter and she steered into the rocks on the reef at the North finish of the Laccadive islands. I traveled to Colombo and joined the Selco pull on rescue backup, cruising that evening.

The boat was vigorously on solid land on coral and had been lifted substantially up onto the reef. It would have been extremely challenging to refloat her, four of her gas tanks were holed and the jumpers couldn't get at them to fix. A genuine dependability issue would happen in the event that any water got on the vehicle deck on the grounds that the vessel would capsize.

The "Salvanguard", towing an unfilled canal boat, was cruising from the Persian Gulf, and when she showed up the flatboat was set close by the setback. We ran ground tackle from the vehicle deck and drove the freight of transports onto the flatboat by means of the side incline. Every one of the leftover fortifications were released into the flatboat and anything mobile was stacked onto the canal boat, including rafts and convenient tween decks.

The Korean team were useful however just the expert talked insignificant English, and I don't talk any Korean. The perceived worldwide language of the ocean is English. Thusly, the team who steer the boat and the officials who complete his directions should communicate in English yet this was not true and correspondences were extremely challenging anyway we managed.

When everything was prepared – the ground tackle hurled tight, the two pulls associated, the gas tanks blown with compacted air, I was on the scaffold of the "Brilliant Vega" with my Selco radio – we made a refloating endeavor. She didn't move. The tide was falling on the tide measure that we set on the reef so I stopped the endeavor and sent the jumpers down to see. No indication of development by any means. The following elevated tide was not until that evening, so I went off on an excursion with Edgar and a portion of the rescue group. We took the zed boat through the tidal pond to a little sand spit island, where we found remaining parts of an angler's camp.

While we were there an open boat diverted up from Kadmat Island, and one of the police officers remembered me from the "Pacifico Everett", specifically the

"Salvaliant" towing the "Majma."

That evening the "Splendid Vega" refloated in the wake of towing at full power with the two pulls – the entire activity being considerably more troublesome in obscurity. The climate was fine so I secured the "Splendid Vega" and drove the scaled down transports back onto the vehicle transporter and reloaded all the versatile gear. At the point when the canal boat was unfilled the "Salvanguard" forged ahead her journey to Singapore. The following day the jumpers fixed the openings in the bottom.

It was a fascinating element that the rescue was performed on the Japanese Form rather than Lloyd's Form, which implied a ton of desk work for me. I recorded each piece of gear utilized during the activity, made up what it was worth and how we managed it. Selco got a generally excellent honor.

The "Sun Aster III" steered into the rocks completely loaded north-bound in the Suez Canal. I traveled to Cairo and was met by Sayeed Hassan, the proprietor of Port Said Navigation and Shipping Co. He was extremely invigorated and was certain we could get the agreement to treatment the boat gave the ideal individuals were cared for. Smits were in Egypt attempting to get the agreement too. The principal thing to do was get consent from the Suez Canal Authority, and he knew only individuals to go and see.

The following month was spent going among Cairo and Port Said, Cairo and Suez, and Cairo and Ismaelia; and on one day we did every one of the three. At last, I got authorization later Alan Bond showed up from Singapore with a short case brimming with cash. When we acquired the consent, the Japanese concurred Lloyd's Open Form. Part of the 'manage' the Suez Canal Authority was a protection from Lloyds with a limitless assurance for contamination which later arrangement was at long last restricted to fifty million dollars.

We eased up the "Sun Aster III", releasing piece of the freight into a contracted big hauler I moved close by. At last, with the "Salviva" associated, I refloated the tanker.

The end function was damaged by the proprietors' English legal advisor needing to qualify the letter, to which I would not concur. It was an indication of the adjustment of the rescue world with legal counselors meddling nearby, which isn't to the advantage of anybody – aside from the lawyers.

I remained in Egypt, with the "Salviva" in Suez. Together we salved the "Gay Fidelity", which had been ablaze and almost sank under my very feet in the Red Sea while under tow. The later deck was flooded when we at long last moored her and put the pull close by to siphon. I was distant from everyone else on the sinking transport while she was being towed. None of the "Salviva" team would join me,

they thought I was frantic and it was a peculiar sensation, particularly around evening time, considering how long she planned to stay above water. I idiotically went into the overwhelmed motor room and slipped harming my leg and losing the main light. Shades of the "Flying Enterprise" rung a bell yet it was not the English Channel so no press inclusion. We secured her external Suez port cutoff points and figured out how to get end. I lived in the Red Sea Hotel neglecting the Suez canal.

I salved the "San Juan", which steered into the rocks on a similar reef as the "Horse." There were two different wrecks on the reef and she figured out how to be in the middle of them. It was a genuine adventure just to arrive at the loss, sanctioning a German engine yacht from Hurghada. We had to discard a large portion of the freight to get her off and take her to Suez with the "Salveritas." The "Salviva" was in the Mediterranean with a tow for Alexandria.

***

I went to London to give confirm and go to an intervention. It was exceptionally fascinating to perceive how the overall set of laws functioned once more, and accentuated the significance of good the evidence.

SELCO SOLD / LARGEST SHIP IN WORLD

When I got back to Singapore it was all change. Mr Kahlenberg was gone. The dynamo, the main impetus, the core of Selco was gone. He sold out to a Chinese, Peter Tham, whom I won't ever meet. Mr K should have stayed as administrator yet there was a line and he was pushed out, and with him the spirit of Selco.

Peter Tham's cohort, Tam Yen Fei, was the overseeing chief; a Miss Wee was the individual director; and a runaway Englishman, Roy Croft, was Tam Yen Fei's associate. An entirely different layer of the board was set up, with William Crafter as director, none of whom knew at least something about salvage.

The former one-story office was deserted and another four-story block worked, with the highest level unfilled – aside from the attorney, Carol Wong. The third floor was outfitted with a rich director's office – with washroom, which was rarely utilized – and Tam Yen Fei; the subsequent floor housed Alan Bond, Dave Warner, promoting, and the seaward individuals; the ground floor with Daniel aid, Miss Wee and their associates. I never saw the senior bookkeeper who worked in the town office.

Elbourne Mitchell, who had been Selco's London attorneys since the start, were sacked and Constant and Constant selected. Their message answerback was 'two cnts' and I pass on it to your creative mind to embed the letter close to the furthest limit of the letter set which is the thing that I considered them. Old Selco was done, the fun and the excitement gone, yet rescue was as yet an interesting game.

I was happy to travel to the Gulf where I joined the "Salvalour" for a rescue in Oman which was effective. I was aground in Fujairah when I got a message to rejoin the pull which was adrift and we continued a maximum speed to Shah Allum reef right inside Iranian waters. The "Wind Enterprise" was on solid land. She was stacked with 357,000 tons of unrefined petroleum and was the greatest stacked boat on the planet ever to have steered into the rocks. At the point when I showed up on location she looked enormous, tremendous, however that was over the water and like a chunk of ice, a greater amount of her was under the water. Her draft was in excess of sixty feet. She was much greater than the "Showa Maru" and I didn't have the offices and accommodation of a headquarters not far off. The conflict among Iran and Iraq had begun however it was a land war and was not yet influencing the waters of the Persian Gulf. I took a full breath and put on my most sure grin when I

went up to the skipper's lodge – a long move from the boat.

The Norwegian chief was extremely quelled, which was not very unexpected in the conditions, and we marked Lloyd's Form. I took on a magnificent obligation, assuming I messed up a la "Tojo Maru" I would bankrupt the organization and perhaps kill a couple of individuals too. A boat stacked with unstable raw petroleum – particularly one as large as this – was not something protected. Assuming that one of the tanks became holed and spilled oil around the boat I would have a likely enormous bomb on my hands. Add to that we were off the coast and in the regional waters of a Moslem country at battle with another Moslem country. It was no big surprise I felt tense.

Selco sanctioned a 100,000 ton easing up big hauler, flew unique pneumatic bumpers up from Singapore, and a rescue group with Captain Ventura responsible for it. Commander Carter was recruited from London as security master. They contracted Gray Mackenzie pulls to ship them out to me and give helping pulls to compartment the easing up big hauler. The Selco pulls "Salvalour" and "Salveritas" were associated toward the back and utilized as ground tackle from the start. At the point when everything was prepared, the big hauler was berthed. I gave each pull a radio code, which we utilized in order to deceive the Iranians. To keep the "Wind Enterprise" immovably on solid land during the release we ballasted her down.

Once enough freight was released I unberthed the easing up big hauler, the pulls got their anchors and the stabilizer was siphoned out. I watched the tide check we put on the reef and, not long before high water, I taught the pulls to initiate towing.

The pulls looked little from the scaffold of the immense big hauler as she began gradually to move. I put the primary motors toward the back and the "Wind Enterprise" slid off the reef into profound water. There was no contamination, which demonstrated that every one of the tanks were as yet flawless. I was in a rush to escape Iranian waters before a gunboat turned up and caused trouble.

The central specialist revealed that the primary motor was intact thus, when the pulls were disengaged, I steered the refloated boat to Dubai at slow speed, leaving the bumpers close by. I reberthed the easing up big hauler and the freight was reloaded. At the point when the easing up big hauler was clear, and all the gear reloaded onto the pulls, end was marked and I hurled an enormous murmur of help. We had been effective – it was a world record.

NAME AT LLOYDS

While surging with regards to the Egyptian desert in engine vehicles during the "Sun Aster III" rescue, I had loads of time to think about and I figured it would be a smart thought on the off chance that I could join Lloyds, the protection market, as a Name. It would give me an incredible passage to the protection world, who at last, were the paymasters of salvors. The earlier year, on one of my excursions to London, Molly Julian acquainted me with the then administrator of Lloyds Peter Green, later Sir Peter, and we partook in a supper together. Assuming that I had sufficient cash he thought it was a smart thought. He likewise disclosed to me the governing rules in the framework to keep salvors and financiers cheerful simultaneously. Salvors were griping the rescue grants were not huge enough to keep them in business. He said the pendulum was swinging and presumably the honors would go up and the general middle figure achieved.

On one of my excursions to Djibouti I remained in the Paris Athénée Hotel, pricey yet excellent. I composed on the lodging notepaper to Edward's dad in-law, who was a Lloyd's Name and inquired as to whether I could join.

Robert Gaynor, Ginnah Borthwick's significant other, consented to second me and I was acquainted with Anne Davison from Willis Faber, who might care for me. I organized with my nearby Barclay's Bank administrator to set up a bank ensure for £100,000 to Lloyds. Anne took me to my rota board of trustees meeting, where it was completely disclosed to me that I was obligated independently for my misfortunes, down to my last metal farthing.

It was most great sitting behind the huge table in that terrific room with the advisory group on the opposite side. The representative implied what he said. I expressed that I comprehended and that was that. I never accepted that I would support such misfortunes, that chapter 11 would turn into a choice, much to My dismay what destiny had coming up for me. I was in transit up, on an exciting ride and I needed to remain with it for the ride – the future looked brilliant and blushing. The main slight puff of a cloud in the far off skyline was my companion Ray Clarke from Elbourne Mitchell who said, with that curious examine his eye, "I trust you know what you are doing."

MANAGING SELCO

I was in Djibouti when I got a call from Alan Bond. "Return yourself once again to Singapore promptly," he trained. "What for?" I asked.

"Simply get in line for once," he told. Bond may take care of business of few words, yet he was not normally so blunt.

I got the following plane to Paris, again remained in the Paris Athénée, and afterward on to Singapore, showing up tired in the workplace. I didn't stay tired for long.

"I'm debilitated. I have malignant growth and been given three months to live. I'm going on vacation and you are in control." And with that he left the workplace and didn't return.

I was confused. It was so totally unforeseen and with the changes, I thought a Chinese would be placed responsible for the rescue and pulls. I stayed there in his seat and thought. What am I going to do? How am I going to do the job? I then thought, well, if I owned the company what would I do? And that is what I did. I imagined to me to claim Selco and worked likewise. Mr K was as yet in Singapore, despite the fact that he recommended we didn't meet out in the open on the off chance that it upset the 'new individuals'. So I met him at his level or Alan's home. I saw Alan at his home and made a settlement with him. I would put forth a valiant effort to run Selco and assuming that he recuperated I would surrender his seat back to him. Alan headed out to the Cameron Highlands, and later to the Bristol Center in England for the in critical condition. I didn't anticipate seeing him again.

It was an unquestionably tense and sensational time for me. The organization was extremely occupied and at one time, I was engineering eight rescue tasks generally in a hurry simultaneously. I was spreading over the world time regions from New York to Tokyo and was called at any hour. The stunt on arousing to the call in my night was to perceive the voice so I could discuss the guest's boat. A proprietor is powerfully insulted assuming that you talk about another person's boat to him. For a very long time I never had in excess of several hours rest at a time.

I was abundantly detested by the Chinese; and P Wee, a rescue expert, and Miss Wee, the work force chief, effectively attempted to sabotage me. They were both wicked and contorted and P was generally so grinning and pleasant, while pushing in the blade. Miss Wee was really harmful that I just overlooked her.

I thought at first that Tham Yen Fei was wise and that his sluggish discourse was an indication of him thinking. He was an exceptionally enormous person for a Chinese however always

looked half asleep, and I realised in the end that he was out of his depth as far as salvage was concerned so I ignored him too. Fortunately he didn't attempt to meddle. What's more I froze out Roy Croft, despite the fact that was very glad to enjoy a lager with him.

The one brilliant star was Captain Chua. He had malignant growth however generally recuperated, and was alive on one lung. He gave me his unstinting help and filled in as hard as I did. We functioned admirably together and confided in each other.

My mom came out for Christmas and remained in the Tanglin Club – the super friendly club in Singapore – civility of Chris Herbert. She met Bill Crafter and proclaimed him a fake. She was taken around by different spouses, going to Sentosa on the trolley, and visiting all the sights.

I was residing in the Orchard Hotel at the highest point of Orchard Road, inverse the Ming Court Hotel where we had a charming Christmas and New Year festivity. I was a Name at Lloyds at the similarly early age independently, I was not obscure in the rescue world, and I was running Selco Salvage, with its huge armada of pulls and barges. I had something to celebrate.

A Greek boat while heading to China experienced a motor breakdown off the North shore of Sumatra. The "Salveritas", with Crowther in order, arrived at the floating boat first and marked a Lloyd's Form with the expert. While interfacing, Crowther announced a Smits showed up on the scene and the expert said they had a Lloyd's Form concurred in Piraeus. I was in Ops and telexed back teaching Crowther to tell the Smit pull respectfully to push off, the expert's mark was superior to any other person's (shades of the "Special Mariner"). Crowther telexed back that they were in progress yet the Smit pull was still alongside.

'Cut his lines,' I telexed back.

Shortly a while later a furious Roy Martin, the Smit director in Singapore, called and asked me what I thought I was doing, somebody would get killed. I asked him frigidly what he thought he was doing muscling in on my rescue. In that followed a contention on the overall benefits of the mark on a Lloyd's Form. Did a Lloyd's Form supposedly concurred however not endorsed in Piraeus before the marking of the Lloyd's Form by the expert take point of reference? I said I was very glad to see him in court, in the mean time advise his pull to stay away from the "Dumbaia" or I would take out a directive against Smits. He rang off and Crowther had no more difficulty from Smits. Selco and Smits were the principle salvors in Singapore and there was a lot of bad blood between them; the

contention and rivalry was intense.

The following day Roy Martin asked me out somewhere else and I concurred, feeling somewhat like the Biblical Daniel entering the lions' lair. We had an exceptionally wonderful lunch with great wine. We concurred line cutting was just plain dumb and the Lloyds Arbitrators may take a dreary view. In future we should talk and forestall a "Dumbaia" episode once more. Smits would make no move over their supposed Lloyd's Form assuming that I concurred. Indeed, I was really sure Selco would win in court yet I saw no damage in forestalling a "Dumbaia" occurrence once more, it was not illuminating to be in the line cutting business. The "Dumbaia" was towed to China on the Lloyd's Form and grossed a million dollars for Selco.

Alan Bond – against all the chances – recuperated and returned, however he didn't entirely reclaim his seat. He passed on me to run things and moved higher up, however not for long.

The Iran-Iraq war took on a new and monstrous turn and moved out onto the perfect waters of the Persian Gulf. The Iraqis were utilizing French made and sold Exocet rockets against transportation in the waterway to Bushire, however they before long moved further afield.

Alan, his significant other and I were being engaged by the Townleys, Keith Townley was the rescue affiliation head assessor in Singapore. We were eating New Zealand clams and drinking a cool, white dry wine. The phone went and a little later Keith said it was Alan Schofield for me or Alan.

"You take it, Ian," said Alan, thus the pass on was projected. It was Alan Schofield the rescue broker.

"There is a big hauler ablaze only south of Kharg deserted. Smits say it's not salvable. Silver Line are offering a Lloyd's Form."

Kharg Island was the fundamental stacking port for the commodity of Iranian oil and indispensable to their conflict exertion. My cerebrum began staying at work longer than required. The boat was in the disaster area, Smits say they can't do it, it should merit a look.

"Concur Lloyd's Form," I said.

"What was going on with all that?" asked Alan.

"I've concurred Lloyd's Form on a consuming big hauler south of Kharg," I said, grinning.

"You've concurred it, you can do it. On your bicycle or, rather, plane," chuckled Alan, clearing the smile off my face.

IRAN IRAQ WAR

I saw the pall of smoke just about forty miles away. The rescue affiliation assessor and I were travelers on an old, not exceptionally quick, Gray Mackenzie boat Selco sanctioned – the "Dark Atlas". The Pakistani expert was not extremely quick to go into the disaster area, however a reward before long put that right.

The pall drew thicker as we steamed nearer, the infertile piles of Iran now apparent. The land war was seething toward the north yet the ocean war was simply beginning and I was tense. I contemplated whether I was on one of the organizations at Lloyds which safeguarded the consuming tanker.

The "Al Ahood" – green bows not yet decided, harsh submerged – was blasting furiously, the convenience a fire, the blazes jumping into the air overwhelming the entire rearward finish of the boat. My heart sank as we cruised nearer and halted a brief distance off – the very water around the harsh of the boat appeared to be ablaze. Notwithstanding, later a period, I understood the fire was not deteriorating and the entire of the front piece of the boat was flawless. Assuming we could put the fire out, perhaps we could balm the boat. For reasons unknown she was not drifting.

'It is conceivable. Send rescue team.' I flagged Alan Bond, presently completely back in his seat yet higher up. I associated the "Dim Atlas" to the bow of the "Al Ahood" quickly to keep the bow up into the breeze and hold the blazes back from spreading forward.

I concurred with Captain Betts, an ex United Towing ace, prior to leaving Singapore that assuming the boat was salvable he would lead the rescue group. In the occasion, Captain Ventura showed up with his group - Juanito was great, he drove his group from the front. The man in the white kettle suit in the photo remaining before the consuming convenience seen from one side of the planet to the other and on the floor at Lloyds is him. As the sanctioned pulls showed up, so I put them close by to battle the flares with their fire monitors.

I boarded the "Al Ahood" before Juanito's appearance for a glance around. While examining the dim forecastle I had this uncomfortable inclination that someone was taking a gander at me. The clamor of the consuming unrefined was plainly discernible. I realized that two group individuals were missing and it was exceptionally creepy. Unexpectedly something fuzzy contacted my leg. I jumped into the air in dread, my heart beating. Sparkling my light down – it was the boat's cat.

The fire kept on seething, took care of by raw petroleum spilling through into the motor room and consuming on top of the water. The commotion was ceaseless. The

convenience was an immense pipe, fanning and ventilating the blazes which jumped high over the consuming big hauler, around evening time enlightening the entire region. I understood that water alone would not put it out. There was a great deal of water power with every one of the pulls we contracted, yet basically no froth. Smits claimed the main froth accessible in the Gulf and they said the boat was unsalvable. The main particular fire and froth pull in the Gulf was possessed by Smits. Later significant thought I consented to sub agreement Smits as co-salvors on our Lloyds Form. Selco sanctioned a large stream to fly out additional froth from Europe in light of the fact that there was insufficient in the Gulf even with Smits supply. Two inventory boats purchased out the 20 tons of froth, which we stacked onto the "Al Ahood." After ten days everything was prepared for the quenching endeavor. The Smit firefighting master assumed responsibility for the endeavor to extinguish the fire. I put one pull on one or the other side of the towing pull and kept the consuming boat bow into the breeze. Aad situated the Smit pull and his group with hoses – the Selco rescue men as back up – and mid one morning the endeavor was made. Huge loads of froth were poured onto the convenience from the pulls' fire screens and the firefighting group went into it with hoses. Practically all of the froth was utilized lastly the fire was out. It was staggeringly quiet later the times of the thundering heater. Everybody was extremely cognizant that we were in a disaster area and assuming the boat had been assaulted once, why not once more? Any untoward commotion had me and numerous others jumping.

The fire was out so presently I needed to tow the big hauler out of the disaster area as fast as could really be expected. Why she was obviously held by the harsh I actually didn't have a clue, however there was no an ideal opportunity to see whether we could move her. I facilitated the eight pulls for towing and the "Al Ahood" began to move. It required steady consideration and directions to keep up with any kind obviously, yet sluggish advancement was made.

I was extremely drained, not having any rest for six days and evenings, and I asked Hans who was in generally charge of the Smits group and pulls, to take over for some time. After two hours I was awoken by Juanito for some crisis, so abandoned rest. I'm actually astonished that I was immediately conscious and alert, risk does amusing things to one.

I was expecting the "Salvanguard" to show up from Djibouti yet she was late. I needed a major, incredible pull ahead to keep control. We gradually crawled our direction south lastly hurled a deep breath of alleviation when we were out of the conflict zone.

Shortly thereafter the "Salvanguard" showed up and associated up. The "Al Ahood" began to improve speed – a little more than two bunches – and we at long last made the position I settled on external Bahrain for the boat to deliver transfer.

After Juanito let exceed everyone's expectations anchor, I sent the jumpers down to check out the harsh of the setback which was as yet submerged. It turned out she was fitted with a harsh anchor and the power of the rocket blast had passed it over, letting all the chain out, so the boat was successfully secured by the harsh. No big surprise she was so hard to tow. The jumpers cut the chain and the "Al Ahood" swung round and lay to her bow anchor.

I conversed with Martin Eve, whom I had not met previously. He was a real live wire, full of enthusiasm, who talked so fast that the words sometimes fell over themselves so he appeared to be stuttering. He was meager and fit.

The past expert of the "Salvanguard" who got her into the inlet funked coming into the disaster area. A portion of the team were changed also, drove by the bespectacled radio official who was a dreadful piece of work. The Europeans had not set a generally excellent guide to the Filipinos and my profound respect for Captain Ventura expanded even more.

Now that the "Salvanguard" was nearby with her radio official I was in direct correspondence with Singapore by means of wire over radio. I excused a portion of the more modest pulls and got ready for releasing the "Al Ahood." She was a disaster area, the motor submerged, the convenience wore out and shifted aside where it had dissolved. Selco flew up the using pressurized water driven siphons for over the top siphoning and pneumatic bumpers. Chris Herbert probably been in his seventh heaven.

I let Martin and Juanito continue ahead with the arrangements while I managed the assessors and all the shore individuals who turn up later a significant rescue. Even the Press turned up and I was interviewed on the deck of the "Al Ahood," with the bent accommodation as a backdrop. The meeting showed up on ITV straight later the visit of President Reagan.

The feline joined the "Salvanguard", becoming fat and sleek.

The "Al Ahood" was loaded with 140,000 tons of crude oil from Kharg Island and about ten thousand was lost in the fire. A Troodos big hauler was contracted to convey the whole freight to objective, however we were unable to put her close by until the harsh had been lifted. So a second little big hauler was contracted and we ran a bus administration. Martin did the steering and pre-stacking investigations with the London advisors; Juanito ran the rescue group and siphons; Smits ran their siphons and team. I was in by and large charge and arranging. At one phase there were 11 pulls, two big haulers and the setback under my

control – 150 individuals. Every one of the key individuals conveyed radios so we had great interchanges, even with Smits.

The climate went bad and it blew extremely hard on occasion. There were so many shore individuals needing to come on board that I sanctioned a different pull for themselves and gave them fixed occasions to come ready so as not to meddle with the salvage.

The bus administration ran well and gradually the harsh rose out of the water, uncovering the gigantic opening which the detonating rocket made. In the end we put the Troodos big hauler close by and finished the release. She took the freight on to destination.

The siphons and rescue gear were gotten together and the disaster area was left with the "Salvanguard" holding on. I then towed and anchored the "Al Ahood" off Dubai. It was scary when I went locally available her, a wore out wreck to understand the submerged "Dara" the wore out traveler boat of my childhood was close by. At long last Selco brought the disaster area and she was towed to Taiwan for scrap.

In Bahrain I gave my proof to the Constant and Constant legal counselor, while staying on rescue reserve with the pull. Commander Crowther, a Selco ace, was our agent in Bahrain and he was because of assume control over the

"Salvanguard" from me. He was negative and apprehensive that I called Bond and said he ought not order the "Salvanguard". That very evening I cruised the pull back to the disaster area where Smits had an agreement on the "Tiburon" – a stacked big hauler greater than the "Al Ahood" hit by an Iraqi Exocet.

The fire was extinguished and I towed the "Tiburon" to the "Al Ahood" 's release area. Nearly when the anchor was down I was off again with Gert Koffeman and his group for the "Compound Venture". ITC showed up simultaneously so they were contracted also and I towed the "Substance Venture" to Bahrain later the fire was put out.

If there was a crisis when a pull is adrift they generally appear to be ready to move away. Assuming the pull is in port there is in every case some valid justification why she can't cruise. The conspicuous answer was to keep the pull adrift thus I took the "Salvanguard" to the ocean and we moored on rescue reserve, being provided by Gray Mackenzie pulls as necessary.

The "Dashaki" was the last field rescue I performed. She was deserted and untied later a supposed assault and her motor room was overflowed. I almost got the pull run over while going close by, having misinterpreted the speed the boat was floating. I towed her to Dubai and siphoned her out while machinery

conservation was performed.

I given over the pull to another Selco Chinese expert and flew back to Singapore. I moved to Bond's old office on the subsequent floor, while he involved the corner office on the third floor. Martin Eve was rescue ace in the Gulf.

BANKRUPTCY

I returned to my old shape and ran Selco Salvage with Captain Chua under Bond's general oversight, which implied I saw even less of Tham Yen Fei, however something was starting to turn out badly. Selco was making tremendous aggregates from the Gulf War yet cash was evidently close. One of my checks ricocheted, which was rationalized as a bank botch. Nobody had seen Peter Tham who, obviously, was in generally speaking charge yet he stood firm on no chief foothold in the company.

The ocean war seethed on and Selco performed many rescue activities which I ran from Singapore, heading out to London for assertions and planning for the "Al Ahood" mediation. Tham Yen Fei went home for the days from the workplace, as missed Wee. There was a demeanor of uneasiness.

The "Al Ahood" grant was the greatest rescue grant ever around then. Cash was pouring through the entryway yet the organization was not paying its bills.

One day the recipients were in the workplace, the organization was in hot water and made bankrupt. The Singapore Stock Exchange was closed for three days, just like the Kuala Lumpur Exchange in Malaysia. It was simply not possible that the rescue organization could be losing cash. Indeed it was the holding organization Pan Electric which were bankrupt yet it claimed Selco Salvage. It worked out that Peter Tham and Tan Koon Swan, the secretary to Dr Mahathir's decision party in Malaysia, were occupied with some obscure arrangement which had turned out badly. Both in the long run wound up in jail.

I progressed forward as regular and went to Spain to finish up an arrangement with Peter Bruce concerning the "Ceyan" and "Vatan" which were hit by exocets and we had salved and were sold for scrap. The two boats were bigger than the "Wind Enterprise" exactly 400,000 tons extra weight. I got him to pay me US$15,000 costs I had paid with my own cash and was unsure the beneficiaries planned to repay me. I was correct. They didn't and I would have been out of pocket.

I attempted to keep the show going yet the collectors' occupation was to gather and acknowledge resources, not run a company.

Nikki Tan was enchanting and amenable to me, yet I was helpful. Staff were being laid off and the organization was running down. Smits needed to purchase Selco and there were other intrigued parties.

Crafter, the director, vanished. Assuming that he realized what was happening he should

have halted it. Assuming he didn't have the foggiest idea what was happening he ought to have, he was the director and in that, twice doomed. He had fizzled dismally.

I rang Harold Rapp, who used to live in the Log House near Thorns Beach and now owned Dukes Hotel in St James Square. He was interested in joining a syndicate to buy Selco and would find more participants. Mr K, who was in Singapore, agreed to join. Harold rang to tell me he had found interested parties and would I fly to the States to give a presentation. I asked the receivers for permission to go at my own expense, but word came back from the Prime Minister's office that if I left Singapore I would not be allowed back in and Selco ownership would not be allowed to leave Singapore in any event. So that was the end of that idea.

Christoph Bettermann, a German who ran an oil support organization in Dubai with boats and a convenience rig, was keen on purchasing the pulls and barges. He talked with me in my office and asked me for a beverage in the evening at the Sheraton Park Hotel, where he was staying.

After supper he extended to me an employment opportunity in Dubai to begin a rescue division for him. I was intrigued on the grounds that it was very certain that the Singapore government planned to dominate and I would have rather not work for the Chinese. I told Bond and he attempted to put me off, notice me that he didn't confide in Bettermann and, in any case, he needed me to stay with him.

Ray Clarke did a recce of IMS in Dubai and it was good. Bettermann sent me a club class return pass to Dubai and I went up more than an end of the week and consented to join IMS at the earliest opportunity. The beneficiaries held me to one month's notification and afterward didn't pay me! I found that my annuity commitments were never paid into the benefits assets, there was no annuity and we were not going to get our rescue rewards, an immense monetary misfortune to me and obviously the wide range of various Selco employees.

I traveled to Dubai and began another period of my life.

DUBAI

It was a beguiling, friendly Christoph Bettermann who was have for the end of the week I spent in Dubai. He was a tallish man with a smooth-cleaned face and extremely smart. I remained in the Chicago Beach Hotel, which was near the manor that he lived in with his wife.

I was acquainted with Captain Baudoy, who was marine-director, and his significant other who lived in the estate nearby; and Herr Schneiders, the German bookkeeper, who lived in the third manor of the complex. We had a pleasant day by the private swimming poor and supper at the Sheraton. I was guaranteed a decent condo, a vehicle and an agreement to be arranged. Everything looked very rosy.

Dubai is totally different from Singapore. Singapore is green, lavish and in some cases wet; Dubai is dry and brown, the sand is all over the place in spite of the fact that blossoms are developed between the double carriageways. A couple of moments' drive from Dubai you hit the desert, but on a double carriageway. In Singapore, when clear of the condos, it was wilderness. Dubai, albeit cosmopolitan, was very Arab; Singapore was westernized Asian. In Dubai the day of rest and love in the mosque was Friday; in Singapore Saturday and Sunday were free. It was significantly more smoking in the late spring and colder in the colder time of year than Singapore. Dubai was a Sheikdom, managed by one man; Singapore was a popularity based Republic and it displayed in the overall air. I generally felt an outsider, my support was liable for my conduct in Dubai. I had no 'freedoms' of my own. The ostracize local area stuck nearer together.

When I showed up in Dubai to begin work my heart sank at the air terminal. It was in the cool of the early morning, the best season of day. Rather than one of the vehicles I was met by a driver with the workplace runabout. I was taken to my 'decent' level and my heart sank further to my shoes. I had committed the most all-powerful error, the German had deceived me. Bond had been correct. The level had no workers' quarters, was little, the view investigated a low lease block, and was basically empty. I plunked down to think on the just clearly second-hand armchair.

I would have rather not work for the Chinese, truth be told I would not work for them. I observed their cash grubbing, selfish, rules and guidelines, vehicle and driver attitude was not viable with a rescue organization. The fun had all gone.

I had two choices. Find success with it in Dubai and set up with the German. I would make a sensible measure of cash to compensate for what I lost in

Selco – pay, salvage bonuses, including "Al Ahood", and pension. Or call it quits and go home to England. I was a Name at Lloyds and would find something to do. The second option was not much of a challenge. The first was a challenge, and if I could control the German I could make IMS a world salvor. The tools were there, it was just a matter of using them in the right way. Bettermann agreed that Elbourne Mitchell would be our London lawyers. I had the right contacts in London and I was sure I would succeed. I decided to stay in Dubai and give it a go.

***

No office was prepared for me. I committed another error. The IMS complex was on the starboard side of the river going in. It comprised of a wharf for the boats, a manufacture yard for the seaward business, a maintenance office for the armada and two office blocks. The square confronting the street was one-story and worked of cement. The Sahibs of IMS worked there: Bettermann; Schneiders; Suleiman, a Pakastani; and the bookkeepers. Across a patio with a substantial floor was a dilapidated wooden structure, with a feeble stepping stool driving onto the subsequent floor. Here was the core of the IMS armada: Omar, the business administrator, a Palestinian; Alain Baoudy marine director, an Englishman; Chris Loat promoting a resigned Royal Navy officer; two secretaries, Dominic an Indian who worked with me and a Sri Lankan; and, generally significant of every one of, the Operations room monitored by Indians. There was space for an office here and I chose – gave a window was placed in and I could see the river – I needed to be there with speedy admittance to Ops. In my sub-conscience it was far enough away from Bettermann so he proved unable 'sit' on me. We concurred that I have a free hand to run the rescue, and I planned that was how it would have been. Bettermann needed me to be in the substantial square close to him and his secretary, an English young lady, Judith. I won. I whined about the level and he said Judith lived in the square and on the off chance that it was sufficient for her it was adequate for me. I planned distinctly to rest there so let it go for the moment.

Wjsmuller, the number two Dutch rescue organization, were utilizing IMS as their base, yet when I showed up on the scene they moved out.

I began with an unfilled table and a phone. The primary thing to do was to tell everybody where I was, which I did – the rescue representatives being the most significant. The following thing was to prefer Lloyd's Intelligence and Lloyd's List. I knew individuals who worked for both which helped.

I set with regards to learning 'my' armada and its staff, what hardware was accessible, and enrolling the help of George, the German specialist administrator, and Gordon, the maintenance man – an Englishman. The Operations room must be extended with radios, another message and more faculty. I began to discover more with regards to Bettermann.

Nothing especially occurred from the get go, there was a break in the ocean war. My absolute first rescue was a fiasco monetarily. I contracted a pull with an IMS ace as rescue expert to go to Salalah in Oman and tow in an Eastern coalition transport however sadly they fixed the motor and steamed in themselves.

Bettermann was extremely irate yet I became used to his annoyance and disregarded him. "Assuming that you don't as it don't be engaged with rescue," I told him.

It was basic to have a huge devoted rescue pull out on station and a decent rescue ace. None of the IMS men had any rescue insight so I enrolled Martin Eve, who had returned to England and began a pizza business which was driving him into his grave with boredom.

When I began to burn through cash Bettermann became troublesome. Bettermann seemed to have a free hand. I say 'showed up' on the grounds that it later turned out that it was not exactly so particularly free as he made out. It was a pity that he didn't confess all and let me know the limitations toward the start since I thought I was managing the one who settled on the choices. I later found that he needed to acquire Mohd al Fayed's authorization for uses over US$25,000 which – in the rescue world – is peanuts assuming you want to contract a boat or large stream at short notification, or concur a significant commission, or even compensation the attorneys' expenses. Mohd. whom I never met possessed IMS. I in this manner faced a super durable running conflict with the German and went about like I possessed the business and contended later.

It was a real shame that there was no mutual trust because if he had acted differently the final outcome would have been very different. It appeared to me he had some vision however not on a world scale and permitted himself to become stalled in the details of life, rather than clutching the vision and pushing all the way to the finish goal.

Meanwhile, back in the shop, I needed to choose how to beat the opposition. Selco – becoming Singapore government's Semco – was practically out of it for the present. One of their pulls was set to be taken to jail in Dubai, and I am embarrassed to say I didn't go to see them. Arturo Brioso was the expert, my main official on the "Salviking."

Wjsmuller situated one pull in the inlet and collaborated with Niko at Al Jadaf, a plunging outfit with supply boats. Smits worked a base in Bahrain and

later in Sharjah, where IMS additionally possessed a base – the following Emirate east from Dubai and an hour's drive across the desert from the spring. Since Selco had fallen I questioned Smits would wish to have a lot to do with Semco assuming they came into the inlet – once nibbled by the Chinese twice shy.

The IMS base was the key, decisively arranged at Dubai. I sent the jobless pulls, out on rescue reserve in the Persian Gulf, to assigned stations with code names. I convinced Bettermann to purchase two versatile firefighting units for use on the pulls without fire screens, and a major heap of froth. He turned down a fabulous arrangement with Frank of Interworld who needed to base a major heap of froth with IMS, basically giving us froth on special or return.

Mr K was quick to sell his pull. He purchased an old Bugsier rescue pull – the "Pacific" of Amoco Cadiz notoriety – renamed her "Intergulf", utilized Dick Jolly as expert and McFarlane as boss designer, and she meandered the world searching for rescue. She was still exceptionally quick and could surpass any pull in the Gulf. I convinced Bettermann to get her and Dick Jolly brought her up from Singapore and into the creek.

I was expecting to utilize all the group since they were generally sharp rescue men and a large portion of them ex Selco. Bettermann made his mark as a mean financial specialist and diminished all their compensation. The people who might not concur were terminated and sent home to Manila. Of course, Dick and McFarlane returned home also. It left an especially harsh desire for my mouth since arrangements were not respected and it was anything but a decent premise to begin a rescue operation.

I selected Dave Stirling, ex Selco, who turned into her exceptionally fruitful extremely durable expert, he was a characteristic sailor and taken care of her beautifully.

With the "Intergulf" on rescue station as the principle rescue pull – furnished with satellite, telephone and message – IMS were starting to look a touch more expert. I figured Bettermann would have blood vessel breakage when the solicitations showed up for the equipment.

"On the off chance that you don't as it don't be engaged with rescue. We are taking on the world's top salvors and it will not be modest to beat the opposition," I told him. Then it started. I was stirred in the evening. The "Medusa" was hit in the North Persian Gulf and ablaze. I despatched the "Intergulf" and quickly thereafter was called by Mr K who let me know that the proprietors' representative was offering a Lloyd's Form gave I concurred a location commission and let me know the sum. My opposition were Smits and Wjsmuller. Nobody had known about IMS, in spite of the fact that they had known about me. I was reached by Samuel

Stewart the rescue agents, who consented to work with me, probably until Semco was fully operational. Bond, obviously, would not have anything to do with me, he considered I had deceived him. So assuming Samuel Stewart worked with me, Bond probably won't work with them.

I was called by the proprietors' representative, I concurred the commission and IMS was granted the Lloyd's Form. I advised Ops to wire Smits and Wjsmuller that we had been granted the LOF.

I educated Bettermann the following daytime regarding our prosperity and the commission. He got exceptionally upset so I let him know that possibly I ran the rescue my direction, which would be fruitful, or he could do it and I would return home. He saw that I implied what I said and withdrew. He didn't have the skill himself and he knew it. He had recruited an example of the rare type of person on the planet who could make it work, and if IMS somehow happened to be a salvor he wanted me. I won however at significant expense. He let me be and I encountered no more difficulty, however it was an uncomfortable ceasefire. As an issue of politeness I kept him informed yet that was all.

The "Medusa", albeit in weight, was a VLCC, yet at the same time important if not very gravely harmed. The "Intergulf" was fruitful and the LOF was terminated.

I was in contact with Ray Clarke on the subject of safety; what amount of cash ought to be set up by the proprietor from which IMS, as salvors, could be compensated? It was nothing but bad salving a boat assuming we were not going to be paid, and, by setting up an assurance, the proprietor kept up with control of his boat. If an owner did not put up a guarantee – or pay the salvors – then I was entitled to arrest the ship. We concurred a figure and Ray managed the proprietors' specialists and an assurance was organized and set up at Lloyds. Bettermann started to acknowledge IMS was presently in the major association when he saw the size of the assurance that was set up. I, or rather IMS were on the way.

Ray came out to take the proof and set up our case for assertion. The framework fills in as follows. I had acquired a Lloyd's Open Form 'No Cure No Pay' agreement to ointment the "Medusa" and carry her to a protected spot. This had been finished. IMS were fruitful, having 'restored' the patient "Medusa", and presently needed to be paid. Salvors are truly specialists of the ocean; in the event that you are debilitated you call the specialist and he fixes you. Nonetheless, when he sends in his charge you tell him, "Jesus, specialist, I was not excessively sick!" So with a boat proprietor, his boat is in a difficult situation and he requires a salvor and when the salvor requests installment, he says, "Christ, it wasn't so terrible, we might have done it without you." If the different sides can't concur they bring in the Arbitrator selected by Lloyds.

The agreement specifies the manner in which security ought to be set up, which had been done, and the arrangement of a Lloyd's Arbitrator. You can't go to the mediator and say, "Mr Arbitrator, I have done a fabulous rescue work with heaps of risks and the boat is overall quite significant and we have been extremely skilful, kindly compensation me bunches of money."

The Arbitrator needs to know the hows and whys, he wants the proof of what you have done – henceforth the requirement for Ray to take articulations from the members. We realize the proprietors' specialists will downsize the rescue, and their members will say, 'Indeed, we truly didn't require them however they turned up with a pull, just provide them with a modest quantity of cash.' So the expertise of the salvor's legal counselor is to show the rescue in the best light, and show the Arbitrator – through the proof – that the activity was expertly done and that the salvors are resolved to rescue with rescue pulls, gear and personnel.

I had known Ray for a long time and confided in his wise counsel. He was no stodgy legal counselor living in an ivory tower offering equivocal guidance, he was sensible, living in reality with an information on the conceivable. He could contend the particulars of the law as well as anyone and did as such when necessary.

Mike Harrison of Clyde and Co specialists, who represented a ton of freight interests, approached Mr Bettermann to convince him to utilize Clydes as IMS specialists. Clydes represented Mohd Al Fayed, so utilized that as a switch. Nonetheless, one of my standards for working with IMS was that Elbourne Mitchell would be our London specialists. I was not going to alter my perspective and change to a lawful 'processing plant'. I met Mike when I worked with Elbourne Mitchell and he was a charmer. Nonetheless, later a decent supper, Christoph needed to stop his huge Mercedes coming back to Mike's inn with the goal that Mike could open the entryway and be wiped out. I heard not any more with regards to Clydes!

In the rescue world nobody had known about IMS. "IM who?" individuals would say. They had known about me and realized I was an expert salvor. Later the discretion, if either party disagreed with the Arbitrator's honor or discoveries, they could interest the Appeal Arbitrator who was the way in to the framework. Mr Gerald Darling QC was the Appeal Arbitrator and had known me since I was a cadet on the "Dara". He represented BI at the enquiry and, prior to becoming Appeal Arbitrator, represented Selco on events. I met him at a gathering during a meeting on rescue and throughout our discussion, he said, grinning, "Progress significantly from being a cadet on the

"Dara", Captain Tew. I have watched your advancement with interest." Emphasis on the word 'Captain'.

I helped Ray to remember this and he said, "That is all well overall, he might know you however he has never known about IMS. The significant thing is to get him to perceive that IMS are proficient salvors and he will not do that later just one rescue. It may take years."

We were having a comfortable supper at Ray's inn, talking about how best to introduce IMS to the rescue world, how to get us perceived as expert salvors. There was a genuine money related thought here. Intermittent or one-off salvors were not paid as much as expert salvors. The framework energized proficient salvors by paying them more, paying them in actuality to have rescue pulls, hardware and staff accessible consistently for salvage.

I set up for an IMS leaflet to be made with photos and portrayals of the multitude of pulls. We made another of the base with every one of its fixes offices and capacity of rescue gear and froth. I said something to Ray featuring my inclusion in rescue during the Iran-Iraq ocean war and the hardships and risks of working in a disaster area. The entire of the Gulf was currently viewed as a disaster area. The British Chamber of Commerce booklet drew out a rundown of the multitude of boats hit and we had our own graph also. I explained to him why I joined IMS, how I had coordinated the organization for rescue, extended Operations, purchased the "Intergulf", recruited a rescue ace, set the pulls at anchor in the bay on rescue station. We were proficient salvors.

Ray was a top oceanic legal advisor, a specialist in rescue law and I knew it. I was a specialist in my field and he knew it. We consequently had common regard and trust for one another and made a decent group. We concluded that

Captain Tew, the expert salvor, would be the 'essence' of IMS and I would go to all Arbitrations. It was basically impossible that we would have been perceived as expert until we had an allure before Gerald. No matter what, we would pursue the primary honor, get our proof before him and trust he would remember us as expert salvors thus get upgraded awards.

The proprietors of the "Medusa" needed to settle, so I concurred a satisfactory figure and in no time a short time later the cash walked into the IMS financial balance. The eyes of Schneiders – the German bookkeeper – opened wide when he saw the size of the settlement and he nearly bowed to me. But he was the puppet of Bettermann; if Bettermann said, 'jump,' he jumped. Truth be told, assuming that Bettermann

had said, 'Sign this, it is your execution order,' he would have marked. IMS were not only salvors in name, we had cash as well.

"Won't help us at Arbitration to become proficient on the off chance that you settle," he said via telephone when I told him.

"No point alienating a Greek proprietor with ships in the Gulf," I answered. "Might get another one."

But it had begun and we were before long occupied with a lot of cases. Beam utilized each legitimate gadget to get our first assertion heard rapidly, and when the honor was out we pursued. We could generally discover some valid justifications to pursue yet it was essential to have sound ones. The Appeal Arbitrator didn't permit unimportance and he would descend with a crushing weight assuming that he thought we were engaging for engaging. We needed him on our side.

In the occasion, the allure assertion went well indeed and he did what we had gotten ready for. Albeit new salvors, we were perceived as expert, so we got an improved honor and later on, the Arbitrators would grant us on the premise we were proficient salvors. In an exceptionally brief time frame for sure IMS had shown up on the rescue scene and was discussed at the same moment as Smits and Wjsmuller. We were no long "IM who?" however "IMS the Gulf salvors!" I was exceptionally satisfied to be sure as was Ray. My fantastic procedure was working surprisingly better than I had hoped.

***

Mohd Saeedi was an Iranian money manager who claimed a transportation office in Tehran. I previously made his colleague before long the upset when I went to Bandar Abbas on the "Salveritas" to overview a section submerged boat so as to rescue. Mohd was in Bandar Abbas and took me round to see the different authorities. The spot was in a disturbance with the youthful progressive watchmen going around displaying rifles. It was anything but a spot for the timid and I stuck out in contrast to everything else as there were no ostracizes left.

The Bandar Abbas rescue didn't fall off yet Mohd turned into Selco's representative in Iran. He had the most incredible associations and consistently appeared to be ready to get authorization for Selco pulls to enter Iranian waters for rescue. I regularly talked with him in the evening. Selco kept outlines of the Iranian and Iraqi 'hits' and I went to Tehran to see Mohd and haggle with the Iranian insurance agency concerning a rescue case. I was traveling with as little luggage as possible with simply a short-term sack and took these two outlines with me in a plastic pack. The conflict was seething ashore and adrift. At the point when I went through movement securely I thought I was home and dry. A man in plain clothes

came dependent upon me and guided me to an office. It was the progressive mystery police whose standing was no greater than the old Shah's parcel Savac. I entered grasping my plastic sack, keenly conscious about the two 'hit' diagrams peeping over the highest point of my plastic pack. I became uncontrollably nervous without precedent for my life and attempted to look uninterested as I remained before my examiner. I put the pack containing the graphs between my legs. The man addressing me didn't grin and had dead looking eyes. I was alarmed yet did my most extreme not to show it, how was I to clarify the graphs? I was 'examined' for more than an hour standing constantly regarding the reason why I was coming to Tehran without a visa. Clearly my answers fulfilled him since he said I could go. I got my plastic pack with the diagrams staying, feeling like they had a winking light on them and checking the practically overpowering desire to run, I strolled gradually and I trusted with pride out into the swarmed, grimy, boring air terminal – the ladies hidden and wearing dark. I shut the entryway and began to shake with help which, fortunately, halted when going through customs. Mohd was there to meet me and I informed him regarding the encounter.

"Misfortune Tehran is dry," he chuckled, "yet I will get you a decent supper." Which he did – heaps of caviar.

I felt somewhat caught; having got into Tehran, could I get out? I was totally subject to Mohd to get a visa in my identification so I could leave via air. Tehran is 4,000 feet high and encircled by mountains, snow covered until late in the year – the main tone, other than the blue sky, among the boring substantial structures and brown brutal mountainsides.

We later flew down to Bushire to see war-harmed delivers, and were postponed for eight hours at the air terminal on our return. The Iraqis had assaulted the thermal energy station, or so we thought, however it turned out later it was most likely the Israelis.

I managed everything well with Mohd and met him in London too. I needed him to be our representative for IMS yet he was leaned to go with Smits, who had been later him for quite a while. He was owed large chunk of change by Selco and had minimal shot at being paid. I traveled to Tehran however Mohd went with Smits thus I lost my best contact in Iran.

I later traveled to Tehran with Bettermann who utilized Salzgitter, his old organization, as specialists, yet they didn't have the course in the rescue and pull world as Mohd, and IMS missed out subsequently. Notwithstanding, soon after Semco were ready for action, the Iranians put out the agreement for rescue in Iranian waters to delicate and Semco were granted it. IMS bid however I was a reluctant

bidder once I discovered the idea of the agreement and I am really happy we didn't get it. Semco were presently inseparably connected with Iran, working solely in Iranian waters, and in spite of the fact that it barred different salvors from entering Iranian waters, it kept them out of the remainder of the Gulf. The Iranians were presently assaulting ships and no boat was protected anyplace in the waters of the Persian Gulf.

IMS currently had a couple of good finished rescue tasks and the cash was beginning to come in. Bettermann showed he needed to purchase more pulls and supply boats.

Gellatly Hankey, the Selco Djibouti specialists, were claimed by an aggregate whose head office was in London. At the point when I was in Djibouti salving the "Go Rider", the new proprietors were there having quite recently eliminated Mr John – the old head man – and I got to know the new brief chief, John, who was currently back in London. I dined with him frequently when I was there and he had acquainted me with his chief, who was an overseer of Inchcape. Inchcape claimed Gray Mackenzie in Bahrain and I realized they were considering selling their armada. I was just about as sharp as Bettermann to build the size of the armada, truth be told I needed to develop a worldwide premise, and I had examined this with Bettermann in extremely broad terms. I let him know that I realized Gray Mackenzie may be available to be purchased and he communicated incredible interest.

I rang London, addressed my contact and put him in contact with Bettermann. I expected to be involved assuming anything was the fate of it yet Bettermann got his retribution. IMS purchased the Gray Mackenzie armada and I was completely barred from having at least something to do with it and Bettermann financed it on the rear of my rescue – vowing the honors from neglected rescue activities. Precisely what Selco had done to get cash and add to the chapter 11, for not just had the bookkeepers acquired against Selco's portion of joint activities they had acquired against Smits also. I presently knew it was basically impossible that I could keep working long haul with the German and it was inevitable before I left, however not while the ocean war was raging.

The conflict would not continue for ever and when it halted we should have been set up if IMS somehow managed to stay in rescue. It was fine being a Gulf salvor when there was heaps of rescue, yet in harmony there was very little and to endure we expected to work on a worldwide scale. Nonetheless, that fantasy was presently broken, and it was only an issue of awaiting my time.

During one of my visits to London I went to see the number three in the Mohd Al Fayed order and he paid attention to what I needed to say about Bettermann.

"I very concur with you however Mr Al Fayed won't hear a word against Bettermann, he is the blue-looked at kid and you are burning through your opportunity to even try."

So that was the start of a thought of removing Bettermann stopped from the beginning. I might have made IMS into a-list organization working on a worldwide premise, rather it shriveled. Bettermann was elevated to a situation in Harrods, just as IMS and at last the blue-looked at kid went wrong – however I am in front of myself.

I proceeded with my nearby relations with Smits. Before long I showed up in Dubai Klaus Reinigert their Managing Director called me and proposed a gathering, he needed to discuss participation. He made customary review visits in the inlet and came through Dubai to meet me. The interest that Smits had in IMS was the armada, and the interest I had in Smits was their staff and ability. Smits would have rather not bring any more costly Smit run pulls into the Gulf, and I expected to take advantage of a pool of aptitude without paying for it. The undeniable straightforward arrangement was to coordinate on the rescue and we came to an understanding that whichever organization acquired the rescue contract they would get the other as co-salvor. So assuming that IMS got the agreement I would acquire Smits as co-salvor as well as the other way around. We thought it was indispensably critical that nobody with the exception of him and I should know about any understanding. It is extremely challenging to leave well enough alone and, in the expressions of the American Benjamin Franklin spoken multiple hundred years prior, "Three might leave well enough alone, assuming that two of them are dead."

The Arbitrators may take a dreary perspective on it on the off chance that they thought we had sewed up the Gulf and made a virtual imposing business model. The counter-contention was that they may remunerate us for being so reasonable and participating. In any case, assuming we asked our attorneys, or looked for insight's recommendation, our mystery would be out, so we consented to tell nobody – and that implied nobody in our own organizations too. Nothing was to be recorded as a hard copy and we would audit the understanding sometime in the future. We settled on it and subsequently began a most beneficial time for both our companies.

Our joined powers beat the opposition in the vast majority of the 'hits' outside Iranian waters, and nobody had some awareness of our mysterious understanding. Louis Keyser, the Smit shore delegate in Sharjah and I partook in a lunch once every month to audit the cases we had close by, and he more likely than not speculated something. It turned out to be more convoluted for Smits when Smit Matsas showed up on the scene,

yet that was not my concern.

Eventually there were such countless cases that Klaus required a gathering. I was in London and flew over to Rotterdam for the end of the week on the city container. I was met by a vehicle and driver and taken to Smits' base camp by the canal boat harbor. It was a huge second for me. The Dutch were the world forerunners in rescue and Smits was the greatest and best Dutch salvor. They were the most incredible on the planet and I was entering their base camp as a visitor of the Managing Director to talk about situations where we were co-salvors, equivalent accomplices. A long, long way from boss official of the "Salvaliant", yet just twelve years on schedule, and I had just begun the rescue division with IMS a little more than a year prior. At the point when I passed on London to join Selco in Singapore, never in my most extravagant fantasies did I envision something like this. Just to enter the primary entryway was to look into rescue history – with a model of a well known Smit pull in the foyer.

Klaus had a corner office with a view over the old harbor and I enjoyed all of Friday with him. We examined with their in-house legal counselors the cases they were managing, and I gave an audit of the cases I was managing. We had concurred that assuming IMS had gotten the agreement then I would run the case to mediation with Elbourne Mitchel, and assuming Smits had acquired the agreement then they would run the case with their London attorneys Holman, Fenwick and Willan. I conveyed a sheet with me that just held back the name of the salved transport, mediation date, security, assessed grant, pulls included, and a one-line portrayal of the rescue – explosive assault, fire, or whatever – and that was adequate for me to recall every one of the applicable realities and have the option to surrender a to-date continue. I observed the legitimate work intriguing and had a decent memory for detail and turned out to be great at surveying what a rescue was worth.

Gert Koffeman, who had been with me on the "Al Ahood" for the freight move, and was presently one of Klaus' two right-hand men, had lunch with us. Klaus was stressed that, with such a lot of cash required between the two organizations, we ought to have the understanding recorded as a hard copy. It was not because he mistrusted me but if I should have an accident – say hitting a camel in the desert – then there was no proof of what we had agreed, and vice versa, say he got run over when riding his bicycle at weekends. I concurred and he delivered a composed understanding for me to peruse, which incorporated the immeasurably significant split which was fifty, independent of who had done what or the number of pulls were involved. It was kept easy to dispose of any contentions. The main issue was that a third individual knew about the agreement

– the individual who composed it. We concurred I would have one unique and he would have another and it ought to stay mysterious. The remainder of the time was spent talking about rescue, Semco, Smit Singapore office and being displayed round the workplace. That evening at supper we consented to the arrangement and I flew back the following day to London. The understanding worked flawlessly until I left Dubai, when I uncovered its reality to Bettermann.

Although the salvage division was more successful than I ever imagined possible, in the accounts it did not appear to be doing so well. The real expense for IMS was me in addition to another in Operations at two or three hundred dollars every month, the "Intergulf" and the convenient rescue equipment.

The pulls on rescue reserve were charged to the marine division at a full business rate, so the marine division abruptly turned out to be entirely beneficial. The net outcome to me was a much diminished reward. Goodness, my naivety while arranging my contract.

The names of the multitude of pulls and supply boats had no shared factor thus, to the rest of the world, there was nothing to recognize them as having a place with IMS 'that notable Gulf salvor'. We wracked our cerebrums to concoct an answer. Selco utilized the Sal prefix to every one of the names, Smits had Smits as the prefix, what could IMS have? It was my mom who said why not use IMS and add the word Salv, so Imsalv turned into the prefix and we renamed every one of the pulls later creatures steady with their capacities. The "Intergulf" turned into the "Imsalv Lion"; the other huge pull turned into the "Imsalv Tiger"; a little yet exceptionally valuable boat turned into the "Imsalv Fox"; another the "Imsalv Lynx" – and extremely fruitful it was too.

The last blow came when I was in England. There was an Iranian assault on the Sharjah Petroleum oil field and the capacity big hauler and oil creation stage were set burning. Smits acquired the agreement and IMS were the co-salvor, so Smits ran the operation.

Bettermann knew the chief and inquired as to whether he could arrange a settlement. It was a fabulous case with extremely high risks and was worth very much of cash. Not long before the intervention Bettermann at last settled however provided that US$900,000 was repaid out of the settlement to Sharjah. I protested unequivocally in light of the fact that there was no compelling reason to pay them anything, we had the agreement and I was sure at mediation we would be granted more than the settlement figure without taking care of anything. All it was doing was to deny IMS of $450,000 and Smits of a similar sum. For reasons I actually don't have the foggiest idea, Klaus consented to this insane arrangement. I told Bettermann I would have

nothing to do with it. It later turned into the subject of a criminal indictment in the Dubai Court with Bettermann in the dock.

The Iran-Iraq war halted in July 1988 with a truce and with it the rescue. Bettermann turned out to be significantly more troublesome in light of the fact that he was adequately keen to see that when the cases were through intervention, the rescue pay would stop and IMS would out of nowhere become not really beneficial, if not unrewarding, and no arrangement had been made for what's to come. My excellent vision was out of the window since I could don't really work with the German and the sooner I left the better, yet first I needed my money.

I remained on for an additional nine months, going to mediations in London. I once traveled to Tokyo and arranged an incredible settlement with the Japanese on one of the last ships hit in the Gulf. I set myself up appropriately and had a case loaded with archives which I used to respond to the inquiries put by the panel of six standing up to me. I was exceptionally satisfied with myself as were Smits.

It was with incredible help later my last day with IMS I traveled to Mauritius in the Indian Ocean for a vacation, cruising side interest sailboats in the tidal pond close to the inn by day and betting in the gambling club around evening time. I flew home through Nairobi, where I went on safari with my mom who showed up from England.

UK ALDERNEY RIO DUBAI

I was back in England for the mid year, a 'liberated individual' with enough cash to fail to help some time, despite the fact that there was cloud faintly not too far off. It was 1989 and the primary exceptionally faint thunderings of difficulty at Lloyds was being heard – asbestos and contamination. In any case, I got a check for the 1986 record and purchased a shop with two pads above it in Alderney, the northernmost Channel Island. I invested some energy searching for an appropriate boat. I sanctioned a Freedom 21, test cruising her for ten days in the West Country. I observed she was a young fellow's boat and I was presently not youthful, yet coming up to middle-age! I at long last chose a Freedom 30, "Opportunity Freyja" (Freyja is the Swedish Goddess of adoration) and cruised off solitary to Brittany for the excess summer. I burned through more than two months all alone and reviewed the Log for the RCC Journal, which was distributed. I kept the boat at the Beaucette marina in Guernsey over the winter.

Peter Bruce rang me up one day in October from Australia and proposed I may like Rio de Janeiro for a difference in scene. I concurred and flew out with US$40,000 in real money emitted around my body, which I got up Airport from Thomas Cook. I should prepare a big hauler for cruising to India for scrap. It was with much alleviation that I put the cash in the protected of the Meridien Copacabana, where I resided for a long time. I'm embarrassed to say I was not extremely fruitful, having invested an excessive amount of energy in the clubs. I flew home later Peter went up to diminish me.

I spent an unsatisfactory few months doing nothing when Mohd Saeedi rang up and asked me to go back to Dubai and work for him. I saw him in London with his right-hand man Christian Bang, and flew to Dubai. Saddam Hussein invaded Kuwait shortly afterwards. I was in Singapore at the time looking at the tug Mohd had purchased. I flew back to Dubai in an almost empty plane to find Dubai with a much reduced expatriate community. I spent six unsatisfactory months in Dubai and went to Sri Lanka for Christmas 1990. I was not very well and flew back to England on New Year's Eve.

The Gulf War was battled and won yet I didn't get back to work in Dubai. The thunderings at Lloyds became truth and I confronted enormous misfortunes, which I didn't think I was in a situation to pay, regardless of my Godmother passing on and leaving me some cash. I cruised "Opportunity Freyja" back to England and a securing on the Beaulieu River somewhere around the Beaulieu River Sailing Club, of which I was a member.

The debacle at Lloyds appeared to be kicking more awful so I off a shop on the Quay at Lymington in November 1991 selling nautical timekeepers, indicators and books – not that I expected to make a fortune but rather it gave me an income and time to figure some solution for Lloyds.

It was very similar to bygone eras when the limo pulled up at 04:00 in the first part of the day to take me to Gatwick for the Emirates trip to Dubai. The club class flight was as great as could be expected with incredible food, and it was a crisp morning so I had the option to check out the view from my seat by the window. It was the first flight I had made for 18 months and I was quite excited – and this from someone who had flown over a million miles in ten years!

I was met at the air terminal by one of the IMS drivers, who carried me in the know regarding the news. Bettermann, obviously, had gone; as had his secretary, Judith; Omar was still there, what a survivor he was; Adnam was VP; and an Arab financier was president. The workplace and base had been moved to Jabal Ali, the enormous port thirty minutes' drive from the creek.

"No energy now, sir, no rescue," the driver said with a smile, going to see me sitting in the back.

My old secretary, Dominic, was still there yet worked in the identification segment; Gordon actually fixed the boats and worked from an office at Al Jadaf, the maintenance yard over the street span over the creek.

The driver dropped me off at the Sheraton Hotel. The gallery from my room disregarded the rivulet, and only downstream on the contrary side was an uncovered land parcel. It had been the IMS base and nothing was left. The spot – with all its sorrow, all its victory – was only a memory.

A driver and vehicle was doled out to me every day so I could go anyplace, which was extremely wonderful. Dubai was all buzzing about, the streets were stifled with traffic, new structures were going up, the spot was occupied. The environment was hot yet not agonizingly so and later November in England was bliss.

Omar took me to see the IMS Dubai legal advisors where I said something concerning my part in IMS and the occasions encompassing the restitution of US$900,000. On one more day he took me to see the Dubai investigator who was arraigning Bettermann. I would show up in court one day one week from now, in the interim appreciate Dubai. I did!

I was in Dubai for north of a month so utilized the vehicle and driver. I was driven across the desert to a little lodging in the lower regions of the mountains for a dip and lunch. We went to Al Ain, the college town of the

Emirates, which is in lower regions of the mountains close to the boundary with Abu Dhabi. It requires over two hours of desert heading to arrive at Abu Dhabi yet I was not doing the driving so it was fun.

I gotten together with Barry Howard, the entertainer, who lived in Bournemouth and drove him to Fujairah to swim in the blue Arabian Sea and eat. The section to the town is stupendous, the street having been sliced through the fruitless mountains.

The Dubai Courthouse is an impressive structure. It was starting to get hot when we showed up at the enormous vehicle leave. Omar and I got together with the IMS legal counselors and we went into the court at the named time. I entered with impressive anxiety; an Arab country, abnormal law, and I was an alien.

Ahead of me was a raised dias. In the gut of the court were seats which were at that point loaded up with individuals. To one side of the dias was an enclosure with bars, very much like the enclosure for a wild creature in a zoo. It was loaded up with individuals standing, and in the front was Bettermann. It was a genuine shock, a culture shock, to see anybody in an enclosure not to mention the pleased German I had worked for. He looked pale and more slender than when I last saw him.

The Dubai examiner came in wearing a red cape, clearly intended to threaten, and remained at a little work area on the left-hand side of the dias. Three appointed authorities came in and the court stood while they sat down on the raised dias, peering down on all in the court. In the court, at the front under the actual noses of the adjudicators, was the observer box.

I accepting a full breath as I was directed to the case and the entryway shut behind me – everyone's eyes in the court, including the appointed authorities', on me. There then resulted a legitimate contention in Arabic with regards to the translator, which allowed me an opportunity to settle down and get my heart beat down. When the contention was over the Dubai examiner asked me inquiries in Arabic, which were then converted into English, in accordance with the assertion I had made. I replied in English in what I trusted was an intelligible consistent voice.

Bettermann's legal advisor protested occasionally, predominantly over the interpretation. The interpretation gave me loads of time to think and recall what I said in my assertion. I gave my proof honestly and truly. Bettermann was yesterday's story as far as I was concerned and much as I might have disliked him at the time I was working for IMS, he was history so I did not try and slant my evidence against him. Out of nowhere it was finished, next case. I needed to return the following week and answer more questions.

It was exceptionally hot back out in the vehicle park and I anticipated a dip at
the Sheraton to unwind.

I seemed multiple times in the court and went through nine hours in the observer box, and afterward flew home for the remainder of the UK winter. Right around a year after the fact I discovered that the three appointed authorities were changed and Bettermann was acquitted.

UK SHOP

I went to London a great deal and partook in gatherings of Lloyds Names and joined three activity gatherings. These were dull days without a doubt; I confronted liquidation or, later, going to see Mary Archer on the difficulty committee.

In 1993 I vowed all that I possessed to Lloyds and expanded my endorsing. Assuming I planned to go belly up I planned to become penniless with a bang. My sibling James was utilized in London with an organization occupied with recondite work to do with venture. I was prompted on a wise venture by a Mr Evans of Grimston Scott, and James accompanied me to meet the asset administrator. He articulated the speculation as strong and it did very well to be sure, so well indeed that I sold out and had cash in the bank!

The shop was very fruitful as a one-man project, however a gigantic tie. I was unable to sell anything assuming that the shop was closed. It was interesting to be behind a shop counter and notice human conduct. To some I was only a shop laborer of no importance hence treated as such with obscurity, or sometimes with disdain, others drew in me in discussion and ended up being fascinating individuals; and others were programs who had no aim of purchasing anything. These I found the most troublesome on the grounds that it was my merchandise they were playing with which, obviously, is some unacceptable mentality to have as a shopkeeper.

One 'program' figured out how to pester me enough so I inquired as to whether he planned to purchase anything or not and he answered, "No, I can't stand to and it is all very well for you residing in a decent spot encompassed by intriguing things. I live in Birmingham and I work in a processing plant and it is a treat for me to be here." I attempted to be more lenient in the future.

Soon in the wake of beginning the shop Wendy turned up requesting a task and she turned out to be extremely useful doing odd hours for myself and days when I went to London. Wendy was a notable Lymington character, brimming with fun and relentless babble, with an undeniable haircut. Substantially more significantly she was great in a boat. At the point when I observed assistance for the shop, she came day cruising with me.

We crossed the Channel to Cherbourg and had the best sail back I at any point appreciated in "Frejya", averaging a little more than six bunches on a wide reach with splendid daylight. Our record for constant prattle was nine hours!

In the colder time of year of 1994 I traveled to Hong Kong with a Chinese companion and did a multi week visit in China, which was entrancing. I flew on to Sydney and

remained with Peter Bruce and his significant other, being bound to the house for four days during the hedge fires. Los Angeles tumbled down in the tremor on the day I rang to affirm my booking to San Francisco. The protection misfortunes turned out bigger than anticipated and affected on a couple of my syndicates.

During the dead long periods of 1996 January and February, I traveled to Singapore and was taken by a companion to see the old Selco base. It was exceptionally frightful and impactful. The 'new' office block was vacant and abandoned. Mr Kahlenberg's office in the bygone one-story building was currently important for a stockroom. The shipyard had gone downhill and in my mind I could hear the voices of Selco faculty. All the perspiration and work, the triumphs and disappointment, all gone into the ether – everything except a memory.

Kahlenberg had passed on and not many went to his burial service; Patani, my old bosun, suffocated; Diotay, my old Salvaliant cook, dead from cirrhosis of the liver; Barros, my "Salvanguard" bosun, killed in the Gulf War; similar to my Chinese cadet; and my "Salvanguard" messman killed when an Exocet hit the motor room of a boat they were salving. The main sign that Selco at any point existed was on the power shed, which had a Selco shipyard sign on it. It was history; the past, it was gone – look to the future.

I tracked down somebody to care for the shop and spent a decent arrangement of the late spring of 1996 cruising. Edward and I cruised "Freyja" to Ireland and back in 12 days, and were granted the RCC Royal Cork container and the record was distributed in the Journal. I later cruised down to the Morbihan in the Bay of Biscay and back with Michael, an Irishman I met who took to the ocean like a duck to the water.

In November I moved the shop to bigger premises with Paul who presently went along with me on a super durable premise. Paul was bright and great at shows, particularly the window. I figured I could make a showcase however by changing only a couple of points, great became splendid. I currently worked with a completely fledged arrangement with Nauticalia and the shop turned into a kind of establishment, albeit still mine. We were as yet on the Quay however presently in the most unmistakable position, and when Chris Murdoch from Nauticalia refitted the premises they stuck out and pulled in the eye.

The seaside disintegration at Thorns Beach where my mom actually resided turned out to be downright terrible that medicinal work must be done or the ocean would get through. Beaulieu Estate, who possessed the ocean side, would not concede any risk, despite the fact that Lord Montagu conceded an ethical obligation. In the end I worked out an arrangement with them by which Beaulieu provided the wood and I provided the labour.

The work was highly deferred in beginning yet fortunately the colder time of year created for the most part easterly storms so minimal more was lost. In any case, simply providing the work was costly and I acquired cash from Midlands and charge cards to pay.

Ralph Montagu needed to purchase the Windmill yet would not offer sufficient cash. Then he was offered a lease but eventually it was put on the market and sold very well. All obligations were paid off and my mom possessed a smidgen more capital.

On Christmas Eve 1996 I got the first of my Lloyds benefits and what a help it was. My resources were presently mine and I had benefits for sure, having paid every one of my misfortunes. The future looked blushing again and I permitted a seed to grow. I purchased yachting magazines and began to check out boats.

Finally M, whom I met in London, turned up out of nowhere and I asked him, "Would you like to cruise round the world with me?"

The practically quick answer was "Yes."

M was the impetus. We checked out and nearly purchased a Freedom 35 yet later the overview turned her down.

Peter Bruce rang up out of nowhere and I drove down to Plymouth. He was preparing a RFA big hauler to sail to India for scrap and needed me to accept her as expert. I mulled over everything except I claimed the shop and my cruising. It was returning the clock not advances so I declined.

CIRCUMNAVIGATION

On 12 October 1997 M and I dominated "Autonomous Freedom" at the metropolitan marina close to Sandy Hook and cruised to New York. I figured out an issue with the traditions at their central command at Newark and we cruised south.

I reviewed our investigation journey to Cambridge Chesapeake Bay, which was distributed in the RCC Journal.

The Intercoastal Waterway was hard motoring and difficult work however it got us down the 1,100 resolution miles to Fort Lauderdale in shielded waters for I didn't fancy the colder time of year North Atlantic in a little boat. Both my senior sibling Donald and my granddad were gotten out in Atlantic winter tempests, and I wanted to be the third in my family.

M and I started many fixes and enhancements including bringing in a self controlling stuff from Canada. A SBS radio and transmitter was fitted also and the flexy airborne fitted right toward the back. The marina was so enormous we recruited a vehicle so we could arrive at the loo without a long walk particularly assuming that it was raining.

M had a court date in Ireland and flew home, while I traveled to England for two or three weeks and saw my auntie who cruised with her dad across the Pacific not long before the War. It was the start of my proposed book.

Edward and Philippa and my Goddaughter, Camilla, and her sister, Olivia, came out to Nassau, Bahamas for Christmas, leaving in Georgetown on New Years' Eve.

M and I forged ahead to Cuba, Cayman Islands, and through the Panama Canal into the Pacific, where we continued following my granddad right around 59 years later him.

Tahiti, August 1998

AFTERWORD

This journal was composed altogether from memory while abandoned in Tahiti, engineless, trusting that another one will be flown up from Auckland. Any mistakes are totally because of my memory. It was an intriguing and animating task important to keep me sensibly on the honest from the enticements of this outlandish and sexual island. My team delighted in Tahiti somehow and befriended an American yacht in the marina. I'm surprised at the sum associated with now I require a brief. There was a period limit, the storm season was drawing closer and when the motor showed up and was fitted we would cruise. The two months spent writing more than one thousand words a day was very intense as I rushed through what turned out to be a varied and interesting life although there is often a lack of detail. It is more an appearance than an inside and out biography.

Tiggs, Nick's Boston terrier, is wheezing as I compose this afterword somewhere in the range of twenty years after the fact in my office watching out over a field towards the Isle of Wight, the gleam of the Solent only noticeable at high water.

The twenty years, aside from the initial two, have not been so momentous albeit nothing could match the rescue years except for the years have been totally different. Running the shop was everyday despite the fact that Lloyds was high danger and for the second time in my life I confronted chapter 11 however got through and presently I am out. I have been all over the planet again yet that was as a charge paying traveler among numerous on a boat so doesn't actually count. I have been to Antarctica and that was truly fascinating there being just 100 or so individual voyagers and we arrived in elastic boats.

"Cruising in Grandfather's Wake" my record of the circumnavigation of the world with "Autonomous Freedom" was distributed by Reeds in 2001 the year we got back to the UK. "Rescue A Personal Odyssey" my record of my rescue years was distributed in 2007 via Seafarers. I have quite recently distributed a novel about with regards to rescue "The Dare" and two books of brief tales "Reflections on The Sea," so I have not been altogether inactive. The shop is a distant memory and is presently a bistro albeit still called "The Boathouse."

I shared for a couple of years an excellent Nicholson forty ketch, "Coral of Aqaba," with my siblings in the wake of being compelled to sell "Autonomous Freedom." We made some great travels including Scotland. Infection has constrained me to leave the ocean yet I have delighted in six years cruising the English inland streams with Nick and our sixty foot tight boat, "Merlot", yet presently we

have been compelled to sell her since I can don't really get onboard.

The ocean, the ocean, goodness the ocean, her call has left me. I never thought in my most out of this world fantasies she would go and she has and removed a portion of my spirit with her. My most punctual recollections are of the ocean, the harbor waters of Poole lapping on the shore before our home Waterfront. The breeze adrift from those most punctual occasions to the practically insensate wail of a storm, the ocean murmuring, to the delicate murmur of a breeze in the apparatus running before the exchange winds. Never will I fail to remember the vibe of speed as Edward and I as youngsters overwhelmed the Yarmouth Lymington ship in my firefly testing the new self bailers, strong, interminable youth, at one with the boat and the ocean, we felt like we were flying hopping from one wave to another. The sensation, so divergent in "Autonomous Freedom" flying up the Red Sea with distinct infertile Abu Ail behind us, the breeze a consistent fifty bunches as we flooded and rode northwards. Thus numerous others to be recollected. The ocean in the entirety of her states from ice like quiet, silver in the twilight, to the white beat breaking waves apparently throwing themselves at yacht or boat, to the flicker of the moving ocean in brilliant daylight or the dim northern oceans dull under dark low cloud where the sun appears to be lost, to the splendid tropical oceans so clear you can see into the profundities, even her actual soul, always remembering the ocean is a requesting escort consistently requiring admiration or she will kill you. My living was made on the ocean, my most noteworthy delights have been cruising on the ocean, my motivation has come from the ocean, the very motivation to live has been the ocean, and presently it appears she has abandoned me and left me bereft.

THE END

Printed in Great Britain
by Amazon

81798845R00096